She Said
God Blessed Us

# She Said
# God Blessed Us

*A Life Marked by Childhood*
*Sexual Abuse in the Church*

GAIL HOVEY

Exposit

Jefferson, North Carolina

*Some names and identifying details have been changed to protect the privacy of certain individuals.*

LIBRARY OF CONGRESS CATALOGUING-IN-PUBLICATION DATA

Names: Hovey, Gail, 1940– author.
Title: She said God blessed us : a life marked by childhood sexual abuse in the church / Gail Hovey.
Description: Jefferson, North Carolina : Exposit, 2020 | Includes index.
Identifiers: LCCN 2020025613 |
ISBN 9781476682778 (paperback : acid free paper) ∞
ISBN 9781476640778 (ebook)
Subjects: LCSH: Hovey, Gail, 1940– | Adult child sexual abuse victims—United States—Biography. | Child sexual abuse by clergy—United States. | Sexually abused girls—United States. | Abusive women—United States.
Classification: LCC RC569.5.A28 H68 2020 | DDC 616.85/83690092 [B]—dc23
LC record available at https://lccn.loc.gov/2020025613

BRITISH LIBRARY CATALOGUING DATA ARE AVAILABLE

ISBN (print) 978-1-4766-8277-8
ISBN (ebook) 978-1-4766-4077-8

Cover photos: The author and the church of her childhood

Printed in the United States of America

Exposit is an imprint of McFarland & Company, Inc., Publishers

Exposit

*Box 611, Jefferson, North Carolina 28640*
*www.expositbooks.com*

For Alex and for Pat

I am trying to hold in one steady glance all the parts of my life.

—Adrienne Rich

# Table of Contents

### Section III—By Their Fruits

# An End to Childish Ways

# 1

# In the Beginning

My first memory of Georgia is in my parents' bedroom, April 22, 1956, Sunday, after church. She had just been hired as the first Christian education director the congregation had ever had, and Mother told me to take her upstairs so she could freshen up before dinner. I did as my mother instructed without complaint and led Georgia up the stairs, past the bathroom, my sister's bedroom, and the linen closet to the master bedroom.

I stepped back to let her enter. "You can put your things there, on the bed."

The mahogany bedstead dominated and darkened the room. The spread was white, the bed perfectly made, and the room immaculate.

Georgia went past me into the room. She was just my height, but only because she wore high heels. She put her coat on the bed, then crossed the room to look at herself in the large rectangular mirror above my mother's dresser. Her forceful step conveyed an inherent authority that led me to believe she was much older than my sixteen years. She was only twenty-four. In 1956, the divide between grown-ups and children was still stark, and we were without question on opposite sides. She took lipstick from her purse and began to apply color. Something about the way she moved awed me; it was as if she had been here before.

I had too, of course, though my parents' bedroom was almost off limits. Still, at three or four years old, I had snuck in to commit my first-ever conscious sin. In the bottom drawer of my father's dresser there was a tin box filled with small brown envelopes, each one labeled: *food, clothing, recreation, tithe*. I stole from those envelopes, as if taking their coins might give me what I needed from my parents. Never more than a dollar, and always from the envelope with the most cash in the hope that what was taken would go unnoticed.

I wanted to impress Georgia and I thought this story would amuse her. How I took money and then went outside and *dropped* the coin in a safe place, returning to *find* it, to hurry home to tell my mother my good fortune, without lying, already exercising legalisms to outwit a guilty conscience. Yet something about Georgia's presence intimidated me. I kept quiet.

She caught me watching her in the reflection. I looked away quickly. She got out her comb and caught my eye again, smiled at me in the mirror. She was about to speak and sensing that made me afraid. She would ask me what I couldn't answer. I told myself she wanted to be alone and backed away, escaping down the stairs.

Later, she told me she knew exactly how I felt and why I fled. She told me this was the moment she began to love me.

# 2

# Whither Thou Goest

Union Theological Seminary in New York City, September 1962. I was a new graduate student. At the first orientation session, I stood at the side of the room to scrutinize the men in my class: young white men in dark trousers, tweed jackets with leather patches at the elbows, navy sports coats. Seminary was a male domain with only four women in our class of ninety. The women didn't interest me.

I studied the men because one of them would be my husband. Georgia, on *her* first day at seminary, had met Sam and had known at that moment that she would marry him. The story was part of her mystique. It was nuts to think this way. I couldn't help it. The same would happen for me, or it ought to, if I had eyes to see. Looking around, I had no idea. Though I hated to admit it, this just proved that Georgia was smarter than I was and more perceptive.

Union required practical field work as well as rigorous academic study. I applied to Chambers Memorial Baptist Church in East Harlem, where the congregation was black and Puerto Rican. I'd studied abroad in Lebanon for my junior year in college. Learning about the Arab-Israeli conflict, I thought seriously for the first time about political and racial struggles for justice. I was ashamed that I'd had to go to Beirut to see that the United States was an imperialist power and that there was rigid segregation back home in Chicago. On my return, I vowed to keep learning, applied to work at Chambers, and was thrilled when they said yes.

Then I discovered that, at Chambers Church, I had to team-teach with Don, a tall Baptist white man from Texas. Not thrilling. Not the man I would marry. He tried to treat me like a lady, but not for long.

"You're pretty fierce when you're mad," Don said, a little awed.

"Never forget it," I said.

With field work figured out, I started to study and couldn't help feeling a bit superior in Old Testament class because I'd been there—to the Egyptian desert, the Jordan Valley, the Dead Sea. When Dr. James Muilenburg stood before us like a prophet, with his white hair and handsome weathered face, I could visualize the places he spoke of, the hot, barren, ancient beauty of the Holy Land. He told us that Moses was talking to his people, instructing them in the desert, and then he intoned:

A wandering Aramean was my father; he went down into Egypt and sojourned there, few in number; and there he became a nation, great, mighty and populous.

The words flooded my imagination. I knew at that moment that the wanderer was my father too. I had done something Georgia hadn't done; something Don hadn't done. I had gone to Lebanon, to join this wandering Aramean's family. I wasn't a solitary soul alone on the planet, or confined to the narrow family of my birth, the homogeneous community of my childhood and its church. I belonged to a multitude, an historic people, shared the lineage of the Israelites, which was the lineage of the people I had come to know and love in Lebanon—Muslims and Christians of many hues and all of us People of the Book.

Now, more than a year and a half later, claiming that wandering Aramean as my forefather, I saw how Lebanon had prepared me for Union and for New York. I left class exhilarated, walked cloistered halls with polished brick and marble floors to James Chapel for morning worship and joined with my classmates in singing praises. "All Glory Laud and Honor/ to Thee, Redeemer, King..."

Most of the seminary felt to me like sacred space—sheltering arched corridors with low, gray ceilings; a central, secluded quadrangle; the chapel with its high, stained-glass windows and imposing free-hanging cross. Don and I met in the Pit, a corner basement room that was unsanctified. In need of a paint job, the room was furnished with cast-off chairs and worn couches. First on Sunday night, then during the week, we sat at a narrow table and began to develop the most arduously organized youth program that Chambers Church had ever seen. Bibles open, I watched how Don held a Winston cigarette in two long fingers, as if it were part of his hand—his flawless, graceful hand.

He was a talker: about the priesthood of all believers, the meaning of the resurrection and his core affirmation that love is stronger than death. I told him about Lebanon, how it had challenged all of my certainties, beginning with religious. My way to worship God wasn't the only or the best way but one of many. He was fascinated by what I told him, and he spoke his own beliefs with facility and conviction. I was ferociously competitive, and my disinterest in him as a possible mate meant that I could admit he knew more theology than I did.

Now, on a Tuesday night in early October, I took out a cigarette, then almost dropped it. His hurried gesture to hold a match for me was just what I did for Georgia.

"You know why it's called the Pit?" He didn't wait for me to answer. "Henry Pitney Van Dusen."

Don had majored in philosophy in college and had already explained to me, without condescension, that whoever asks the questions controls the conversation. He wanted to tell me about the seminary president, a powerful, ecumenical, patriarchal leader. It seemed funny to me that this humble room bore his nickname.

"When Van Dusen was ordained back in the twenties," Don said, shifting in a wooden chair that was too small for him, "there was some controversy among the faculty because he refused to say he believed in the virgin birth, the literal, biblical account."

I'd never given the virgin birth much thought. Don's animated seriousness made me smile.

"Don't you see?" he said. "It's allowed here, encouraged, expected that we challenge orthodoxy, that we maintain our intellectual integrity. We have to find faith that works for us. We have to teach the kids that it's not about believing this or that. It's about loving God and each other and finding ways to make that real."

He was earnest to a fault when he talked about love. I'd had enough for one evening and said goodnight, walked the dark corridors to Lampman Chapel for the late-night service. What the hell did Don know about love? I could tell him a thing or two—only I couldn't. I couldn't say I loved Georgia or that by now our love was both a blessing and a curse. When, exactly, I lost the simple magic and caught Georgia's guilt I couldn't say, only that her guilt was infectious and I carried it now, a chronic disease like malaria that flares and subsides and flares again.

I reached the small sanctuary below the refectory and sat on a tall-backed, reed-bottomed chair in the soft candlelight, surrounded by the stillness of others at prayer. The enormity of Georgia, of our transgressions—I couldn't think about them clearly, what we'd done wrong. I just hugged myself and tried to keep from weeping there in the silence.

When I'd left for college four years before, Georgia had given me a letter that I read again and again like a prophecy.

> You will grow in your understanding of yourself as a sinner until you detest yourself. And you will grow in your knowledge of God's eternal love for you as you are—until your heart breaks with the need to somehow humble your pride and serve him above all.

These words had helped me know I would go to seminary myself, like Georgia had.

In the bookstore, I bought a woodcut by a German artist whose name I can't remember and hung it opposite the foot of my bed. Bold black, red, and brown lines made a man at prayer, his large head and shoulders deeply bowed, giant hands clasped above his skull, pulling it down into abject submission and anguished supplication. The words across the poster read, "God be merciful to me a sinner." I sat on my bed and stared at this image of myself. Someone else knew exactly how I felt, desperate for mercy for offenses too heavy to name.

I had to translate the Book of Ruth for beginning Hebrew. I'd learned the alphabet without too much difficulty: א ב ג ד. I knew the story because Georgia taught it to me. "Where you go, I will go; where you lodge, I will lodge; your people will be my people and your God my God." Ruth and Naomi. Gail and Georgia. We understood that the passage was an expression of absolute loyalty, for the whole of life, even unto death when we would be buried in the same place. Obviously, we didn't mean this literally, and used the old language of the King James to joke, "Whither thou goest..." when she set out to get groceries and I agreed to go with her.

But studying Hebrew was hard. I couldn't make the letters into whole words. Whether I was in my room or in the library, after about fifteen minutes, I might as well have been trying to read Urdu. The text blurred; my body began to tremble. I knew I would fail. Impossible. Maybe pride was a sin, but I was too proud to fail. I didn't understand why Hebrew eluded me or that what I really feared was the attention failure would shine on me.

Jake sat next to me in Hebrew class and asked me out. I said no but he kept asking. What I remember is his room, his narrow bed, and the two of us caught in a strange push-me-pull-you tangle. We were seminary students, and we were not married. But my body was hungry and knew what it needed. A hot boy from the Southwest, he wanted to take me, but was frightened by his desire, and then by mine.

He pulled his hand away too soon. "If you come like that, you'll ruin yourself for marriage."

I was underneath him, my sweater bunched around my neck, my skirt bunched at my waist. My body screamed for him to finish. Pulling his hand away, as if my coming would burn his flesh, he damned me. I had my eyes closed. I did not touch him. He did not ask me to touch him. We were seminary students; we had not wed.

I think I wept. I know I fled. He gave me a present for Christmas—a short, slender book on Picasso, which I read only once but kept for years, creating a little romantic lie to blot out the rest. The rest he had no way of knowing. When he took his hand away and spoke those words, leaving me there on his narrow bed, unmet, he gave me confirmation of my worst fears. What my body cried for, craved, I could not deny. Those things sullied me, made me contemptible. I could not take in that this had anything to do with Georgia. Georgia loved me. And who else could I ask for help?

I called her from the phone booth at the opposite end of the hall from the Pit. "I'm going crazy. I can't study. I don't know what's wrong with me." I wanted to tell Georgia I was haunted. The people from my childhood, if they knew what I'd done… I wanted to tell her how I kept seeing myself back in that church, marching down the center aisle, singing. All those people who respected me, if they knew…

It wasn't judgment in her voice that made me uneasy, but too much assurance.

"Is it that you have doubts?" she said. "You shouldn't be alarmed by doubt. Any thinking person has them. Mine still—"

"It's not that," I interrupted her. "It's like a pressure builds in my body." I struggled for words. "If I don't release it, it feels like I'll explode." Madly I would wiggle my toes inside my shoes where it didn't show when I was with other people and agitated. It kept me from screaming, barely. "I'm frightened," I said. "I can't make myself… I'm coming apart."

I didn't remember, then, that Georgia hadn't been able to study when she entered seminary either, that she'd escaped to the movies, three or four in a day sometimes. When she'd told me this, I was innocent; it sounded sophisticated, rebellious, free. Now her silence was making me uncomfortable. Had I said something I shouldn't have?

"If you're that unhappy, for heaven's sake go talk to someone." It was more an order than a comfort.

It would be years before I took in what was at stake for Georgia in that cold, hard giving of permission. Did she have such trust in professional confidentiality, or did she lie awake terrified that she'd be found out? I never wondered. I wasted no time. I went to see the dean who was responsible for the well-being, academic and otherwise, of all women students.

I went in shame and defeat. Georgia had never needed a counselor, never confessed what Virginia, her religious teacher, had begun when she was twelve. Georgia said that telling me had been sufficient.

"Get married and have children," Georgia said repeatedly. "Don't do what I did." I understood. She loved me better than Virginia had loved her. I didn't need someone younger, enthralled, to whom I could safely speak. It was easy to be obedient to Georgia. I hadn't yet been tempted.

I sat upright in front of the dean, a white-haired, strait-laced woman in her sixties who wore silver-rimmed glasses and had a warm if proper smile. She sat behind her desk and listened without expression. I focused on the words I had to speak, as armored as could be against what she might say.

"Georgia was the best thing that ever happened to me."

Georgia came to me like the *Gloria.*

Each Sunday morning, when I was four, five, six years old, I stood with the congregation of adults singing for all I was worth, the melody I had learned by heart and the nonsense syllables that only later would ungarble themselves into the creedal words of the *Gloria.* I didn't need the text to be joined with the others in adoration.

In church when I was young, I didn't know that everyone around me was singing, "Glory be to the Father..." and that what we sang was an articulation—honed over the ages by the people of God—of the deepest meaning of the Christian faith. For me, as a little child, this special singing filled my heart. I sang along, ignorant, but sensing anyway that I was part of something oh so much larger than myself.

Just so, Georgia came to me, taking me like the music took me, for all I was worth. I hadn't known I yearned at sixteen for what she offered any more than I was searching as a six-year-old for sacred song. With Georgia, I entered a place apart, parallel to, but beyond the reach of normal, daily life, free of the strictures of common existence, common sense. It's the only way I know how to say what happened.

That day with the dean, I didn't yet know how to say this.

"Georgia was the director of Christian education in my church. I wouldn't be here if it weren't for her. We came to love each other very much."

The dean nodded. "Go on."

I must have said something more about Georgia but I don't remember. All that mattered was to tell her the truth. "We even," I said, "we even made love."

I said it out loud, that plainly. She didn't gasp in horror.

"We don't anymore," I said, quickly. "Not for a long time. I love her still."

I watched the dean carefully. She smiled at me.

Now I wonder if it was a nervous smile. At the time, it puzzled me. Maybe what I said wasn't important or unusual. Maybe what I'd done wasn't so bad and I was just stupidly anguished over nothing. We loved each other. Could it be, as Georgia said, that love was all that mattered?

I waited for the dean to question me. She didn't ask what now seems obvious. *How old were you? How long did it go on? Did you say that she was married? Do you know if there were other girls involved?* She didn't comment on the fact that both of us were women though, consciously, I was troubled most by this.

I went to see the dean only twice. It was 1962. Sexual misconduct on the part of clergy would remain invisible and off limits to public discourse for decades more. I thanked her very much. For what? Had she understood exactly what I told her but saw that I was not yet ready to question anything about Georgia? I don't think so. I suspect that she was simply not equipped to take in what I was telling her. I think I persuaded her with my facile tongue that all I needed was to share a complicated secret. Georgia had told me her secret. I told the dean my secret. Now that I had, it would lose its fangs. I could get on with my life as a regular young woman who was interested in men and expected to find a husband among her classmates.

Every Sunday morning, Don and I took the bus to East Harlem. We got off at 125th Street and Third Avenue, walked past the flimsy furniture stores that lined the block, and turned into 123rd Street where Chambers Church was located. The sanctuary was on the second floor. Don went upstairs and sat at the piano to play for the service. He also played organ, clarinet, and several other instruments. Impressed by all his music, I did what I'd done countless times for Georgia, stood next to the piano to turn pages. His long fingers gave him a wider reach on the keys than Georgia had. I noticed this; I liked it.

More and more frequently, Don and I ate our meals at the same table, studied next to each other in the library, walked together to class, and sat in adjoining chairs. He talked about love all the time, how it was the core of Christianity. He spoke of it theologically, his supple mind laying out for me the deep meaning of words I'd known since childhood. *God so loved the world that He gave His only son. Greater love has no man than this, that he lay down his life for his friends.* He wanted to live like that, a life for others.

It took until late February for me to realize that I was falling in love. Far too anxious to let love develop slowly, naturally, over the course of the semester, I telephoned Don and insisted that he meet me in the Pit that very night.

Don tossed his jacket onto a couch and joined me at our regular table. Quickly, nervously, because he didn't know why I'd summoned him, he lit up a cigarette and held the match for me like a gentleman. His light-blue dress shirt was smoothly pressed under his gray wool vest, his dark tie knotted neatly. The harsh overhead light shone on his broad forehead, exposing his gentle features and mottled brown eyes which were magnified by his big glasses with their black frames.

"I have to ask you something," I said bluntly. "I think I'm falling in love with you."

Don's eyes got bigger, as if my remark had caught him completely by surprise.

"You talk all the time," I said, "about love. I think you include us. I think you're shy. I think you mean us, towards each other."

Sitting stiffly in my chair, I waited while he took a long drag on his cigarette.

"I want to know if you feel the same as I do. If you love me too. I need to know, so I don't get carried away if it's just me. If you don't reciprocate."

He blinked as if to make sure he wasn't imagining what he'd heard. He smiled. He turned away and back again. He was still smiling. I didn't realize how odd my question was, how desperate, really. He had never taken my hand; we'd never kissed. It was all talk that made me feel this way, talk that never bored me, that showed off his lively mind, the kindness of his disposition. Just talk, and his beautiful hands on the piano.

"You love me?" He sounded slightly bewildered.

"Yes, if you'll let me."

He reached across the table then, timidly placing his hand over mine. He grinned. "Thank you. Yes. I mean in answer to your question, yes."

I don't remember if we kissed. I do remember that Don went home skipping. He lived two blocks down the street and after we said goodnight, he skipped all the way home. He told me the next morning at breakfast.

"I kept saying to myself, 'Someone loves me. Gail loves me.' And I skipped."

Don was gawky tall with a large head, narrow shoulders, long arms and big feet that turned out a tad when he walked. I see him still, skipping down Claremont Avenue, taking it in that someone loved him, that I loved him. It's a miracle he didn't trip and fall on his face, and a sweet memory, even now.

# 3

## Suffer the Little Children

The Sunday my father hired Georgia to be the director of Christian education at our church, she came to dinner with her fiancé, Sam Cartwright. She left her coat on the bed upstairs and I fled from her. Now she sat in my chair, Sam on her left, my parents at the head and foot of the table. Mother had covered it with a white linen tablecloth and set it with her mother's Haviland china, the good crystal, the sterling silver. From where I sat next to my sister Carmen, I could look out past our guests, through the screened-in porch to the back lawn, the birdbath sheltered by a curved hedge, and behind it, thick evergreens shielding us from the neighbors.

"When we moved here in 1940," Dad said to our guests, "the congregation was tiny and the only one in town."

"Except for the Catholics," Mother said.

"We wanted a town with a church," Dad said, "and committed ourselves to this one, though neither of us grew up as Presbyterians."

The familiar litany: How the city was no place to raise children and we'd moved from Chicago when Carmen was two and I was three months old. How families, including ours, prospered, as did the village, as did the church, which in time became too small. My father, an engineer, was modest, playing down his role in the construction of the new building.

"We hired an architect," he said. "Money was pledged."

Then, with pride he couldn't hide, he told how, just the year before, the small, steepled, white-framed church I'd gone to all my life had been lifted from its foundation and turned, making room for a new stone sanctuary.

"It's much to my liking," Georgia said. "Spare, powerful space because of the simple concrete walls and raw beans."

Her intensity, which had made me run away from her, was focused now on my father. I had never heard anyone express an opinion about architecture and she was exactly right. I loved those raw timbers.

"Our next project," Dad said, "is to tear down the old church to make room for an education wing. We have to go step by step." He paused, as if embarrassed. "For now, you'll have to make do with the corner office in the old building."

"I like that office, tucked away at the back," she said. "I played the piano in the old sanctuary. The acoustics are excellent."

"We're grateful," Sam said, putting his hand on Georgia's arm as if to claim her in this setting, "grateful that you'll hire her for just a year." His voice was deep and soothing. He explained that after he graduated from seminary the following spring it was most likely that he would be called to a church that would require them to move away.

I studied him across the table. He was a good match for Georgia—taller, his hair darker brown, better looking though not outrageously so, and a little older. He exuded the same urbane air. They lived in the city, experienced what people in my town didn't know of or hid from.

"I'm a conservative man," Dad said, his eyes full of mischief. "We've never had a Christian education director before. If you aren't any good, we aren't stuck."

"Wise indeed," said Georgia, "and of course it works both ways." She seemed to know exactly what to say to please him.

"Touché!" He became serious. "There are those who say we don't need a director."

"You know the type," Mother said, "the ones who want everything to stay the same, who don't want to spend the money, who are frightened by new ideas."

Mother was as taken with Georgia as Dad was. Though I can't remember what she wore that day, my mother would have wanted to make a good impression as she always did when clergy came to dinner. She would have selected something to bring out the luster in her dark brown eyes and her brunette hair which she braided and pinned up like a crown, something pale green or soft yellow, patterned. She knew how to do this because years before, in a rare act of self-indulgence, she'd gone to a stylist, one with the most exotic name I'd ever heard: Celeste. Mother spoke of Celeste shyly, as if she were a guilty pleasure. I looked from her to my father. He was fair, with clear blue eyes, and they shared a quiet handsomeness.

"You'll know you've done a good job," Dad said, "if we hire someone to succeed you."

Mr. Cartwright folded his napkin carefully. "It's possible that I'll get a church close by." He smiled self-consciously. "Even so, we're going to want to start a family."

I turned away. I disliked babies and everything about them, going way back to when I was one. I couldn't help that I was the baby in my family. Baby meant the *pleasingly-plump-blue-eyed-dimpled-blonde-curly-headed-cherub* my mother and father saw me to be. I couldn't help it that I had those looks, which were more like my dad's than Mother's. When I was finally allowed, age ten, to cut off my golden ringlets, I began to look like myself, and I was not and had never been angelic. Carmen was like Mother, straight dark hair, dark eyes, and Mother loved to dress us in matching outfits, Carmen in peach and me in baby blue. We went to church every Sunday in that little white building my father had spoken of.

I had no idea what a director of Christian education would do or what I might learn from her. My belief was born on Easter. Carmen and I sat with our parents, were swept up in resurrection hymns, and because Jesus rose, we got petunia plants to put in our garden. Year after year I learned my faith from the songs we sang: Jesus loved me, and climbing Jacob's ladder, we were soldiers of the cross, though I couldn't say exactly what that meant.

I was only five and at Vacation Bible School when we acted out a story that would stay with me and show me how I should live my life. A man fell among thieves and was left by the side of the road. A priest and a Levite saw him and walked by on the other side. Only the Good Samaritan stopped and did what was required. Faith had consequences. We were to care for the injured stranger.

Not until Mrs. Benkhe died, when I was seven, did I think hard about God. Mrs. Benkhe was our first babysitter, and I wanted her to go to heaven. Sitting on the step in front of our house, brow furrowed and fists clenched, I wondered if I should pray for her. If God was all-powerful, as I had been taught, her entrance into heaven should have nothing to do with the prayers of a seven-year-old. What if, I reasoned, someone just as good as Mrs. Benkhe died but no one prayed for that person? If Mrs. Benkhe got in and the other person didn't that wasn't fair. *Fair* was the foundation on which our family stood. Though my heart told me to pray, I would not let myself. Already I imagined God out there judging the dead instead of up close with a little child who might need Him to comfort her as she dealt with death for the first time.

If my parents' bedroom was the scene of my first sin, stealing coins from small brown envelopes, it was also the room in which, when I was ten, I had my first epiphany. Why I chose to sit in the little black rocking chair between my parents' dressers, I have no idea. It was Good Friday. Mother had planned an outing for us, to go to the city to visit old friends, since we didn't have school. It didn't seem right. I rocked vigorously, thinking about the death of Jesus. Dying on the cross, had He really saved us from our sins? Then the doubt, the question, went away, and I believed. Believing, I had to confront my mother. Since Jesus saved us on Good Friday, Good Friday must be the most important day of the whole year. How could we just go off and have a good time with some old friends of Mother's as if it were an ordinary day?

Usually the trouble between Mother and me was more mundane. She wouldn't let me go out and play until every single job on my list was completed. She said I came down the stairs like a herd of elephants. When my hair was long, I wanted braids; she wanted ringlets. She was a *should* person, attaching moral meaning to each of her instructions. I argued, but the expression of anger was not allowed in our house and Mother punished me for my outbursts.

Carmen was the obedient one, two years older, and we shared a room until she turned sixteen and decided she wanted a room of her own. I was hurt when she moved into the guest room, which was smaller, had a double bed with a dust ruffle, a white vanity and pale pink wallpaper. You couldn't have paid me to live in that pretty feminine room.

Our room became mine. The twin beds with their matching dark green coverlets were okay. I got new wallpaper, a pattern called "spatter-dash," with tiny, dense drops of color thrown all over it. Mother did good, finding me that perfect wallpaper. I got to keep our old dresser, only now all the drawers were mine. Dad hung a mirror above it, and with his help I put the deer antlers I'd picked up in Colorado on the wall too and hung my cowboy hat there. I spent a lot of time in front of that mirror, liking how tough I looked in that hat.

Nineteen fifty-four and I was fourteen. Sitting at the desk in my room, I had an epiphany as powerful as the one I'd had when I first believed in Jesus, only this one wasn't religious. I had to lead a double life, separate myself from my family, their black and white expectations, their tidy respectability. I couldn't leave home until college. I could make of our house a hotel with public and private rooms. In public—at meals, in the kitchen—I'd act as if all was well. In my room, I'd have my real life. Coming to this realization was a culmination. I had tried to tell them who I was, the *me* captured in a photo Dad took. Me in my Levi jeans and Levi jacket, up on Willie, a Morgan horse I rode for a year while my parents decided whether or not to buy me a horse of my own. Mother actively disliked the photo. I didn't look ladylike. She couldn't understand that the last thing I wanted was to look like a lady. I didn't even want to look like a girl, which is why I loved the picture. Perhaps it sounds contradictory. I cringed if there was any suggestion of masculinity in my appearance. Masculine girls were disgusting.

If I could just *be* a boy.

The memory of that vow to live my secret life is vivid, and it played out in complex, nuanced ways. No one could ever say my parents didn't love us or that they were not conscientious. I got their work ethic, and I got their absolutism. Yet by the time Georgia arrived, I found them, especially Mother, intrusive in a way I could not bear. Sometimes her company, always her touch. I recoiled when she tried to hug me or hold my hand.

Looking at our family from the outside, this trouble was invisible. I did well in school, attended church and sang in the youth choir with all my friends. One night a week we had choir practice, and since the congregation had grown enough for there to be two services, the youth choir sang every Sunday morning at nine o'clock. Dressed in our maroon robes, in a double line, we came down the center aisle of the sanctuary. I knew all the verses, sang with my head up, and wanted everyone in the congregation to notice that I sang with my whole heart.

Then I realized I was proud, and pride is a sin. I didn't want to sin. It wasn't about breaking the commandments, which seemed too extreme to be a temptation—*you shall not kill, you shall not steal, you shall not commit adultery.* Okay, I had stolen but that was a long time ago when I was little. Not sinning meant I had to be perfect, like it said in the Book of Matthew: *You, therefore, must be perfect, as your heavenly Father is perfect.*

I was fifteen when I opened the door to our powder room and went inside. A small space, decorated in a manner that fit its name, it was very private. I turned on the light and locked the door. I washed my hands thoroughly. Then I raised my head, looked at myself in the mirror, straight in the eye, and gave a command. "You shall be perfect as your heavenly Father is perfect." In a ritual cleansing, I washed away my sins—my anger and my pride. I would never sin again. I wiped my hands on the linen guest towel and went out.

Mother sat in her chair in the living room, mending socks. I sat down on the couch, took a deck of cards from the drawer in the long, low coffee table and began to play solitaire. It felt just fine to have a secret from my mother. Only I wanted her to see me, to notice that I'd changed. I didn't like our fights any more than she did. From now on I would pay attention. I would stop myself from sinning by force of will.

Of course, it didn't take. Later, everyone I told would laugh with me at my pious young self. Everyone except Georgia. She didn't want to believe I could ever have been such a fool.

# 4

# Your Cloak as Well

Summer 1963 and now I was the religious teacher.

"Matthew five, beginning at verse thirty-five." Mrs. Waters began to read. A small dark woman, her short hair was hidden by a faded blue and pink kerchief. Because she was older, married, and had been in the church longer, the other members of our Bible study group, Florence Tanner and Clara Lewis, deferred to her. With a cigarette-scratchy voice, she read without confidence. "You have heard that it was said, an eye for an eye…"

I squirmed. Yes, everyone needed to participate, but her hesitant reading diminished the power of the text. I should have read it myself. My year of fieldwork at Chambers Church was finished, but this small group of women I'd met with for Bible study had asked me to keep coming through the summer. Every Wednesday night I made my way to Wagner Houses in East Harlem, pushing aside my fear of the neighborhood because they wanted to continue meeting.

"…and if anyone wants to sue you and take your coat, give your cloak as well." Mrs. Waters read more steadily now. "And if anyone forces you to go one mile, go also the second mile. Give to everyone who begs from you, and do not refuse anyone who wants to borrow from you." Mrs. Waters looked up. "Is that the end?"

"It is. What do you think?"

She put her head back down. Clara sat next to her on the oversized tan sofa across from the huge gilded mirror, and she exchanged a nervous glance with Florence who sat on her left, opposite me in a matching overstuffed chair. They lit cigarettes and I knew they were stalling. I got out my cigarettes. Florence held a match for me, but she didn't say anything.

"This passage," I said, "doesn't it seem like nonsense?"

"Thank you!" Clara said. The good-natured extrovert of the group, she laughed. She wore an old man's shirt with rolled up sleeves, tails tied around her waist, worn jeans, and rubber slippers, which made her look like a cleaning woman, though she worked for the post office. I felt comfortable with Clara. Florence and Mrs. Waters put me on a pedestal. With all of them, I felt like I had with my friends in Beirut. I needed to be accepted, was amazed and relieved when I was.

"I give to everyone who wants to borrow, I can't pay my rent!" Florence said. She wore a light magenta shirt, tight black pants, and carried herself like a model. Even sitting she was statuesque.

"Why you think we have rent parties?" Mrs. Waters said.

"That's right," Clara said. "You can't trust nobody to pay back. But if you come Saturday night to my party, buy my liquor, I make the rent money."

We talked easily then, ate the sugar cookies Florence offered, drank coffee, smoked. They listened respectfully when I explained that Jesus spoke to people who lived under foreign occupation. A Roman soldier could grab a Jew and force him to carry his load for a mile.

"During the first mile," I said, "the Roman's in control. But think about it. When the mile's up, and the load could be surrendered, the Jew says to the soldier, 'I'll carry it further for you.' It shifts the dynamic between them, gives the Jew a subtle power. Does that make sense?"

"Sure," Clara said. "But it frustrates me. How can I read the Bible by myself, if I don't know that stuff you tell us?"

"It's why we meet," Mrs. Waters said, to my surprise. "So we can learn more."

Abruptly, at eight-thirty, Clara stood up. "I left my teenage daughter home alone."

Mrs. Waters, who had six children, left with her.

"You can stay awhile, can't you?" Florence asked.

Flattered and nervous, alone with her, I knew I'd have to carry half the conversation.

"More coffee?"

As she came across the room to fill my cup, I admired her natural elegance, and I wished I was comfortable enough to tell her that her skin made me jealous. A rich brown color, it was more beautiful than mine.

She treated me like an equal, even looked up to me because I was in seminary. She must have been at least ten years older, knew things about life—all the women did—that I, from my safe little suburb, had never had a chance to learn. I didn't think about what safety in my suburb had actually entailed.

"I'm…. I need to ask your advice," she said, biting her lip. She crossed her arms, then uncrossed them and held her hands folded tightly in her lap. "My son doesn't like it. He gets real mad, when I have my man friend over."

I made eye contact because I knew I must, hearing Florence the way the women had just heard the Bible reading, taking in the words but not the meaning. Except the women wanted the meaning. What Florence said shut down a part of my mind.

She smiled a bit sheepishly, but spoke quite plainly. "I need to have him stay over. You understand." If the seminary student sanctioned what she did, it must be all right.

I must have shrugged or made some other dismissive gesture. Whatever I did satisfied. Florence relaxed and began to tell me more about her only child.

Why have I remembered, sharply and for decades, this awkward exchange with Florence Tanner? I could not take in what she was telling me. Understanding, I would have had to disapprove. They weren't married. That was the simple truth, except I couldn't let myself think even that. Florence was a black woman. White people were always judging black people. No way on God's green earth would I judge her. Not about anything, especially not sex. I believed that God blessed Georgia and me. I wasn't ready to face the contradictions.

I did that night with Florence what my parents must have done. Seeing what was right in front of them without seeing, hearing without hearing, so they didn't have to do anything, didn't have to intervene. It was the same incomprehension that Georgia's husband Sam must have cultivated. We all kept what we couldn't face in hermetically sealed compartments, protecting ourselves from the splendidly, frightfully obvious.

I'd sublet an apartment on 111th Street off Broadway for the summer. Friday night, when Don came over after work, I told him right away about Bible study but stopped before the conversation with Florence.

"Don't you get bored?" I said. "Going up and down all day?"

For the summer, he worked as an elevator operator on Wall Street and still had on his uniform: short-sleeved white dress shirt, narrow black tie, and black pants. They made him look even more pale, a creature who lived indoors and underground. I put two cans of beer in front of him and gave him the opener.

"I'm still trying to get the hang of it. It's an old elevator and some-times I don't hit the floor right. Then I'm in trouble. The men get irritated if it takes one extra minute to get where they're going. In the slow times, I study Greek vocabulary."

"I don't think you're smart enough to do my job," I said. I worked in the dietary office of St. Barnabas Hospital in the Bronx. "You know, when you're a patient, they bring you a menu for the next day and you have to check off what you want. I get to count the marks." I made lines in the air with my finger: one, two, three, four verticals and a diagonal. "It requires genius intelligence. Peas, peas, peas, carrots, carrots, chicken, chicken, meat loaf." We laughed.

"You're right," he said. "I'll stick to Greek."

I took two plain cream-colored plates from the orange cupboard next to the stove and set them on the table. "You know, it pisses me off that you get to stay all summer in Mel's apartment without paying a penny." Mel Schoonover was senior pastor of Chambers Church, a white man who, like us, had gone to Union. A genetic disorder made his bones brittle, and we were in awe of what Mel had accomplished, getting around in a wheelchair. He had taken his wife and daughter away from the city for the summer, leaving his apartment to Don. Don had been invited to work at Chambers a second year. Mel and Don were American Baptists; I was a Presbyterian; Don was a guy. I had no way to compete. But Mel didn't respect me the way he respected Don. I didn't want to think about why, and it wasn't fair.

Don looked up at me from where he sat at the kitchen table to see if I was really angry. He grimaced, as if he understood he'd gotten special treatment. The air was sultry and I pressed the beer can against my fore-head to cool off. I put the food out, a simple meal of macaroni and cheese, and a salad. When I sat down with him, we bowed our heads while he said grace.

"You've got yourself a great apartment," he said, "for cooking, I mean." He pointed to the high shelf with its pots and pans and large crock-ery bowls.

"I can't use those. The students I sublet from keep kosher. I mustn't defile those dishes with my Gentile hands."

Don started to smile, mischievously. "If they don't know…"

"You don't mean that."

"Why not? What's the meaning of a blessing? If the rabbi blesses the dishes, they are changed. But how? In a material way? In the mind of the believer?"

"If the believer doesn't know, what's the harm?"

"Exactly."

It had never occurred to me not to honor their request. I was happy with Don's little heresy but afraid to ask if he really believed that what you don't know can't hurt you.

We did the dishes and went into the living room. I sat on the couch in front of the coffee table, where I'd placed my copy of James Baldwin's *Another Country.* I expected Don to sit next to me; he chose the chair opposite by the philodendron. He told me how he'd tied tarantulas on his mother's jade plant to frighten her guests.

I was ready to make out with him, like I had with boyfriends in Boulder and in Beirut. Unlike Jake in my Hebrew class, men I had dated before were unafraid to complete what they began, bringing me to orgasm, self-hatred and relief, all mixed up. Don kept his distance, which strangely was okay. I picked up Baldwin's book.

"Have you read this? It's more emotionally alive, violent, and passionate than anything I've ever read."

"Sex and race," Don said. "Yes, I've read it. It's like Chambers Church. Without hypocrisy. Another country."

"Love is another country. I want to live there."

Talk. Talk was safe, even about these things, and so we did, endlessly.

Two months later, on Monday, August 28, Clara Lewis and I sat next to each other on the long bus ride to Washington. We were wound up to be marching for jobs and freedom, and so was everybody on the bus. We talked, we dozed, we shared the fried chicken that was passed up and down the aisles. Then, we struggled as a group to stay together amid the crowds that gathered before the Lincoln Memorial and stretched out in a dense mass along the reflecting pools all the way to the Washington Monument. Holding on to each other, we settled ourselves under and in the trees to the right of the Memorial where the speakers' platform stood. I was the only white person in our group, special and accepted. Unconsciously, I knew my place: to be obedient, ready—as I had been in Beirut—to perform, quickly and without complaint, whatever was asked of me. I'd had a master teacher.

I was exactly where I wanted to be, surrounded by members of Chambers Church. We sang freedom songs. I knew the words because we sang them in church. We cheered the speakers until we were hoarse, clapped until our hands hurt, embraced each other, and made our way home. On the bus, I swore to keep the vow I'd made to Dr. King, to rededicate my life as he called us to do. I kept repeating the most important parts of the speeches to tell Don. Dr. King said that even militant black people should understand that because white people were present, it showed that we understood that our destiny and freedom were inseparable from their destiny and freedom. That was right. I would be part of this urgent, irresistible struggle for justice.

For me, the struggle offered a secret bonus. I could hide. Thelma told us that she didn't want to hear anything about guilt. Thelma was the assistant minister's wife at Chambers, and at the beginning of the year she had gathered all the field work students, all of us white, in her living room.

"If you're here because you're guilty, for all the deeds white folks have perpetrated against black folks, if that's why you're here, get on out. We've got enough to worry us without having to take on white folks' guilt."

I got it. I was a pro at hiding guilt. Never mind the source—sex or race or both—I would not speak of it. What they didn't know couldn't hurt them or get in the way of the far more important work at hand.

Every time there's an anniversary, when the music is played and Dr. King's "I Have a Dream" speech is rebroadcast, I thank my young self for getting on that bus and Chambers Church for welcoming me. It would take more years than I like to admit before I could see how it had hurt me to hide from what made me guilty, hurt me and the work I wanted to accomplish.

It was the roses that did it, the dozen red roses Don brought me on his way home from work the night after the march. Narrowly conscientious, he'd been too timid to ask for the day off. He was an elevator operator on Wall Street; it was just a summer job. For once, I'd had the grace not to ridicule him for his priorities.

Don understood. "I was a fool not to go with you."

"Don't worry. There will be plenty more marches for us to go on together."

I woke in the night. I had to tell Don about Georgia. If we were going to be married, I had to tell him. If I didn't, he couldn't know who I was and I would be guilty of deceit. The last thing I needed was something more to feel guilty about. But what did I have to say, how much?

# 5

# Putting Away Childish Things

July 1956, and I couldn't wait to tell Georgia everything. I'd been away at camp. When I thought of how she'd sent me off, my face still flushed. She'd driven me home from church and we were in the car in front of my house. I was bold and teased her.

"I'm going to be gone two whole weeks. Do you think you can stand it?"

Her answer was one I'd never imagined, not a word but a gesture, a simple one that sent shivers through my body. She took my hand. That's all. She took her right hand off the steering wheel and reached across to take my hand. I didn't want her to let go, ever. Now I was back and I burst into her office without knocking. She turned from her papers on her desk to look at me, squelching her pleasure.

"So, it's you," she said sternly, setting her pen down. "Serenity ends."

Insulting endearments, what she called reverse psychology, were known to me now. I launched right in with my stories.

"Boone, my counselor, told me that when the sound of an axe rings in the forest, she can't tell if it's a man at work or if it's me. It's the best compliment I ever got in my whole life!"

I squatted to show Georgia how I balanced on the gunnels of the canoe, pumping like on a swing, sending the craft bumping across the water, until the counselors yelled at me to stop because it was dangerous. She picked up her pen again, and turned slightly away from me, as if I was going on too long.

"That sounds exciting," she said, but her voice contradicted her. It was flat. She pointed to the papers on her desk. "I made progress while you were away, on my Isaiah curriculum."

I sat down abruptly. She had no interest in what I loved most.

"Look here," Georgia said enthusiastically, holding the outline of her project before me.

25

The room seemed to stretch out long and narrow and I sat much farther away from her than would have been possible in her little office at the back of the church. I watched myself capitulate. At camp, we had nicknames. Mine was Gee Jay and, sheath knife on my belt, matches and jackknife in my pocket, axe in hand, I lived happier than I ever lived at home. To have Georgia I couldn't be Gee Jay. I could only answer her unspoken ultimatum. She would decide what we talked about and I could take it or leave it.

Georgia continued excitedly, as if she took it for granted that I would be enthralled by what she'd learned about Isaiah in my absence. She enveloped me with her enthusiasm and took my hand again while she drove me the short distance home. By the time we parked under the giant elms in front of my house, losing Gee Jay didn't seem important anymore.

A couple of days later I wrote a poem for Georgia, a poem called "Fire."

> *At first it starts as a tiny flame*
> *bright in color yet weak in*
> *warmth and glow.*

My poem described how fires burn, how they need to be tended. If ignored, I wrote, they will die, and all that will be left

> *is a heap of ashes*
> *to remind you of what could have been.*

I wasn't trying to find a way, surreptitiously, to tell Georgia about camp. I just wrote what came to me that evening as I sat at my desk. I didn't know about metaphors, didn't think about what I was saying or how she might receive it. I'd gotten in the habit of leaving her a note at night. This note was better than usual.

I told Mother I was walking the dog, put Skody on her leash and headed down to the church where I tied the dog to a small tree and went inside. Fighting my fear of the dark, I made my way through the passage behind the choir loft, feeling for the light switch on the rough concrete wall. I had placed the poem in an envelope and written her name in my best handwriting, *Georgia (almost) Cartwright*. They were to be married in August. I slipped the envelope into the corner of the large blotter on her desk, where in the morning it would be the first thing she saw.

I was out in the driveway shooting baskets in the late afternoon, a very predictable place to find me. When Georgia pulled up, I pretended not to see her and sent off a long shot from the side, praying it would swish though the basket. I hadn't seen her since I'd left the poem, which made me nervous, but not enough to miss the shot.

"Showoff!" she called as I walked to her car. "You're pretty hot stuff, aren't you?"

"Ah, just luck." We both knew I didn't mean it.

"I have something for you."

She handed me a folded piece of white paper and, with a quick good-bye, drove off before I could do anything but wave. I hurried to my room, closed the door and sat at my desk. Carefully I unfolded the single sheet, which was typed, double spaced and unsigned. I read it; I read it a second time. Over the years I would read it again and again until I made six perfect holes in the paper where the folds came.

*Indeed, it is a joyous thing to hit the spark which kindles a flame....*

She took up my description of fire, asserting that *flame* stood for something, a deep meaning which *'twixt us no longer seeks definition*. I see now that her language is overblown, even pompous—*in truth, I would speak of else besides*, and so on. She was playing, I suppose, enjoying herself, but she made awkward, even illogical transitions. She took herself and her position with great seriousness, spoke as my senior, my superior, interpreting my thoughts. Her statement ends with declarations: *Be adventuresome—trust in the "source of all fire"—and dare to burn, and live, and give light and warmth without fear of neglect.*

She'd found me out. I hadn't known what I was asking but she could see. I smoothed the paper on the desktop and took an involuntary deep breath. From that day forward, I believed that Georgia knew me better than I knew myself.

I went back outside, dribbled without shooting, dodging imaginary guards. Finally, I stood at the free-throw line, bounced the ball three times as I always did, and then sent it off to drop neatly through the basket. I could trust her. She told me so herself.

It was Georgia's last day at work before she left to be married. I had to see her one last time. When I pushed open the door to her office, I found it empty. I panicked, furious with myself that I'd missed her. Then I heard music; she was at the piano in the old sanctuary, and I hurried to her side, stood happily, watching her graceful hands on the keys, her intense concentration. I didn't know what she played. It didn't matter. All I wanted was to be near her.

We went back to her office; she had to make sure everything was in order as she'd not be back for a month. Purposefully, she tucked her purse under her arm and was about to pick up a pile of papers when she stopped. She sat down, fingers tapping the armrests of her chair, an expression I couldn't read masking her face. A fan hummed in the window. I sat too, stiffly, directly before her on a metal folding chair.

"I want to tell you something."

The silence that followed made me anxious. Was I supposed to ask her what?

Then, making up her mind, she looked at me directly. "When I speak to you and the other kids, I know what to say because of Virginia."

Georgia was a brilliant teacher, making what could be boring stories from the Old Testament pertinent and sometimes even awesome. I didn't understand why her face was troubled in a way I'd never seen before, as if she didn't know if what she said was good or ill.

"Virginia was my teacher. She came to my church when I was twelve. I adored her." She searched my face to see if I understood. "I was young, but I soaked in everything she taught us. Now, I teach. I speak, but the way I do it, it is Virginia." She put her hand to her forehead, pushing her hair back. "I followed Virginia into seminary. I'm going to marry a minister, just like she did." She smiled at me then, as if what she'd said was a secret between us. "I have to go now. Oh, my dear."

She stood and stretched out her arms to me, her palms open and I knew to place my hands in them, her fingers against my wrists, warm and steady, her eyes locked on mine, entering and holding me.

Happy that my parents approved of her, I went with Mother and Dad and my best friend Amy to Sam and Georgia's wedding on August 18, 1956. I wore my best dress, one that Mother had bought for me. It was pink and sleeveless, and I hated pink. I hated sleeveless because I looked fat in sleeveless, because sleeveless showed too much flesh. When Mother first showed it to me, I screamed at her, "I'll never wear that stupid dress!"

But it really was the prettiest dress I had for summer, with its pleated top and billowing skirt, and, strangely, to Georgia's wedding I wore it gladly. We drove to the town where she grew up, a wealthier version of our town. The church was Presbyterian, larger than ours, and every pew was full. I met Georgia's mother, a Scandinavian blonde, and later I would wonder what it might be like to have such a mother, one so much more beautiful than her daughter. I met Virginia, and I was disappointed in Virginia, her dowdy, conventional appearance. I wanted someone more splendid for Georgia to adore.

I don't remember the ceremony. What I've never forgotten is Georgia's face, radiant as she came down the aisle at the close of the service, her arm linked with Sam's, her joy at being married spilling over and filling the sanctuary. Then she turned her splendid smile on us. Of all the people she might have waved to, she waved to us, as if we were the most important people in the church.

September, the beginning of my junior year in high school. Georgia began our study group with prayer, swiveling in her chair to face us. We had gathered in her office, the small, corner room with just enough space for folding chairs to be set up in front of the floor-to-ceiling bookcases on the two back walls. A map of the Holy Land was pinned to the wall to the right of her desk. She kicked off her shoes.

"I trust you don't mind if I'm a bit informal."

Even in her stocking feet she retained her not-to-be questioned authority. We were girls who belonged to the church, serious students, some of us good at sports, all of us Girl Scouts, something the in-crowd had given up in junior high, and we didn't have boyfriends, which meant we had time.

I studied Georgia, assessing her not against some external standard of beauty but only against herself, her own familiar attributes—plain brown hair swept up off her forehead, intense gray-blue eyes, and a serious, even sober demeanor that could break into mischievous scheming or heartfelt laughter. She'd already taught me that a person in her position must not wear big earrings or other adornments that might draw attention and distract from what she was saying. Today she wore a simple blue blouse and small pearl earrings. She was beautiful.

We closed our eyes and bowed our heads. Georgia prayed confidently, as if she expected God to be paying attention to her request for openness and insight. She had us open our Bibles to the Book of Jeremiah and nodded to Doris to begin reading.

Doris was sitting at the end of the row, a self-conscious smile on her chubby, freckled face. The youngest girl in the group, she was happy to be included in this company. She began tentatively. "The words of Jeremiah…"

When we finished, with a commanding voice for God and a stricken cry for Jeremiah, Georgia read the call again. I swallowed the story whole, committing it to heart.

> Now the word of the Lord came to me saying,
> "Before I formed you in the womb I knew you,
>    and before you were born I consecrated you…"

Hadn't I just experienced something like this? Smaller, to be sure, on an entirely different plane, but not completely different. Georgia, almost like God, had, when she read my fire poem, the ability to see what I could not. Georgia understood my affirmation and my plea, interpreting me to myself. Surely this text referred to a related, special kind of knowing. Jeremiah's anguished attempt to avoid being a prophet was a cry with which I could identify because it expressed the terror of being young. *Ah, Lord God! I do not know how to speak for I am only a youth.*

How many times would I claim these words as my own? Georgia wasn't God. But she knew God, his work, his teaching. I could be tongue-tied in her presence, desperately wanted to please, terrified that I would say something wrong. Jeremiah felt the same, didn't know how to speak any more than I did. And God refused his excuses, as Georgia refused mine.

> But the Lord said to me,
> "Do not say, 'I am only a youth';
>    for to all to whom I send you you shall go,
>    and whatever I command you you shall speak.
> Be not afraid of them,
>    for I am with you to deliver you,
>    says the Lord."

The words comforted and thrilled me. *Do not say, "I am only a youth."* Youth was to be taken seriously, right now. I would be taken seriously.

Georgia drove all the girls home before she pulled up in front of my house and parked in her regular place. It was September, almost six. There would be another hour of daylight.

"Come, sit close to me." She patted the seat beside her.

I obeyed. She made me uneasy; a passing car might see us, and what would its occupants think? Why couldn't we just secretly hold hands like we had before? Still, my mother would be in the kitchen and my dad wouldn't be home for another twenty minutes. We were safely alone.

I looked through the windshield to the gray pavement which stretched out ahead of us and curved slightly north. The old elms arched to meet high about the street, a natural soaring like that of a cathedral. I wanted to say this to Georgia, how the trees moved me. But I was afraid I'd sound silly and searched for something else to say, not yet comfortable with silence.

"Nobody ever made the Bible real to me before. You know. That God would call Jeremiah when he was young."

"A youth. Like you."

"Yeah." I wasn't wrong to identify with that passage.

"It still happens," Georgia said. "God still has work to be done. Already I see how he is acting in your life."

"Well, I don't." I was thrilled and embarrassed.

"Look at me." She pulled away, shifted in her seat, her back against the car door, and studied me intently. I thought she could see right through me. I looked away, anxious. I didn't know what she wanted.

I was sixteen years old; it was 1956. Mother had been conscientious and years before, when I was eight or nine, she'd warned me about men, to stay away from the crew working on the railroad. There was a steep incline from the tracks down to the widest street in the village, and I rode my bike there, pretending I was on horseback, charging down the narrow valley, out onto the broad plain. The men on the tracks were friendly, and I told my mother about them.

"You mustn't talk to them," she had said firmly, and she explained to me that I had to be leery of strange men. She never said a thing about women.

"I have to go now," Georgia said softly.

"I know." I turned to her again.

"I want to kiss you goodbye."

She dumbfounded me. I loved holding hands, her confidences, the sweet affection and closeness I found I'd longed for. But they hadn't prepared me; my imagination hadn't known how to go forward to this. I couldn't think clearly, and then I didn't want to. I let my eyes answer her, the flush that rushed to my cheeks.

She did kiss me then, in the dim light of the late afternoon, the shadowed, silent street empty, the arching elms our only witness. She kissed me fully on the lips. I closed my eyes. I let that kiss enter me, all the way down to my toes.

"I love you, Gail," she said, her voice low and sure.

"I know." It was all I could say, but I knew it was enough. I walked up the driveway, into the kitchen and I found myself in my room without quite realizing how I'd gotten there. I hugged myself. Georgia loved me. I loved her. I could say it at last.

Thanksgiving weekend, my parents sent me to visit my sister Carmen at Carleton College in Minnesota where she was a freshman. It was time, they told me, to start thinking about where I would go to college.

Carleton was a serious place. We went to Carmen's history class; we went to the library. Saturday night we double dated. But the details got lost because nothing remarkable happened and what happened next was remarkable beyond belief. I took the train home on Sunday, and halfway there, it started to snow. When we arrived at my station, the final one before Chicago, it was already dark. Descending the stairs, I could make out three people standing on the platform, their shapes blurred by the large flakes falling through soft, yellow station lights. No one else got off. Somebody was with my parents.

Georgia. I was thunderstruck. Over the weekend, and even more on the train, I'd been thinking about her, and here she was, as if I'd made her materialize by the power of my mind.

I hugged all three of them.

"The weather was too bad for Georgia to make it back to the city," Dad said.

"She'll be staying over," Mother said.

"I hope you don't mind," said Georgia.

When we got home, we had a light supper. It was 9:30 already. I put on my pajamas and went to sit on the bed in Carmen's room which was now the guest room where Georgia was staying. I was eager to tell her whatever she wanted to hear about my weekend, even my date the night before, though I knew I'd never see him again.

In her cream-colored dressing gown, her hair not yet unpinned, Mother came to stand in the doorway. She didn't tell me to go to my room as I'd expected. "Georgia, please don't let her bother you," she said. "Send her to bed when you're ready."

"Of course," said Georgia. She was sitting at the little vanity combing her hair, and she thanked Mother for her hospitality.

"Our pleasure," Mother said. "Anytime. Goodnight, now." The two women smiled, and I could tell they really liked each other.

"Goodnight, Mother."

I closed the door so our talking wouldn't disturb my parents, whose bedroom was catty-corner across the hall, and I climbed in bed with Georgia. I was about to tell her my adventures when she put her arm around me and pulled me close. I let myself slip into the quiet she created, lay in her arms like a child, hungry for the affection I hadn't gotten, hadn't known I needed. This was all I wanted, more than I'd dreamed of, this absolute safety. I didn't need to tell her anything, only to stay like this for as long as she'd let me.

When Georgia kissed me that first time in September, it was my first kiss since Jimmy in the cloakroom in kindergarten. With my junior high boyfriend Robin, I just played cards. At a sleepover once, in the eighth grade, Sharon and I had danced to a slow dance. With mutual, silent consent, we danced close, and my body stirred in a new way. But when the song finished—maybe two songs—that was the end of it.

Georgia switched off the light. In the dark, she began to unbutton my dad's old shirt that I wore as a pajama top, the old shirt with the new collar that my mother had attached. I held my breath. With great tenderness, she caressed my cheek and she kissed me, longer than she ever had, her fingers then finding my breast. She did nothing without asking my permission. She was in no hurry. Just as she had read my poem and then my mind, now she read my body, knowing what I wanted before I knew myself.

She whispered, "Don't be afraid. Touch me too."

I unbuttoned silk pajamas, found skin as soft, and felt her nipple rise under my finger. I had never touched my own.

"Don't make a sound," she said into my ear. It went without saying that my parents mustn't know. Not because we were doing anything wrong but because what we did was beyond their understanding.

"My sweet, do you know how I've longed for this?"

Instead of speaking, I snuggled even more tightly against her, and I felt her hesitation. But by this time there was no turning back. Not having words for what I wanted, I asked for it anyway. I took her hand. I couldn't stop myself. I took her hand and put it where there would be no question but that I wanted her to finish what she had quietly, audaciously begun.

She sighed, almost as if I'd frightened her. "My love, are you sure?"

"Yes."

"I love you, Gail. I will never do anything to hurt you."

She sighed again, as if giving up, giving in, as if my action, my affirmation, undermined and then dissolved whatever resolve, whatever constraints she'd sworn to herself to retain.

"Take off your pajamas," she said, her voice calm, accepting, taking charge. I did as I was told, as quickly as I could, fell back on the bed, more than obedient, frantic for her to finish. With the same deep tenderness, full of love, Georgia claimed me, carried me away.

Next morning, I walked in the sun-lit snow to catch the school bus, singing silently with all my heart:

> *When morning guilds the skies*
> *My heart awakening cries*
> *May Jesus Christ be praised.*

# 6

## Will Set You Free

Saturday morning after the March on Washington, after the dozen red roses, I walked down to 110th Street to get the crosstown bus to East Harlem. I had to tell Don the truth, the truth of Georgia. I could think no farther than that.

Don buzzed me into the building and opened the door to the apartment with a big smile. I'd never asked to come over before like this. Even in his bare feet, I had to stretch to hug him. I followed him down the hall into the living room. A big brown easy chair, a high-backed yellow chair in the corner by the windows, and a rust-colored couch against the inside wall stood on the bare linoleum floor. Don and I sat down on the couch.

So as not to lose my courage, I blurted out, "I have to tell you something."

I stared at the opposite wall, the pale, institutional green that covered every interior surface in the entire apartment complex. I wanted him to encourage me. Instead he offered me a cigarette, then lit one for himself when I shook my head, no. I let the burning tobacco smell fill my lungs and kept my face averted. I did not want to cry.

"Is something wrong?" he said, alarmed. "Did I do something…?"

"No!" I said with relief. "It isn't anything to do with you. It's about me. Something you should know about me."

Eight years I'd kept the secret. Eight years. I didn't think of the dean; she didn't count. This was the first real telling, and I saw that it was difficult, like talking to Georgia was sometimes difficult. I could say it wrong. I could wreck everything.

"I have to tell you about a friend of mine. Her name is Georgia." My mouth felt dry and I ran my tongue over my lips. "It's about why I'm in

35

New York, at seminary. It's about why I want to marry you. It's about everything." I laughed to keep from crying.

Don sat very still and waited.

"Georgia Cartwright was the director of Christian education in my church. She came when I was a sophomore in high school. She's had an unbelievable amount of influence on my life, and it's really important that you understand that." I turned to face him, brought my legs up to sit sideways on the couch, putting a little distance between us.

"Okay," he said, puzzled.

"Maybe this will sound weird, but Georgia is married to a minister, and I knew I would marry a minister. Our lives are like that, interconnected. I experience a kind of inevitability in what happens to me. Because it happened to her first." I was evading. "Georgia used to stay overnight at our house—when she had late meetings or the weather was bad. When it was hard for her to get home to Chicago."

Don looked perplexed, as if he didn't understand why I struggled so to speak. He'd also shifted, pulled his left leg up under him and sat sort of off balance, his shoulders at a slant. I thought he looked like Picasso's old guitar player, all angles, bones, and tendons.

"You can't stop now," he said, the tremor in his voice belying his effort to sound casual. "What you have to say can't be that awful."

"It's not awful!" I looked away from him. "We loved each other. We even, for a time, we were … we made love to each other."

I glanced at him. His expression hadn't changed from its puzzled frown. It was as if he expected me to go on. As if he hadn't heard.

"We were *lovers*," I said, meaning to be emphatic, but my voice failed and I could only whisper.

"It's okay," he said simply. His jaw was firm, not tense, as it was when he was anxious or upset. His pale brown eyes were magnified slightly in his thick glasses, and he was looking at me directly, his expression free of shock. He reached for my hand. "It's okay," he said again. "It doesn't matter."

"It's not that I wish it hadn't happened. Knowing her is the most wonderful thing in my life. Before now. We loved each other. We still do."

"Don't worry," he said. "It's good you told me. I guess there's something I should tell you too." He did what I would learn people always did. When I told them about Georgia, they didn't know what to say. They changed the subject, talked about themselves. Told secrets. Don shifted again, stretched his legs out, then slipped down to sit on the floor in front of me.

"What you're saying isn't so unusual. You shouldn't feel bad about it. When I was a kid, I did the same thing with one of the kids on my block. I stayed overnight at his house, and we tried it once. Lots of kids do that. It doesn't matter. Honestly."

I stared at him, astonished. How could he compare his experience—playing in the dark a single time with a kid down the block—to Georgia and me?

"It's not the same," I said, urgently, angrily. Georgia, I didn't know how to make him understand. She was my secret joy, my secret shame, my guide, my keeper, and for years; only I couldn't even say it that clearly to myself, not then, not yet. Suddenly, it didn't matter that he didn't understand. What I said hadn't changed anything. We would hold no secrets from each other. In time, he would come to understand more fully. What mattered now was that he knew.

That night I called Georgia.

"My dear," Georgia said when she heard my voice. "You've been making yourself scarce." Before I could explain, she continued. "You've picked a perfect time to call. The kids are in bed, and Sam's still at a meeting."

Hers was the voice that entered my bones. We chatted easily for a while about the March on Washington. She and Sam had gone but we hadn't even tried to find each other in the crowd.

"Don brought me a dozen red roses," I said. "He was proud of me for going, especially because he couldn't."

"So, he's smitten," she said lightly. "What a lucky, lucky guy."

I gripped the edge of the table. "Georgia, I told him. This morning I told him about you."

I thought I heard her gasp. I rushed to reassure.

"It's okay. He doesn't care. He said it didn't change anything."

I definitely heard her sigh.

When Georgia finally spoke, her voice was calm, as if it came from the part of herself she wanted most to be, as if she was saying lines she had rehearsed a thousand times, preparing for this moment. "My love, get married. Have children. Then I'll know I haven't ruined you."

The tone of her voice—earnest, caring—mattered as much as what she said. I would marry Don. Children were the last thing on my mind. She hadn't ruined me, but I would have to show her that and didn't argue.

We said goodnight and hung up, but she remained with me in the room, her admonition a kind of blessing. She had not been angry with me for telling Don.

# 7

# Becoming Obedient

I had a slumber party on a Friday night in February, and I invited all the girls in Georgia's study group, Sharon, Margaret, Doris and the others. My best friend Amy and I were also in the group, of course, but we were in a secret category. Georgia was staying overnight at Amy's house too.

"It would draw attention to us," Georgia said. "If I only stayed at your house."

I stiffened, not knowing how to react. Everything about Georgia was uncharted, without antecedents, without warning, without rules. She must have seen my confusion.

"This changes nothing. I love you no less. Trust me."

Whatever loss I felt when I learned about Amy was compensated for in a strange way by the gain of a confidante. Amy and I talked about Georgia. Did Georgia do this on purpose? Did she figure that if Amy and I talked to each other we'd talk to no one else?

At the slumber party, I didn't talk to Doris. I kissed her; sweet Doris with her freckles and her fresh, clear laugh. She would save me a seat on the bus, let me crash the lunch line, come to the gym to watch basketball when I was on the court. I liked her attention, returned it, teased her, included her. I'd been well taught. We were in our basement, which we called the rec room, with its pine paneling, Ping-Pong table, and built-in bar.

When I kissed Doris in the dark, underneath the Ping-Pong table, she kissed me back. Somehow, I knew before I did it that she would kiss me back. I liked kissing Doris. It felt like kissing Georgia. Then I knew I needn't stop. I liked knowing that just as much, just as much as kissing her. If I'd continued, she would not have stopped me. I only kissed her.

Did I stop because I had to tell Georgia everything? I was babysitting the next time I saw her, in a house on the other side of the village from my house. The two little boys were asleep, and waiting for her, I imagined what we might do in this elegant room when she arrived. Cold air blasted in when I opened the door. She put icy fingers on my hot cheeks and kissed me before she even got her coat off. Anxious, I told her immediately what I'd done with Doris.

Georgia stepped back from me in the small vestibule where we stood, flattening herself against the outside door, her face lit by the small overhead light as if she'd been arrested and would be interrogated. Her silence sucked my breath away. It couldn't have lasted but a matter of seconds, but it seemed an eternity.

"Never do that again." Georgia looked at me, the affection I was accustomed to replaced by a hard, defensive stare.

"I was just trying…" She'd told me to be nice to Doris.

"I don't care. Never do that again."

She rebuttoned her coat. "I can't stay." She glanced around, as if to make certain that we were alone, and then she was gone.

I stood in the entranceway looking into the interior of the house. The rooms I'd thought modern and sophisticated just minutes before were cold and empty now. I'd never upset Georgia, not like this. Terrified of losing her, I vowed that if Georgia forgave me, I would never risk disappointing her again.

But I couldn't apologize because the next day I got the flu and went to bed, the twin bed on the far side of the room, away from the door. Mother brought me soup, toast, and ginger ale. She was kind to me, as if such indulgence couldn't spoil me when I was sick. I slept and slept, woke to worry about Georgia, if she was still angry for what I'd done. I had no way to let her know I was sick, that I was sorry. I was such a jerk, such a complete and total jerk.

By the fifth day I was feeling better and thought I'd get up after a good nap. Coming out of a hazy dream, I heard voices, the sound of footsteps coming up the stairs.

"You have a visitor," Mother said cheerfully.

Georgia stepped into the room behind her, frowning. Her hair was swept back off her forehead making her face prominent, commanding. "I've come to visit the sick," she said with what I thought was mock seriousness. "Like our Lord taught."

Mother laughed lightly. "Georgia can keep you company. I'll be downstairs making dinner if you need anything."

I held my breath, ecstatic that she'd come, and listened to Mother's steps, down the hall, around the corner, down the stairs. Georgia came slowly past my dresser, my antlers and my cowboy hat, past my desk, around to the side of my bed. Her expression was pious and severe, and it frightened me.

Standing over me, she said, "I've brought my Bible. Would you like to hear some scripture?"

"Sure." She could do whatever she wanted.

Still unsmiling, she pushed with her hand against my legs, which were under the covers, to get me to move so that she could sit down on the side of my bed. Settled, she directed her gaze at me. "You really want me to read the Bible?" Her tone was incredulous, and her face broke into a smile.

"I thought you were serious," I said. She wasn't angry.

"I'm always serious with you. Oh, my dear, how I've missed you."

"Me too." Earth returned to its right orbit. Georgia hadn't banished me.

"Listen to me, my sweet," she said, taking my hand. "There are things I need to tell you." Her voice was insistent. "I have broken it off with Amy, and with Louise. You know I also … with Louise?"

"Yes, you told me." I only knew Louise slightly. We'd met at a regional church gathering. She lived in another town.

"I've told them that I have stopped with all of you. I love them, your smart, silly friend Amy, and sweet, lonely Louise. But it's over with them."

"I understand."

She tightened her grip. "You must keep our secret. Amy mustn't know. I told her it was finished."

"I understand," I said. Then, gathering my courage, "You're not angry?"

She shook her head slowly. "You gave me a scare."

"I'm sorry. I didn't mean—"

"Never mind now. Maybe you saved me from…" She frowned, leaving the sentence unfinished. She let go of my hand. "May I?" She touched my cheek with cool fingers.

I nodded, leaning towards her. Gently, she pulled the covers back, slipped her hand under my pajamas and caressed my breast.

"How are you feeling?"

I just looked at her, knew she would see in my face what she wanted to know, my total adoration and surrender, my body hers, its need now urgent. I was completely beside myself. She had given up the others, cho-sen me. She would make love to me now.

Georgia cocked her head, alert to the possible approach of my mother coming up the stairs. She didn't kiss me, but her hands eased themselves tenderly over my bare skin. I groaned softly; she quickly put a finger to my lips, moving on to satisfy my desire, which she did, sitting on my bed, her Bible beside her on the dark green spread, making a house call, visiting, comforting the sick.

I didn't learn until much later that I was allowed to meet Georgia at the Art Institute because Mother intervened. It was late March, a month after my flu. Georgia had been working for the church for almost a year, and Dad had begun to have doubts about her, that she held me too tightly, had too much sway. Mother was still Georgia's champion, captivated by her intelligence, her knowledge and her magnetism, just as I was. Mother expected Georgia, with her deep commitment to her calling, to be a good influence on me, to calm my anger, to pass on to me her high standards of belief. Mother got more than she asked for. Georgia instructed me in matters small and large.

"You keep your hymnal open, pay attention until the very end, the last words of the last stanza." Once Georgia pointed this out, I could hear what annoyed her, the quiet slap of books being closed long before we'd reached the end of the hymn. When I saw my parents among the offend-ers, I aligned myself with Georgia, judging them and not always silently.

What troubled Georgia even more were the childish beliefs she'd dis-covered in many members of the congregation. "Grown men who run businesses, intelligent women like your mother, their faith is stuck on lit-eralisms they learned in Sunday School. They lack even basic knowledge of biblical scholarship. It's shocking. It's why I went into this field." This I did not repeat to my parents.

On that Saturday in March, Dad dropped me off at the Art Institute on his way to his office on Chicago's South Side. Earlier in the week, I had yelled at him, tears streaming down my face, when he said I couldn't meet her. "When are you going to stop treating me like a child?" He said back in his falsely calm way, "When you stop acting like one." Mother's interven-tion changed things; Dad and I pretended it never happened.

Georgia was standing by one of the big stone lions that guarded the entrance. She greeted me with her knowing smile, her face open, as if she had nothing to hide, and hurried me inside. I'd never seen what she was wearing, a gray wool skirt, long-sleeved white blouse, red blazer, and tiny gold leaf-like earrings. I liked how she looked—casual, relaxed, and with understated wealth. Her running lecture began with the place of David (pronounced the French way, "Dah-veed") in art history as we passed a large painting on the way to the Impressionists. My whole body thrilled. I'd never spent an entire day alone with Georgia. Then, I was afraid. What if I disappointed her?

I followed Georgia into a room which, for the museum, was of modest size with no more than a dozen paintings on its four walls. Two of the walls had doors leading in and out. No one came. It was as if the room were ours, for a private viewing. I didn't question this. I never questioned when I was with Georgia, what she did. I was years away from examining anything about her, the liberties she took, the lies we had to tell, or how we loved each other.

Georgia stretched out her arms, turning slowly as if offering me each painting. "Tell me," she said in a carefree tone, her skirt flaring slightly as she spun, "which is my favorite."

I had no idea. I didn't know how to look at paintings, hadn't had an art class since elementary school. My faced slipped into its deep, worried frown as I began to walk slowly around the room carefully studying each painting, the click of my leather soles against the hardwood floor the only sound. I was conscious that Georgia was standing by the door watching me. I didn't look at her. I could not afford to select the wrong one. Georgia said that we were attuned to each other. Georgia said we knew things about each other we couldn't know if we weren't so attuned. She'd told me that being with me was as good as being alone. I learned that was a high compliment. We didn't need to speak to understand each other. It should have been simple for me to pick her favorite.

Though I have little memory of the others, I can still see one painting, a painting I wished was the one. The colors I remember were deep browns and greens, but it was the subject matter that caught my attention, the startling directness. Lovers, women lovers. They had straight cropped hair. Did Georgia see it as the two of us, here in this public place, on canvas, an image of our intimacy? The figures were fully clothed, but I thought the artist wanted me to know they wouldn't stay that way. I was deeply conscious of prerogatives and suggesting this picture seemed to me to cross a line I was meant to stand behind. I looked at her helplessly.

"Over here, love," Georgia said kindly. She had seen my anguished indecision. She pointed to a painting on a different wall, a woman at a piano. "The artist is Renoir." She smiled at me, acknowledging my silence. "It's all right, my sweet."

Stunned by relief that I hadn't pointed to the wrong picture, and, even more, astonished and grateful for her generosity, I couldn't move for a minute.

We stood together in front of the painting. How could I be so stupid not to figure this out? A young woman sat tall on her piano stool, her full, almost white dress flowing onto the floor around her feet, her hands on white keys, before white sheets of music lit by two white candles. A narrow ribbon ran around her neck, down the front of her dress and around to the back, making a large loop on the pale blue cloth. The piano was dark and upright. We saw her in profile, her cheek rosy, and her eyebrow strong.

Georgia was in profile when she played. I'd watched her again just yesterday.

"I was never good enough for my teacher," Georgia had said. "Miss Petite was an exacting perfectionist with great expectations. She told me I could be a concert pianist if I would work hard enough. She flew into fits of rage if I didn't meet her standards."

George spoke in a way I'd grown accustomed to, her voice losing its authoritative tone when she confided in me.

"The unforgivable sin was playing with emotion she said I had not yet earned. For that I was chastised, banished from her good graces until I played again with proper restraint."

Georgia's hands had gone back to the keyboard, but she didn't play. "Miss Petite also taught me that freedom and discipline are inseparable." She had turned to me, her eyes probing, as if she wanted to make sure I understood. "Who is freer than the virtuoso, a freedom born of decades of diligent work?"

"Is it you?" I asked now, nodding to the painting, grinning. I'd lost my fear of her. She would always come to my rescue.

Georgia laughed quietly. "Well, hardly." Then, after a pause, "Aren't you glad we don't live when women had to dress like that! But you read me well. I wouldn't mind sitting for a painting, a painting like that one."

I met her gaze, held steady. I wanted to say what I'd said a hundred times, that I loved her, that she could trust me. I just looked at her, knowing it would please her more. I didn't have to say it. My eyes brimmed with adoration.

A May afternoon in Georgia's car, parked on a street in the southeast section of the village, a part of town where no one I knew lived. We had three weeks left before she moved. I'd always known; she'd always known this time would come. Sam would graduate from seminary and be called to serve a congregation. They would move away.

Georgia had asked me to come with her as she had an errand to run. She stopped in front of a house. I expected her to get out. She didn't.

"Say it out loud," Georgia said quietly without looking at me. "I want your voice to remember. Say what we do."

Hunkered down, I did what I was told, at first reluctantly, incredulously, and my speaking made the place we sat in, not of this tidy world, this still, spotless, sun-lit street in a part of town where the trees were not yet tall.

"First, I take your face in my hands..."

We sat there, the two of us, as far from each other as any two passengers would normally be, she in the driver's seat, I in what was called, before seatbelts, the suicide seat. We didn't look at each other but out at the clean, empty street.

"I unbutton your starched white blouse, slowly..."

Though my voice was almost without inflection and unnaturally low, I began to sense its potency, kept going.

Georgia said God blessed us.

Georgia said the body was God's good gift.

"I bend down and kiss your nipple..."

What was pornographic, transgressive, I wondered darkly. What I spoke had become like a fire I could not, did not want to douse, yet I was vaguely troubled that this disembodied coupling, however irresistible, was somehow, in a way I did not understand, perverse.

"Then I slip my fingers..."

There in the car, my voice deep down, my words brought us to the end. She wanted to remember everything about me. I never forgot how vulnerable she looked when I finished, or what she said.

"It will be better. You can come visit me. We'll have more time."

# 8

# With Those Who Rejoice

Don and I began our second year of seminary as a couple, which helped to keep my anxiety under control. A Wednesday afternoon in October found us in the library reading Augustine, a section of the *Confessions* for church history. Don was on my left at the long table. It was raining outside; the tall, opaque windows that lined the east wall of the high-ceilinged reading room let in little light. I struggled to concentrate.

I kept reading, paragraph after paragraph, dutifully turning pages. I could not leave until I finished. Conscious of Don's presence, the silence, and the hard, wooden table, I watched the hands on the big clock mark the passage of an hour and a half.

> … happiness is known to all, for if they could be asked with one voice whether they wish for happiness, there is no doubt whatever that they would all say yes. And this could not be unless the thing itself, signified by the word, lay somewhere in their memory.

I sat with my open book. What did this have to do with me, this pursuit of happiness? What about justice? Happiness was for little children. Don saw me looking up and leaned over. I saw him frown before I could tell him I was finished.

"What's wrong?"

"Why are you reading that page?" He showed me the assignment sheet.

I'd read the wrong section. This simple error tapped into what I had no words for, rage and blame. I jammed the base of my thumb into my mouth and bit down as hard as I could to punish myself, to keep from screaming. There were only two ways to be in my moral universe: right and wrong. And I was wrong.

I don't know what Don thought when he saw the deep tooth marks in my hand. He never said. He was not like other men I'd dated. They were manly in monotonous, conventional ways, physical and self-assured. Luke, my college boyfriend, might play football and have the physique of a Greek god, but I was smarter than he was. Onnig, whom I dated my whole year in Beirut, was solid as a rock and would have protected me, but protection can seem like control. What tall, gangly, bespectacled Don had was a mind and hands with long graceful fingers. I came to take pride in his tall frame and to share his disdain for the narrow, crippling definitions of masculinity that prevailed in the culture. Rejecting conventional roles, he would teach music to our children; I would teach them how to throw a ball—though we had many things to do before we would think seriously about children.

In the formal Gothic sanctuary at Union Theological Seminary, its free-hanging Celtic cross above our heads, Don and I wed in May 1964, the pews filled with family and friends, many of them from Chambers Church. The congregation represented where we'd come from and where we were going, in ways we couldn't know yet. James Ault, who was the seminary dean of students, stood ready to conduct the service and lead us in our vows. Melvin Schoonover, pastor of Chambers Memorial Baptist Church, sat in his wheelchair, ready to preach, and Don stood next to them with his best man, his brother Gordon.

Before she preceded me down the aisle, I hugged my sister Carmen. She was my only attendant. Her wedding at Christmas six years before had been Mother's wedding, perfectly staged in our hometown church. This one Don and I planned ourselves and our parents came as guests. Still, I wore my sister's wedding gown, and Mother was astonished that her pleasingly-plump little daughter had grown up to fit into it.

On a visit home, just weeks before the wedding, Mother sat me down on the bed in their guest room, to talk about sex. She was supremely conscientious, and duty required that she teach her daughters the facts of life, which she had done when we were little and then not another word to me until the month before I wed.

Assuming my virginity, she said, "He'll want it. Give him what he wants. You'll find you usually enjoy it yourself."

Knowing a thing or two about enjoying sex, I could have found her ludicrous, her assumptions, her instructions. But we were in an unfamiliar safety zone, my mother and I, given us by my choice of a husband, my gratitude for my parents' approval and for their generosity, and so I found it sweet, what Mother told me, and touching that my parents still did it and enjoyed it. They were fifty-seven years old.

I waited with my father at the back of the sanctuary, took his arm, and we began our long, solemn walk between smiling faces on both sides of the aisle. My father had had to be persuaded that we could wed before we graduated, which wouldn't be for another year. He let himself be swayed because he approved of Don and because saying yes to our marriage relieved him of worries I didn't know he carried.

I hadn't realized what a baffling daughter I was to Dad, and not just because of Georgia, her overpowering presence in my life. I loved things he thought belonged to boys. He had been troubled by my anger. He, and Mother too, had feared I'd never wed. Now he could leave such worries behind. When we reached the front of the sanctuary, before he turned to join my mother in the pew, he kissed me on the cheek, his eyes full of affection.

Don and I were seminary students, which meant that this would be no ten-minute exchange of vows but an hour-long service of worship: hymns, prayers, a sermon, and four passages from the Bible beginning with one from Deuteronomy which includes the happy affirmation that the Lord our God is a devouring fire, a jealous God. What were we thinking?

I did not invite Georgia to our wedding. Ever since I saw her marry Sam, I'd known what I wanted when I wed—a man like Sam and a full church ceremony. It's what she wanted for me, as she told me repeatedly. What pleasure it would have given her to witness our vows. But I did not invite her. I don't remember how I explained to my parents, who were still in touch with her, that she wasn't coming. I do remember my intuition to keep her away, one I trusted instantly, without any second guessing or need for reasons.

Georgia would not have done to me what Virginia did to her. Virginia, her religious teacher, who took her to bed when she was twelve. On the day Georgia married Sam, Virginia asked for sex one last time. "If we do it now that you're an adult, it frees me from having seduced an innocent child." I didn't fear that but I also didn't want Georgia's presence to remind me of that legacy.

Though the paper is stained with time, I can still read our Order of Worship for a service declaring that this faith we'd been born into was to be taken with the utmost seriousness, more radically than our families took it. We had Communion, something not expected at a wedding between a Baptist and a Presbyterian. *Donald and Gail have chosen to celebrate the Lord's Supper as part of this service because it is their belief that through the love of Jesus Christ their marriage is possible.* If this was rebellion, it was rebellion into the fold, into what our parents had claimed to believe, only we would take the faith far more seriously. At Union and at Chambers we had experienced a Christianity that spoke to our minds and our emotions more profoundly than the tidy Protestant practice of our childhoods. That we were sanctimonious in our newfound ardor, we could not see, though we felt free enough to point fingers at the self-righteousness of our parents in their comfortable, segregated, hypocritical churches.

On my wedding day, I was not thinking about Georgia, not even that I was glad she wasn't there. This was for Don and me. We sat together in the front pew to hear Mel preach to the gathered congregation the unbreakable bond between the church and the world, personal faith and public action, love and justice. When it was all done, we rose to sing the hymn adapted from Beethoven's Ninth Symphony, the hymn for joy, "Joyful joyful we adore Thee / God of Glory, Lord of Love." I sang with my whole heart, with the pure innocent elation I had sung with as a child in church, leading the youth choir, marching down the center aisle of the sanctuary.

The first night of our married life, we booked ourselves into the Robert Treat Hotel in Newark, New Jersey, and watched a movie on television, some adventure story set in an unnamed African country. Later, remembering this, we would see it as an omen, but that night we hadn't a clue that within two years we would be living in South Africa ourselves. We watched TV because I'd gotten my period and we decided to wait to make love. I cried when it came, as if the bad timing were my fault.

Lying in bed with Don for the first time, my distress had dissipated. We had just experienced a wedding it was hard for us not to call perfect. I couldn't know how prescient it was to take comfort that night in simple affection. We were on our honeymoon; we had a week; there was no hurry.

The next morning, giddy in love, we drove to Rehoboth Beach, Delaware. Don wore Italian sandals—loosely woven black leather—that made his feet sexy European. He was reading Updike's *Rabbit Run*. As a wedding gift, he gave me *Poems of Doubt and Belief*, co-compiled by our professor Tom Driver, and he wrote in the front, "…our hearts are pounding. I Love You, I Love You, I … Love … You." He read me his favorite, "The Windhover, To Christ our Lord," by Gerard Manley Hopkins.

> *I caught this morning Morning's minion king-*
> *dom of daylight's dauphin, dapple-dawn-drawn Falcon…*

I had a peignoir. I had let Mother buy me a layered, soft, sexy white peignoir. I hadn't even known the word; they didn't teach it in French class. The third night of our honeymoon, when my period was over, I put it on, the skimpy nightgown, the long sheer over-garment, amazed at how it transformed me into a beauty.

"You look, uh, gorgeous!" Don said enthusiastically. He wore brand-new pale blue pajamas, and we got shyly into bed to take off our special garments. We'd filled our days with reading and walking the beach, the boardwalk, going over every detail of our wedding—the service, Mel's sermon, conversations at the reception, including the one in which my mother wished Don well, taking on, as he was, her difficult daughter. I wondered about virginity. I'd never had intercourse with a man. Don was a virgin. He would come to me in his innocence; maybe I could salvage mine.

I wasn't thinking this directly in my overactive brain that night, just that this was ordinary, what people did, marry and make love. We went slowly, and I let him take the lead, as he was the man, after all. Under the covers, lying on our sides, I stroked his back, waiting. I'd never had a lover who was shy like this, who seemed not to know what to do.

"It's not going up," he said, so faintly that it took a moment to register what he meant.

I touched his cheek to calm him.

"I'll go to the bathroom," he said. "I'll see if I can get it to go up."

The rush of affection that filled me can only be called maternal. "No, no, no."

I held him tight to keep him with me, picturing him under the bright bathroom light, masturbating madly to make himself hard, then racing back to enter me, shocked that he would suggest such a thing.

"We have to do this together, love," I said.

"I'm so sorry."

"It's okay."

"I love you," he said, in the voice of a child.

"In the morning," I said. I turned my back to him to snuggle against his long lean body, and we fell asleep like that, like little children.

At dawn we tried again, coming together out of sleep, before gods or goblins could get in our way. Happiness entered our bed, that we could do it, simply, in the morning. We went to breakfast. Walking the boardwalk to our favorite eating place, he grinned like he'd conquered Everest, holding my hand. We ate eggs and bacon, fresh squeezed orange juice, fried potatoes, and the best cup of coffee we'd ever tasted, anywhere.

# 9

## With You Always

I visited Georgia in June, the week after school ended. Sam's new position as assistant minister was in a large and prosperous Presbyterian church just three hours away. I took the train. Sam met me at the station, drove me through winding, tree-lined streets with attractive homes set back on wide green lawns. I was shy with him and happy when we reached their house, which was red brick and substantial.

I sang in my head that song from *My Fair Lady*, about being on the beloved's street and soaring up seven stories. They had a house that was worthy of them. It was like my house—solid red brick with white trim, only it was larger and more square. I almost didn't notice that there were two front doors; from the street one might not even see that it was a duplex.

Georgia was waiting at the front door, arms crossed protectively over her chest, lips closed in a vulnerable, shy smile. She gave me a quick hug. She kissed Sam. I felt no jealousy. I had no name for Georgia and how we loved; I only knew my place, though secret, was secure.

We sat in the living room in chairs opposite each other while Sam ran an errand. She got out her Salems. I reached over quickly to grab the matches, held one for her and tried to keep my hand from shaking. I could see my chivalrous gesture amused and pleased her. She looked lovely, in a neatly-pressed green cotton shirtwaist with a V-neck, a dark green belt at her waist.

"The furniture is all gifts from the congregation," she said when I complimented her on the room. "I'm a poor preacher's wife now. When you don't have much, it doesn't take long to get settled. You can help me unpack the last of the boxes, books mostly." She wanted to get everything in place; she wanted to work.

"They expect the minister's wife to be an unpaid employee," she said.

"I have to tell you that annoys me. Still, I like writing curriculum, and nothing is more important."

When it was time to make lunch, I followed her into the kitchen, emptied the ashtray, rinsed it out, and returned it to the small table. I knew how she wanted to keep her house.

Not until after lunch, after she'd made egg salad for sandwiches, toasted the bread just as Sam came in the door, and we all ate, had an apple at the end, chatted as if the three of us had lunch together all the time, not until after we'd cleared the table and washed the dishes, until she'd kissed Sam goodbye and watched him drive away; not even until sometime after that, when she was certain we would not be disturbed, only then did she take me upstairs to her bedroom, their bedroom. What I remember about that afternoon is the sunshine streaming through white diaphanous curtains that billowed in the soft breeze. We were floating, somewhere in a world all our own. We had hours, and her hands on my cheeks when she first kissed me were sure and warm. A faint trace of perfume lingered in the air. It was as close to perfect as anything I'd ever experienced, making love in the light of day when I could see her face, how innocent and strong it became, lovelier still when I reciprocated, giving her what she'd given me. I knew that afternoon what it was to be completely happy—body and soul one, and satisfied.

Except for the slight stirring of the curtains, the room was silent. It was the quiet I treasured, when nothing was expected of me but to lie with her, to wait for her to determine what we'd do next. I almost dozed so her voice startled me.

"Do you have questions?" she said, stroking the top of my head as I was snuggled down against her breast. "Questions about sex, I mean."

I shook my head. Nothing about this was puzzling.

"Do you have questions," she repeated, "about what it's like with a man?"

She wanted me to talk. It was like the art museum, where I was supposed to know her Renoir. I was as baffled. Sex with a man was the last thing on my mind.

"You can ask me anything."

I didn't see what Georgia needed. Years before, Georgia had had questions and Virginia wouldn't talk to her. Georgia was going to do better by me, but how could she if I wouldn't play my part properly?

Finally, because I was stubbornly, protectively still, she said, "Well, it's very different. Sex with a man is very different."

I had no idea what she meant. But I would remember her comment, which really told me nothing. A decade later I'd wonder what she'd have said if I hadn't been such a coward, if it possibly could have helped us.

The next morning, after Sam left for the church, we sat on the living room couch, she with her coffee and cigarette, her new recording of *La Boheme* on the phonograph. With the libretto open on our laps, we followed along, Georgia singing out her favorite lines.

> *Chi son? Sono un poeta*
> *Che cosa faccio? Scrivo...*

And how do I live? Like *da gran signore.*

Her pleasure in the music made me happy. She stood to turn the record over, held the disc above the player carefully in both hands, then hesitated and set it down. She turned to me, an expression on her face I couldn't read.

"Love, I have something to tell you." She came to where I sat and looked down at me. "I'm going to have a baby."

"That's wonderful!"

"Yes, it is wonderful. But … I don't know what to do."

"About what?" Had I said the wrong thing?

"Are you sure…?"

"Tell me."

She lowered herself carefully, looking away. "My guilt has become almost unbearable."

She had never said anything like this.

"Sam. It's worse because I'm pregnant. Loving you, I'm unfaithful, betraying him."

I was seventeen years old. It was 1957. I was simply, impulsively ingenuous, without a clue. "Tell him," I said. All I could think of was that Sam was no threat to me. I was no threat to him. Especially now, with a baby coming, if she could just tell Sam she loved me, we could all live happily ever after.

Was it punishment for my foolishness? She couldn't tell him. What she could do, did, was to pressure me to stay longer than I'd planned. She talked me into calling home, provoked an argument.

After Mother heard me out, she said, "Do what you want." She didn't mean it, but she was afraid of my anger and wouldn't insist.

If she said I could do what I wanted, I would, and did. It was the beginning of a pattern. Near the end of every visit Georgia made me demonstrate that I would defy my parents and choose what she wanted. I wasn't ready to wonder why she made me suffer my parents' displeasure, or what good it did her to alienate them.

November, my senior year in high school, I went for a weekend to meet the baby, little Joel, just three weeks old. Joel, asleep in his crib in the guest room, while Georgia and I made love on the bed beside him and she insisted that we stay completely under the covers.

"He might wake," she said. "You never know what might make an impression on him."

Her caution seemed extreme, though I did what she said. She was attentive to her little boy, tender, not exactly anxious but absorbed in a way I had never witnessed before.

The next afternoon while Joel slept, Georgia sat on the stairs and I sat above her. I liked the feel of her red jersey, the soft fabric against my fingers as I worked to loosen the tension from her shoulders.

"I look at my baby sleeping," she said. "I watch him in Sam's arms. How has it come to this, that I should know such grace, when I committed...?"

She didn't finish her sentence but I knew the ending. "Don't," I said. "Don't do that to yourself."

"I'm living a lie with Sam." Her voice broke as if she was close to tears. "It's worse now that Joel..." She bent forward, out of reach.

If Joel made it worse ... I said what sprang impulsively to my loving, logical mind. Nothing to do with morality, adultery. I couldn't stand to see her suffer.

"Let's stop," I said strongly. "Our love's not dependent on that."

Georgia sat up straight on the stair below me. Georgia got quickly to her feet. My mind raced. She could become an honest woman, without secrets, for the first time since she was twelve. She would turn now, utter a gigantic sigh of relief and embrace me for setting her free.

Leaning heavily on the hand railing, Georgia descended the stairs. At the bottom, she turned and looked up at me, confusion and alarm on her face.

"You don't want to make love anymore?" she said slowly.

"Not if it hurts you so."

She turned her back. It took me a minute to realize that I had said the wrong thing. The next hours were as long and heavy as days and weeks.

She didn't speak to me, and her shunning took away the ground I stood on and the air I breathed. We went out in the car, but driving, we might as well have been in different vehicles, different cities. I didn't know how to reach her or how to defend myself. *Can't you see that my intention was loving, to ease your pain? Why do you need sex with me? Is what you need all that matters?* I could not say any of this.

I don't remember what happened when we got back to the house. I only know that we continued to be lovers and that I learned, again, never to assert myself until I was certain of what she wanted me to say.

"Don't read this until you're on campus," Georgia said.

I was about to head off to the University of Colorado at Boulder, the only school I applied to, Georgia's alma mater. She'd just presented me with a red-and-white-striped flannel nightshirt she'd worn in college, and now she handed me a letter. Though I would tell people I chose CU because of its stellar history department, I chose it because Georgia went there; Georgia studied history there.

I wore that nightshirt until it shredded and I read the letter she gave me that day in late August until I knew parts of it by heart. Obedient still, I waited to read it for the first time until I got to college.

> You will know days of despair, desire, and desperate seeking; you will be lonely even in groups and with many friends; and all this will grind you and mold you and crush you with a capacity for compassion for your fellows that will almost excruciate you.

Sitting in the protection of my dorm room or walking across campus under the big sky in view of the Flatirons at the foot of the range, Georgia's words played in my mind, explaining me to myself. I didn't know what to do with how I felt, and Georgia showed me. Yes, I wanted to have compassion for my fellows, and if it took that—despair and desperate seeking—so be it.

I understood Georgia's words rather like the foreign films I saw with Luke. We started dating in November, after the football season was over. He played second-string and was movie-star handsome—Gregory Peck with big black glasses. Not only that, he was older, quiet, and more mature. On our first date, Luke took me to see Bergman's *Wild Strawberries* in black and white with subtitles. Afterward we drank beer in a popular gathering spot called The Sink and struggled with the film's meaning. I liked sitting with Luke because people noticed us. My roommate Tami said he looked like a Greek god. This gorgeous guy was my date.

"Tell me about Europe," I said. He'd been in the army, traveled.

Luke shook his head in disappointment. "The guys on the base just wanted to hang out. I could never get anybody to travel with me. I went alone—Munich, northern Italy, Switzerland."

He told me about castles and cuckoo clocks, German forests and Italian motorbikes.

I told him I wanted to go overseas. "I'm going to apply for a junior year abroad program. I want to go to Lebanon." I wanted to impress him and didn't say that when it was first suggested to me at church that I go to Beirut, I had to run home to look it up in the atlas. Anyone could go to Europe. The Middle East sounded exotic, and I liked it that Luke knew where Lebanon was.

"When I traveled," he said, "I must have gone inside a hundred cathedrals."

"You're joking!" It impressed me that he would visit churches.

He shrugged, smiled. "Not a hundred. But lots. I'm studying architecture."

He walked me to my dorm. He kissed me goodnight and he left. I sat right down and wrote Georgia that I had a boyfriend.

Georgia wrote right back. She was delighted and had happy news of her own. A new friend had come into her life, a woman named Rose. Rose was a nurse. She had a lovely voice and sang in a chorus. She was engaged to be married. Georgia told me that I had to come to visit at Christmas. She couldn't wait for Rose and me to meet.

Two days after Christmas, I took the train to Georgia. Rose and I sat at the little kitchen table while she made coffee, and I could hear in Georgia's voice, see in the affection in her eyes that having both of us in her presence made her immeasurably happy.

I watched how at ease the two women were with each other. Rose was older, maybe thirty-five, and graceful, with long blonde hair wrapped around her head in a thin braid. Her skirt was long and her blouse buttoned tightly at the neck and cuff.

I wanted to tell her that except for the diamond engagement ring she wore, she looked like she belonged on a nineteenth-century homestead. As if she were reading my mind, Georgia said, "Rose is a Mennonite."

"Music brought us together," Rose said. "Our friend Anna, the cellist, introduced us."

They chatted about Anna and chamber music. I thought Rose was beautiful. I already knew from Georgia's letters that although they were deeply drawn to each other, Rose was no threat to me. They were not and would not be lovers. I understood the power of this friendship for Georgia. Love without sex, so love without guilt.

And then Georgia's little boy Joel, fourteen months old already, cried, and the three of us went to him, Rose holding him as if she had held hundreds of little people. We sat while Georgia got him a bottle and fed him. A quiet peace settled on the room, mother and child and two adoring friends.

I carried all this back to college with me, reread the letter Georgia had sent me off with.

> I don't know, Gail, why we have come together as we have. But I believe most sincerely that God is active in our relationship. I will always honor it. I will never understand it.

I took her at her word, and right then I understood what Georgia needed to assuage her terrible guilt without denying her terrible need for me. I wrote to her immediately. *If you need to, tell Rose about us.*

Georgia blessed me for giving my permission. She told Rose everything. Rose listened without judgment. I was thrilled that I'd gotten it right, giving permission. It was the beginning of a new time. Rose would become almost a member of Georgia and Sam's family, like I had naively thought I might be. Sam would counsel Rose about her fiancé who had put off marriage for seven years, and Rose would finally find the courage to break with him. She helped with Joel and the other children as they came along, Georgia's anchor and Sam's friend too.

I have no clear memory of when, but Georgia and I ceased having sex, maybe just a few months later, before I went to work at camp for the summer. I didn't connect this change to Rose's arrival, her presence somehow making it possible for Georgia to let go of me, at least sexually. What I do remember is that in the winter of my freshman year I was glad that Rose knew about us. For the first time, someone else appreciated my place in Georgia's heart.

Descending a hill near the CU student union on a snowy Saturday morning, thinking about Luke, his unassuming steadiness, I wasn't watching where I stepped. I slipped, fell backwards on the ice and whacked my head on the pavement. I got up slowly, brushed myself off and kept going. It wasn't until I sat in the theater that night and needed to read the program that I felt queasy. Luke and I were seeing a live performance of Graham Greene's *The Potting Shed*. The queasiness only got worse as the play unfolded, and I wondered for the first time if I might have hurt myself when I fell and hit my head.

Fighting nausea, I was determined to stick it out until the end of the first act. Right before the curtain came down for intermission, I heard a line of dialogue that I never forgot. Someone has died, and a woman character speaks: "I am not yet strong enough for sympathy."

Once we were outside, I grasped Luke's arm, dizzy. "I was afraid I'd be sick."

He took me to the health center.

I did have a concussion, which in time healed itself. I never forgot that line from the play, though it would be years before I figured out why I remembered. To be strong enough for sympathy, one has to acknowledge that one has suffered something—loss or harm—something calling forth compassion. I could not do that, not for years. I would be strong enough to do many things. I had a big voice, a big personality, and people often thought, as I wanted them to think, that I was strong. But to be strong enough for sympathy, I had to acknowledge what had happened to me, find language for it. That line from the play, remembering it, was a beginning.

For months, I'd ignored the fact that I stopped menstruating when I arrived in Colorado. At the beginning of my sophomore year, after nine months had come and gone, my roommate Tami decided I was having a baby elephant since elephant gestation takes twenty-four months. By this time, I was having trouble zipping up my skirts, and it could have been said that I looked pregnant. She organized a baby shower with funny animal presents and suggested that I get myself promptly to a doctor.

At the campus health center, I told Dr. Winter, an old rumpled man, why I'd come.

He said immediately, "Do you have any reason to be worried?"

I looked at him, puzzled.

"Do you have a boyfriend?"

"Yes."

Not until I was back in the dorm did it dawn on me. He wanted to know if Luke and I…. Of course not. Once, on a long, late night drive home from a visit to his parents in Nebraska, Luke pulled off the road.

He had one of those cars with seats that went flat like a bed. The highway, the land around us, was empty for miles and miles. We'd never had such privacy, had only danced close and kissed. Now we both struggled to open jackets, find flesh, only Luke wanted what I'd never given.

"We're not married," I said, stopping us.

I would have claimed pregnancy, the danger of it, if he'd insisted. My deeper, hidden fear, despite my desire for him, was something else. I was not yet prepared to discover what sex was like with a man.

Dr. Winter examined me and told me to see my doctor as soon as I got home for Christmas. He suspected an ovarian cyst, something the clinic was not equipped to handle. His diagnosis was correct, and I had surgery during semester break to remove the cyst, the ovary it had destroyed, and my appendix while they were at it. After a week in hospital, I rested at home.

Georgia brought Rose with her when she came to pay a sick call. Mother had never met Rose, and they seemed to like each other immediately. At lunch, Georgia and Rose filled the house with warmth and laughter. I lay on the couch and told them to stop their joking. My vertical scar was four and a half inches long and it hurt like hell to laugh. Just before they left, as if it had been planned in advance, Rose engaged Mother in conversation in the front hall so that Georgia would have a minute with me alone.

She sat on the coffee table next to the couch and smoothed out the afghan that covered my legs, looking away from me. I thought she was going to tell me that my surgery had scared her because she couldn't stand the thought of losing me. Something like that. I wanted to take her hand; I was afraid of Mother.

Georgia lowered her head to face me. "You must never think that what we did, this surgery. It has nothing to do with what we did."

I sensed what she needed me to say. "Of course not."

Later, I wondered if she blamed herself. I never asked. I never told her that what she accomplished that winter afternoon was to make that crazy notion real. I might have been coming to this myself, but her saying it hurried the process, planted the idea in fertile soil where it took root, went underground, spreading, hibernating, coming back to life at unpredictable times and places.

I flew back to Boulder on Friday and moved into my new room, which I would share with Tami and Pat. The three of us had been counselors first semester in freshman dorms. We were all on the dean's list and members of SPUR, the sophomore honorary association. They were the best friends I would have in college though only one friendship would endure. At graduation, I couldn't have guessed which one.

While I was away having surgery, Pat and Tami had taken the bunk beds and left the single for me. On Sunday night, I sat on my bed, pulled off my slacks, and discovered that my left leg was deep red in color and badly swollen. In the morning, I went first to the administration office because it was closer to my house than the clinic and reported in to the new dean, the one who had approved my application to the junior year abroad program that would send me to Beirut. He'd given me permission to miss two weeks of class. More than that, I would have been required to drop out for a semester. I couldn't drop out if I was going to go abroad.

I walked from the dean's office to the health center with my schedule in hand, all papers properly signed, across the snow-covered campus, alert to patchy ice on the walks. Dr. Winter took one look at my leg and admitted me to the clinic; I had a blood clot in my left thigh. I couldn't grasp that I suffered a real threat to my heart any more than I had been able to appreciate the seriousness of my surgery. A kid I'd known from my summer job at camp wrote me a get-well card. "How can you be in the hospital? I thought you had a wrought iron stomach?" I howled in delight. Exactly what I wanted people to think of me.

I started receiving Coumadin, was released from the clinic and returned daily for a blood test to determine how much of the anticoagulant I needed. My arms, with blue bruised veins, came to look like those of a junkie, though I didn't know the word yet. Hungry for sympathy, I didn't know what to do when I got it and insisted I was fine, as if the surgery, the clot, the daily taking of blood didn't faze me. Then, one night when I was getting ready for bed, I discovered my arm was still bleeding from the needle that morning. I tied a wet washcloth over it and went to sleep. In the morning, the cloth was blood saturated, and I was again admitted to the clinic.

It went on like that all semester. I went to class; I was readmitted and missed class. I had to drop one course, but managed to earn twelve credits, the required lower limit and I got A's because all I could do was study. Tami had a car and could have driven me to the clinic when it was hard to walk, but I called a taxi. I didn't know how to ask for help, was afraid of offending, presuming. Why was all this happening to me? Better not to get anywhere near that question. Tami didn't visit me often in the clinic and neither did Pat, which hurt me though I said nothing. Luke was my most faithful companion, which increased my affection for him, though I'd come to realize something was missing in our relationship. I knew what it was to be in love. I wasn't in love with Luke.

When I was in the health center, my parents phoned regularly, but Mother did not come. I think she didn't come because she was afraid I didn't want her. I wanted her though I couldn't ask. I'd turned twenty. To be able to ask for my mother, I would have had to have a different childhood. Maybe, if Georgia hadn't come to town, Mother and I would have grown closer as I grew up. I know it's what she wanted. Years later, when we spoke about this time, she chastised herself. "Why didn't I come to be with you? What kind of mother was I?"

I had to wrap my leg—my calf and thigh—in Ace bandages. In the summer, I would be fitted with a thick, expensive, elastic stocking that I would wear for several years. I was told I would never ski, that my athletic days were over, but I didn't take that seriously. I had to walk slowly and with care.

On a bright April day, coming down Broadway to our house, I saw Tami standing in the entranceway, waving at me.

"You have a telegram!"

I ran. For the first time since surgery, swollen leg be damned.

CONGRATULATIONS ACCEPTED BEIRUT COLLEGE FOR WOMEN
   LETTER FOLLOWS

I shrieked. I laughed. I sat down so I wouldn't jump up and down. I was going to Beirut for my junior year in college.

I phoned my parents who were happy to hear such good news. I called Georgia, who couldn't stop saying how proud she was. I remembered her letter, how she'd ended it.

> And one day you will bless God even for the wretchedness you find in your life for with it will come goodness. You will have a big life, Gail. Hard, demanding, but satisfying your desire for meaning and beauty and courage.

Would it have been better for me if Georgia hadn't written that letter? I cherished the letter: I loved her for writing it, and in so doing, I again gave myself away. Reclaiming myself would require wrestling with cause and effect. To the extent that what she said was true, I'd have to first discover and then accept that her saying it wasn't what made it so. Not only that. I'd have to discover and accept that her having said it didn't make it a lie. It would take decades to trust that it was not her prerogative to validate nor was it in her power to falsify whatever meaning and beauty and courage I would, indeed, find in my life.

That April day in 1960, when the telegram arrived, all I could think of was that, yes, my big life was about to begin.

# SECTION II

# In the Wilderness

# 10

# Neither Jew nor Greek

In 1966 in the Northern Transvaal of South Africa, we had to assume that our mail might be read. As *Mufundisi* and *Jefro*, chaplain and chaplain's wife, at Lemana Training Institute, we were the only Americans and we were watched. When a box containing *The Autobiography of Malcolm X* arrived some months into our tenure, we were amazed it got by the censors.

Lemana was a high school and teacher training college which had been founded by Swiss missionaries in 1906. Don was in class teaching church history. I sat in an old canvas director's chair on the back veranda of our sprawling old house and read *The Autobiography*. My last year at seminary, with other students from Union and Columbia University, I'd helped organize a Southern Africa Committee. Students who'd been engaged in work on civil rights expanded our concerns to include the liberation struggles in southern Africa. It was work on this committee that had gotten us to South Africa. But nothing I did seemed an adequate response to the brutal presence of apartheid.

One thing I did was teach catechism, and I was supposed to be preparing for the next day's lesson in Shingwedzi, an even more remote school an hour to the east. I couldn't put the book down. Malcolm zeroed in on what it was like to be the only black kid in a white town in Michigan, the obliviousness of his so-called friends and neighbors. His town could have been the town where I grew up. There was one black girl in our class. I wanted to identify with Malcolm, since we were the only Americans at Lemana. I understood, reluctantly and sharply, that Malcolm's solitary experience and our own were fundamentally different. No matter how much we were outsiders, we couldn't escape that we were white, identified, like it or not, with the powerful, the privileged, even the oppressor.

Malcolm's book was an urgent message from a teacher. I was well trained to get from a teacher what I was supposed to think, but Georgia was back in a place like Malcolm's town, unable, I thought, to imagine our life. She couldn't answer what I needed to know—what could I do here that mattered, and was there a role for me in the revolution brewing back home?

The veranda where I sat was screened, and just outside an elephantine tree struggled against the rope-like vines that bound its limbs. Beyond a small lawn and sloping rock garden, the high escarpment dropped down to farmland. It was impossible to tell from where I sat that the land had been carefully divided by the government to separate the Tsonga from the Venda and both from Europeans. I didn't pay attention to the knocking, just a branch against the zinc roof. I read in a state of guilt and anxiety, needing to find out if Malcolm would spurn all of us who were white and had grown up with advantages. Except that the knock came again, faint but insistent. Grudgingly, I got up and went to the side door off the living room. Two girls I recognized but did not know by name stood close together, heads bowed, and eyes to the ground, presenting to me the tops of their skulls, barely covered with close shaved hair.

"*Avexeni,*" I said. I was having as much trouble learning Tsonga as I'd had learning Hebrew, afraid to draw attention to myself in error. But I could at least say hello.

"*Avexeni, Jefro.*"

By now I knew that requesting a favor from a white person was, for most students, an abnormal, terrifying prospect. My job was to figure out what they wanted, and I guessed correctly that they needed to use the telephone. They came to me because the only phone on campus that wasn't controlled by the school authorities was on our veranda wall. I cranked the phone, got the operator, and helped them make their call.

Returning to my chair, I wanted to throw something. The girls thanked me with the curtsy that I knew was meant to show respect, but to me was servile and obsequious. I didn't want their excessive gratitude but something that was impossible: their friendship.

Don and I had come to South Africa at the invitation of Francois and Molly Bill, South Africans who had spent the previous year studying in Chicago. They belonged to the Swiss Mission/Tsonga Presbyterian Church and knew Lemana needed a chaplain. They also understood that the position would give us cover for our real work: learning about race in South Africa and American complicity with apartheid. They lived just down the road from Lemana, at Elim Mission, and they would become our closest friends.

We were not missionaries; we emphatically rejected the title. But few at Lemana, black or white, understood this. South Africa was like that then: things were and were not what they seemed. We lived in the mission house, after all, a long, low building with red waxed floors, plastered yellowed walls, that wide veranda encircling the house with its worn red zinc roof.

Bright purple bougainvillea bloomed just outside the window above the kitchen sink. We did the washing up ourselves, to the consternation of our closest neighbors, single white women, one a teacher and one a Swiss missionary who told us washing up was servants' work. From the kitchen window, we could see the rows of aloes which separated the dirt road from the avocado grove and grape arbor. Our Swiss predecessors had been serious gardeners.

We may not have been missionaries, but a demanding array of duties came with Don's title, Mufundisi, duties previously performed by missionaries, and then by white South African pastors. My sometimes shy, anxious, awkward husband had status bestowed on him. From the first day, he took up his tasks with enthusiasm: teaching, preaching, and leading worship, in addition to overseeing Lemana's buildings and their maintenance.

Just before school started, I joined a group of women to clean the chapel. A substantial European-style stone structure with a pitched roof and bell tower, the pews, pulpit, floor, and lectern were covered with bat droppings, and there were huge spider webs in all the corners, as the church had been closed over the long summer, Christmas holidays. When Molly Bill introduced me to the gathered women, they seemed surprised that I'd come to help and incredibly shy. I was happy to be useful and amazed when Molly made something of it.

"You've broken a barrier already by taking up a mop," she said, "and getting your hands dirty. European women don't do that! It means a great deal to the African women."

I may not have been supposed to take up a mop, but I quickly learned what no one bothered to tell me ahead of time: I had a set of required duties that were as obligatory as Don's. On the first Wednesday after classes began, mid-afternoon I responded to a knock on the door. Five village women greeted me and came right in. Mrs. Khosa, whom I'd met when we cleaned the chapel, and who spoke English, came next and entered just as boldly. I stood numbly to the side as more and more women made themselves at home in my living room, filling all the chairs and spreading out onto the floor—village women with bare feet, metal bracelets on arms and legs, colorful blankets pulled around their shoulders, and educated women from Lemana. I counted twenty-three before Mrs. Khosa called the meeting to order.

"What will you teach us today, Jefro?"

It took a minute for me to grasp that they expected me to teach knitting and crochet. Why had no one told me about what was obviously an institution at Lemana?

"I don't know how to knit," I said. "I don't know how to crochet." I didn't say I thought it rude of them to just burst in like this. I didn't say I considered handcrafts a kind of feminine work that was beneath me.

Mrs. Khosa translated what I'd said and had to explain to me the collective shock. The women had never met a white woman without these skills. Then, the shock was mine. They all brought out their handwork; they didn't need anyone to teach them. What was going on?

Next day, I knew I was expected at the chapel because Mrs. Nkhondo had been kind enough to tell me, to explain to me that I, as Jefro, was president of the women's prayer meeting, *Vamanana Va Xiknongela*. Mrs. Nkhondo was the wife of the science teacher and she'd given me a list of speakers for the month. I was number one.

Many of the women who filled the first two pews below the lectern had come to my house the day before. They were Lemana women, teachers' wives and members of staff and village women from up the road, and everything was in Tsonga. After a Bible reading, it was my time to speak.

I told the story of Mel Schoonover, pastor of Chambers Memorial Baptist Church in East Harlem. Mel's story was a way to introduce Don and me to the women. Mel was white like we were. He'd taken over a dying church—the white congregation had fled the city—and brought it back to life with new members from the neighborhood who were black and Puerto Rican. In the church, we all believed, race didn't matter.

"Mel is in a wheelchair," I said. "He has a condition from birth that prevented his legs from growing normally." I waited while Mrs. Mathebula translated. "He was so determined to meet people that he left his wheelchair at the bottom of the stairs in a tenement house and bumped himself up the stairs on his behind. Then he'd reach up and knock on doors and invite people to church." I told Mel's story because it let me talk about race relations in the United States and how the Civil Rights Movement was working to overcome prejudice and inequality.

Mrs. Mathebula got into it, speaking with great feeling and expression, making the story her own.

"I am so grateful," I concluded, "that you have welcomed me into your circle and I look forward to working with you."

Mrs. Mathebula asked if anyone wanted to respond.

An older woman rose up, gripping the back of the pew in front of her, a white kerchief wrapped round her head, her face stern. She began to berate the women. "The cripple did so much and you do nothing!"

Stunned, I wanted to object. Mrs. Mathebula and the others looked chastened. Then three women prayed for rain. We closed with song.

"It's worse than I thought," I said to Don at dinner. "This woman at the end was full of judgment and shaming. Who did she learn that from?" I said sarcastically. "I can't stand these hangovers from the missionaries. I can't stand it that they expect me to be the president of the prayer meeting even though I can't speak a word of Tsonga. And why do the women assume they can barge into my house like that? Didn't the previous women set any limits? Are missionary wives supposed to be walked over without complaint?"

We were not missionaries but we did what many missionaries do: Bible study. When we issued the invitation, we hadn't known if anyone would come. We'd waited until the rains—desperately needed and late to arrive—had finally let up. On a Tuesday night, we opened our home and come they did, Mr. and Mrs. Nkhondo, Mr. and Mrs. Mabyelane, Louise Ulrich, and Adrienne Lambercy. We were never more than eight and sometimes as few as four, but at Lemana it was the only time we were with Africans and Europeans in about equal number and, we believed, on equal footing.

The night was dark and filled with the steady strum of invisible creatures outside the room where the eight of us sat around our low table at the back of the house, hidden from view of anyone passing in front though no one passed by at this hour. I served tea and what I had learned to call *biscuits*.

Louise, our nearest neighbor, who was from Zurich, worked with village women on small income-generating projects. She sat in a low chair that suited her short stature, her black hair falling from a loose bun, giving her an untidy appearance. Alternately patronizing and generous, she offered to begin reading. "From the first chapter of Galatians: 'I am astonished that you are so quickly deserting him who called you in the grace of Christ and turning to a different gospel—not that there is another gospel, but there are some who trouble you and want to pervert the gospel of Christ. But even if we, or an angel from heaven, should preach to you a gospel contrary to that which we preached to you, let him be accursed.'"

"Do you see what I see?" Don said, smiling. It was safe to smile because Mr. Mabyelane was nodding his head quietly, and everyone seemed engaged. Wondering who would speak first, I knew it would not be Mrs. Nkhondo or Mrs. Mabyelane. Though we'd cleaned the church together and been in prayer meetings, they remained diffident, waiting, I imagined, for their husbands to begin.

"The Afrikaners call themselves the new Israel," Mr. Mabyelane said. "God's chosen people." He taught math in the secondary school and was a man of modest temperament, at least in our presence. Handsome, his skin touched with gold in the lamplight, his voice was neutral, but his eyes were angry.

"We are all equal children of God," Adrienne said, "but here, well, we all know how the government separates everyone into categories." She was sitting next to me so I could only see her sharp-featured expression in profile. Also a Swiss missionary, she was the opposite of Louise—tall, slender, pale, with gray hair cut short, and French-speaking from Geneva. An expert seamstress, she taught sewing and pattern-making at the school.

The silence that followed was awkward. I passed the plate of biscuits.

Mr. Nkhondo, a friendly, homely man, came to the rescue, wanting to make sure that Don and I understood how separate development worked here at the school. "Lemana used to have students from the whole Northern Transvaal—Tsonga, Venda and Sotho," he said. "Now only the Tsonga are allowed." He lowered his voice. "They pit us against each other with their perverted Gospel."

By hour's end, it seemed our ability to be together was reaching its limit but everyone was glad to have come. Don closed with prayer, expressing the collective sense of gratitude.

"Thank you, Mufundisi," Mrs. Nkhondo said to Don, making the little curtsy that women always made when they shook hands with someone. "Thank you, Jefro," she said to me. Her quiet way reminded me of

Mrs. Waters in my Bible study group in East Harlem. I had worried that those women were too deferential. I hadn't begun to appreciate the possibilities of deferential.

"Please," I said, "call me Gail." Though I kept asking, no African woman at Lemana ever did.

Once we were alone again, Don and I lit cigarettes and evaluated the evening. We took the study of the Bible with the utmost seriousness since it was, we believed, the word of God. We were learning what the Europeans in the room had known for decades and the Africans for their whole lives, that social intercourse between the races was deeply curtailed and often reticent when it did occur.

"I keep thinking," I said, "of that day we cleaned the chapel. Molly told me how significant that was, absolutely not what the women expected. Maybe that's why they were free to come."

I had rolled my eyes when Molly said what she did, as I'd done nothing praiseworthy, was grateful that the women didn't reject me outright because I was white. Having Africans in our home, against all expectations and at a risk we did not yet understand, did for me the same thing that working with the women had done. It validated that I was a good person. That I needed such validation was complicated enough, but only half of it. I didn't speak of this to Don because I didn't consciously admit it to myself, but I loved being told that I had done something extraordinary, that I was different, better than other Europeans.

Not at Lemana, but years, decades later, I would finally see something else. Georgia taught me and I believed that God chose us, blessed us especially. Just like the Boers believed.

Don and I took turns driving the sometimes cattle-clogged, rutted dirt road to the closest town, Louis Trichardt, which was seventeen miles northwest of Lemana. It was my week to shop, and I climbed into our little blue Datsun pickup and headed out, driving through the school campus, past the brilliant flame tree, the fragrant oleanders, down the steep road by the mill, passing women coming up with staggering loads of mealie meal on their heads.

The drive to town gave me time to think. When the government had taken over all the mission schools in 1954 to tighten control over African education, the Swiss had negotiated to continue providing the school chaplain. Although it had been my connections that had gotten us to South Africa, and although Don and I had identical qualifications, I had to accept what everyone had assumed: he would have the post at Lemana. Though I continued to have my two weekly meetings with the women, that was the only time I saw them and none of them were becoming friends. I hadn't understood the obstacles to friendship. I was Jefro. I was white. I spoke only English.

Molly, who was becoming a real friend, spoke fluent Tsonga and knew how to knit and crochet. I thought about her as I drove toward town, watched a distant rain squall spread streaks across the sky like stains on a gigantic mirror. Molly had asked Angie, the woman who had worked for her for years, to send her baby, who was crawling now, back to her village. Molly made the request, which was really an order, because it was a nuisance to have the baby underfoot. As shocking as this seemed to me, I fought back my judgment because I knew where Molly came from. At her parents' home in the city, Africans were not allowed to enter, except if they were servants, and only through the back door. Marrying Francois, the son of Swiss missionaries who had grown up in the bush, whose playmates were African kids, and who always knew the language, Molly had had to change her life radically.

I pulled over to pick up a small group of people walking along the road who flagged me for a ride. An older man and a teenage boy climbed in back, and I managed to convince the old woman to ride in the cab with me and helped her up. She was barefoot, with slim metal bracelets up her legs, layered cotton skirts, and a thin shawl tied at her shoulder. When she spoke to me, I thought it was Venda, not Tsonga, and we settled into silence as we drove past clusters of cattle and fields of mealies. After about twenty minutes someone banged on the roof of the cab to tell me they wanted out. They thanked me and headed off on an almost hidden path toward the mountains. Getting back in the cab, I thought that perhaps this was the most important thing I would do all week, give a few Africans a lift.

I struggled with Molly's decision to send Angie's child to the village. In the coming years, she and Francois would grow in courage, grappling with what they'd inherited and deepening their commitment to change. Molly would expand her remarkable linguistic skills, training teachers to teach several African languages. And Francois, using the power of the prophetic church to fight apartheid, would finally be imprisoned on the pretext of a prayer he'd written. I couldn't know this yet. Driving to Louis Trichardt that morning, I wanted there to be a special place in heaven for people like Molly, a place where one was judged not by an absolute standard of right and wrong but by how far one had advanced from where one began. Molly wasn't the only one who needed such consideration.

When I reached Louis Trichardt, I went first to buy a saw blade before getting groceries. And then I felt stupid because I didn't know what size blade we needed. I had to call Don. I remembered that the phone booth was in front of the post office. I can see it now with its glass sides, wooden frame of dusty red, and a sign over the door as clear as day: NIE BLANKES, NON-EUROPEANS.

I looked around. It was the only booth. I was hot and thirsty. The drive to town had made me see how little I did that mattered. Now my failure to know what I needed to buy put me in a foul mood. I walked up and down the block, but there was no other phone booth. People walked by me on the sidewalk, both black and white, but I couldn't ask for the European booth without feeling complicit with the system. I lost my patience, marched back to the phone booth and pushed the door open. What difference did it make that this was for non–Europeans? It was bloody stupid to have segregated phone booths. Besides, I wasn't a European. Screw them all. I closed the door.

Where they came from, I have no idea, but suddenly the phone booth was surrounded. People banged on the glass, beckoning to me to come out, their dark faces free of hostility but full of alarm. I realized they wanted to help me, to prevent the sure catastrophe that would occur if a white woman made a phone call in a black people's phone booth. Amazed, I pushed the door back open.

"Madam, there." They pointed up the stairs to the post office. "Inside there." Their insistence sent me quickly up the stairs and through the door. Indeed, safely inside was another phone booth, marked with the same big letters in fresher paint: BLANKES, EUROPEAN. I slipped into it, suddenly self-conscious, furious, and humiliated.

Everybody in Bible study laughed when I told my phone booth story. But then an untypical hush followed the opening prayer. Something was wrong.

Mr. Nkhondo didn't keep us waiting long. "You have made life more bitter," he said, abruptly, his plain face with the buck teeth made homelier by his deep frown. He didn't look at us but it was clear he meant Don and me.

No one moved. Then Mr. Mabyelane put his cup down and the clink of the china sounded to me like something breaking. Louise picked up her cup and stared into it as if to read some truth in the tea leaves.

He had to say more. Sometimes Bible study was the only real conversation I had all week. We were always nervous ahead of time, wondering who would come, but people did. The week before we'd spent the whole evening talking about sex and sex education, about *lobola* and whether or not paying a bride price should be required.

"Please go on," Don said. He sat opposite me, his left ankle resting on his right knee, his foot twitching.

"Before you came," Mr. Nkhondo said, looking at the floor, "we had got used to things. We knew what to expect. We understood how we would be treated. We accepted. Now we see how we are treated here. Tomorrow at the school nothing has changed only it is more bitter."

"We're together in our faith," Don said with quiet passion. "We are neither Jew nor Greek, male nor female, black nor white."

Although of course I agreed with him, Don's formal way of speaking annoyed me. "Thank you for saying that." My voice trembled with emotion. "We have to be community for each other, here and now. We have to find a way." I was elated because what he said meant that Don and I were not making it up. Once a week there was a safe place to talk. Then the elation turned to doubt. If all we accomplished was to make life more bitter, would it have been better if we hadn't come? I was afraid to ask. I wanted to hug Mr. Nkhondo when the meeting was over for being brave enough to speak. I shook his hand.

# 11

## Sojourners in a Strange Land

Sitting at the big table in our little dining room, I carefully folded the articles I'd clipped from the *Rand Daily Mail* and slipped them into a large envelope along with a document explaining Bantu education. Religiously I sent such packets off to the Southern Africa Committee in New York. While we had been waiting for visas back in the fall of 1965, Southern Rhodesia had declared itself independent from Great Britain. By that time, the members of our committee knew enough to be appalled at the lack of coverage in the American press of this important story. Rather than a negotiated independence agreed to by Britain as was happening in country after country across the African continent, the whites in Southern Rhodesia unilaterally seized power to avoid African majority-rule. We were provoked enough to establish what would evolve into *Southern Africa Magazine*, a journal that for fifteen years reported on the liberation struggles in the region. Now the existence of the magazine gave me something to do on a weekly basis; I supplied New York with information they wouldn't have access to otherwise. But after a year, it felt like sending things off into the ether, as I never heard if the packets arrived and New York seemed to exist in a different life. I glanced at my watch. It was too early to wake Don.

Going outside, I stood looking out past the overgrown rockery where once a showcase garden of succulents thrived, out across the distant open expanse of land—small plots, open fields, grazing cattle and clusters of rondovals—to the green mountains far beyond. I didn't know those mountains; I had never thought of exploring them. We were trapped here on our escarpment, locked into a rhythm dictated by Don's schedule and the church.

But wasn't this exactly where we wanted to be? A letter from Georgia the day before was full of what seemed like the privileged and pedestrian troubles that came with an affluent suburban church—a student failing to get into the college of his choice, a woman in the church going through an ugly divorce. Since we'd married, Georgia wrote all her letters to both Don and me, and in this one she wrote that perhaps the four of us could be friends, couples in ministry. I'd read it quickly and dismissively, too absorbed in my own frustration to wonder at the extravagant denial embedded in her suggestion. She annoyed me by making judgments about who was in the more important ministry. I wanted to be free of such comparisons, except I made them myself. I would live fully where I was—in the midst of the oppression and pain that were the daily bread of everyone here at Lemana. I said this as an earnest vow, believing as I did, that being in South Africa, trying to find ways to be faithful in the face of such deep injustice, made our work more important than anything Georgia and Sam might do.

I looked at my watch. An hour had gone by, time enough. Coming back into the house, I walked quietly down the long, cool interior hallway past empty bedrooms on either side to reach our room at the far end of the house. Love in the afternoon. That long-ago time, in Georgia's bed, when she wanted to teach me about sex with a man. What would she have said that could possibly have helped us? The first year we were married, Don's impotence came frequently, and I wasn't able to be loving the way I was that very first night. I went crazy, digging my fingernails into his back, drawing blood, screaming, "You do it on purpose to punish me!" If only he could have stopped me, taken me in his arms and asked, "What is this about punishment? For what?" If he'd been able to do that, could I have answered, could we have teased out what it had to do with Georgia? Instead, terrified and tearful, he confessed that my unbridled desire frightened him and his impotence was there to prove it.

I slipped under the sheet without waking Don and began to rub his back. He stirred, turned, and took me in his arms. We'd learned that if he slept first, his anxiety could be kept at bay. I reined myself in. What else could I do? We needed each other, especially here. In our isolation, I was grateful even for the little he gave me. We kissed each other and declared our love. Don went to his office to write a sermon.

Then it was my turn to write a sermon. Don had a preaching engagement away from the school, giving me the opportunity to speak at the late afternoon service on Good Friday, March 24, 1967. All of Lemana would be required to be in attendance. I threw myself into preparation, believing as I did that preaching mattered.

I was a good preacher. At Union Seminary, I got an A in homiletics. My sermons were down to earth, tangible, not airy abstractions like those given by too many of the men. Our professor, Dr. Edmund Steimle, said so, defending me against my classmates' complaints that I was too political.

The fading late afternoon light gave the chapel a feel of shadowy gloom, appropriate for Good Friday. I couldn't speak directly about what a bleak time it was in South Africa. Decades of opposition to white minority control had escalated after the Sharpeville Massacre just seven years before. When unarmed protestors were shot and killed by police, the decision was made by the liberation movements to take up arms. As early as 1963, key movement leaders were arrested. A number of them, including Nelson Mandela, were sentenced to life in prison in 1964. Others escaped into exile or went deeply underground. Not until the next decade would opposition against apartheid again rise up in powerful ways. We were in the country at the time of deepest repression when the ruling Nationalist Party encountered no serious threat to its power.

Speaking at that time and place, I used the biblical text carefully to make a contemporary statement and spoke on power and responsibility. Though I was not thinking of Georgia, it was with her that I had first become aware of how power operated in relationships. Now I spoke of the most powerful player in the crucifixion story, Pontius Pilate, who saw that Jesus was innocent and tried to free him.

"He had the power in his own hands to set Jesus free," I said, strongly. Instead, coward that he was, Pilate washed his hands of the whole affair and turned Jesus over to the chief priests and scribes who were, the text says, all too happy to take responsibility. But Pilate, the most powerful, remained most guilty of his death.

Now I can see that the verse which has the people say, "His blood be on us and on our children" is mightily laden, justifying as it has, centuries of anti–Semitism. Then I tried to show a scale of blame, from Pilate to the priests and scribes, to the mass of people, and finally to the Roman soldiers who nailed the spikes into Jesus, but who were least of all guilty of his death.

Looking out as I spoke, I saw in the dusk that most of the students were alert and paying attention. They kept me going. In this carefully controlled environment, where it was almost impossible for me to make friends with individual students, and where students were required to go to chapel, attention was not something I could count on. I saw that many students seemed to be trying to get what I said, to understand that I was pointing fingers, laying blame for the calamitous conditions under which they lived, exonerating them for being forced into complicity. I don't think I imagined it, that they sang the final hymn with full conviction.

> *See, from his head, his hands and feet,*
> *Sorrow and love flow mingled down.*
> *Did e'er such love and sorrow meet,*
> *Or thorns compose so rich a crown.*

The days were getting cooler and we had to decide whether or not to stay in South Africa. We'd come for two years, but the Swiss Mission/ Tsonga Presbyterian Church wanted us to make our lives with them. Hard times were surely ahead as apartheid would not be eliminated without a fight. I gave it serious thought. If we stayed, we had to give up our U.S. citizenship and become South Africans, without any safety valve or special protection. Thinking this reminded me of the best compliment my friends in Beirut had given me: "You don't seem like an American." Meaning I listened, I did what they wanted me to do, like I did with Georgia.

Then a letter from New York made up our minds for us.

"Mel Schoonover is leaving Chambers Church!" Don said. "They want to know if I'd be interested in applying for his job."

It was a dream job he had never imagined for himself. Chambers was where we'd gotten to know each other, fallen in love. It would be like going home. He answered immediately and by August was offered the position. He accepted. We would leave South Africa at the end of December as originally planned.

Except in early September another letter arrived. Francois brought it to us but hesitated in the doorway before coming off the veranda into our simply furnished sitting room. He came slowly, as if he would avoid this encounter if he could, and his dusty shoes left marks on the red polished floor.

Puzzled, Don and I sat down. Francois never came to see us mid-day, and he settled into his chair before pulling a letter out of his pocket. He looked away from us, away from the letter in his hand, his sparkling blue eyes angry. His trim, pointed beard ordinarily gave him a mischievous, elfish look. Not today. Today he looked like a man burdened with responsibility.

Francois held the letter where we both could see it and he read the meat of it aloud.

Departement van Bantoe-onderwys
Department of Bantu Education

6 September 1967

*CONFIDENTIAL*
Rev. T. Schneider
Chairman, Field Committee,
Swiss Mission
61, Rose Street
Reviera,
Pretoria.

Dear Sir,

… The Department has at its disposal information which indicates that both Rev. and Mrs. are using the opportunity given them to communicate with the students to propagate their own critical views of the generally accepted policies and established customs in the country. It will interest you to know that the Reverend's behavior has aroused a feeling of repugnance which may have a harmful effect on the work at the institution.

You will appreciate that the Department cannot allow such a state of affairs to continue at an institution under its control and your church is requested kindly to withdraw Rev. and Mrs. from Lemana as soon as possible.

You are also requested in future not to entrust the religious education for which your church assumes responsibility to strangers like Rev. and Mrs. who might not be fully acquainted with conditions and principles underlying human relations in the Republic of South Africa.

Your co-operation in this matter will be appreciated.

Yours faithfully,
Dr. Van Zyl
Secretary For Bantu Education

Flabbergasted, I blurted out, "What does this mean?"

"It means, as you well know, that you are being spied on and reported on." Francois' voice was flat but rose in intensity as he continued. "They have no right to tell us who we can hire. They call you strangers who don't understand South Africa. The trouble is you understand all too well. They make me a stranger in my own country."

He lit a cigarette. "There's another letter, Theo's response to this one that he's sent to the church leaders." Theo was responsible for foreign staff which explained why the Department had written to him. Theo had replied with one sentence: the letter was receiving attention.

"Theo suggests that we do nothing until our synod meeting at Valdezia next month, when all the pastors will be present. We can draw up an answer to the Department when we're all together."

"What do we do in the meantime?" Don said. He got up and began to pace nervously.

"All we've done is talk," I said. "If that's enough to get this kind of attention, this is an even bigger police state than I thought it was."

"Indeed." Francois smiled at me sadly. "I think Theo's right. We decide what to do when we're together, if we should protest this intrusion into church affairs. Think about it. In the meantime, carry on as usual."

We walked him to his truck. "One more thing," he said. "Don't speak of this to anyone."

"Why not?" I was angry.

"I suspect that this matter is related to things beyond Lemana, to the land and the farms. Jaeger may not even know about this letter."

Mr. Jaeger was Lemana's principal, an ineffectual Dutchman we didn't respect. But it seemed very odd that he wouldn't have been told about something at his own school. "We need, at least, to tell the study group," I said.

"Least of all them," Francois said.

"Why?"

"There are people in that group who cannot be trusted to keep their mouths shut."

I considered. "Who?"

He shook his head, unwilling to accuse, and got in his truck.

Don and I watched him drive away, past the row of aloes, the avocado trees, and down the road through the school. We looked at each other.

"Don't worry," I said, seeing Don's anxious expression. Uncertainty alarmed him. I took his hand. "We'll be fine." I couldn't believe they'd actually remove us. We weren't important enough to bother with. The letter confirmed what we'd come to understand about how the system enforced itself. Fear of consequences made people self-censor. That left the government free to do its dirty work without resistance. But I couldn't help smiling. Mostly I felt extraneous here, and unchallenged. This could be interesting. And did it mean that we had actually done something of consequence?

It was hard to wait until the synod at Valdezia in October. The government was toying with the Church, threatening the future of the school, Elim mission, and Elim hospital. Nothing had yet been decided, but if the Church's land was designated white instead of becoming part of the Tsonga Bantustan, several thousand African farmers would lose their homes and Lemana, the mission house, and the hospital would be off limits to Africans, emptied and forced to close. I could not imagine such an outcome, overly consumed as I was with our situation. But at Valdezia, the pastors deliberated only ten minutes about our case. They instructed Theo to write the Department saying that we had done nothing contrary to the duties of servants of the Church.

The government's response came quickly and Francois again came to tell us. "We have been instructed to withdraw you forthwith," he said.

"What does that mean?" I said.

"You can go ahead with Sunday's service, as scheduled. After that, you can have nothing to do with Lemana. If you disobey and Don preaches the following Sunday, nothing will happen to you but the Church will pay. If the Church protests publicly on your behalf, then you will be served immediately with deportation orders."

"Well, that's clear." It infuriated me that we would have to do exactly what they instructed.

"Does it help to know," Francois said, "that the information the Department has about you did not originate with Bantu Education but comes, presumably, from State Information, the Special Branch?"

"Why should that help?" Don said. "Students get paid to spy. I even had one come and confess as much. His guilt got to him. He didn't know what to do. I told him to make his reports interesting."

"But we didn't do anything," I said. "Nothing changed."

Francois smiled at me almost condescendingly. "You are such an American. You think you have such powers."

"Ouch!"

"You've done more than you realize," Francois said. "More than you can measure."

Sunday morning, Don and I walked the short distance to the church for the last time. We walked slowly and I kicked stones from the road into the spiky succulents that lined our path. Inside, to my surprise, the Vamanana Va Xiknongela were seated together in the front pews and they beckoned for me to come and sit with them. I did with pleasure, squeezing between Mrs. Khosa and Mrs. Nkhondo.

Then Mrs. Mathebula, who was speaking on behalf of the prayer meeting, called me to the front. Because the village women were present, she spoke in Tsonga, generous words, I gathered from her expression. They had a gift for me, an African blanket from Khoja's store. I wrapped the blanket, with its bold black and turquoise pattern, around my shoulders, the kind of blanket all the village women wore. Utterly surprised, I had to fight back tears.

Suddenly the women began to laugh, a friendly laugh that puzzled me. I made my way back to the pew.

"Why are they laughing?" I whispered to Mrs. Nkhondo.

"They were giving you your Tsonga name."

Only when the service was finished could I ask what it was.

"*Ximbitani*," Mrs. Nkhondo said. "They named you *Ximbitani*."

"What does it mean?"

She smiled but wouldn't look me in the eye. "It means 'the little pot that boils.'"

I laughed. I cringed. I thought it meant they knew I was angry all the time.

I told her that.

"No, Jefro," Mrs. Nkhondo said. "No. It means you are active. It means you do everything yourself."

Smiling, I pulled my blanket closely around me. *Ximbitani*. Little boiling pot. Maybe they did know me. Better than I could ever know them.

# 12

## Neither Death nor Life

"You are too impetuous to be my friend!" Carolyn's slightly shocked expression made her face open and vulnerable. Then she laughed.

She sat with Don on the couch across from me in our living room in East Harlem. I had just announced that only beautiful things would be allowed in our home; I had just held a hideous green-glass ash tray above my head and dropped it. A wedding gift, it broke on the linoleum floor exactly as I had intended. Making Carolyn laugh was the point as she rarely did these days. Her husband, Charles, had just died.

Charles was my colleague on the Southern Africa Committee. Charles and Carolyn had come from New York and Don and I had come from Lemana to Zambia just the year before. A group of us, all working in or on Africa, had gathered to strategize about how to stay connected with each other and affect policy change on southern Africa in the United States. Charles and Carolyn had then visited us at Lemana. Seven months later, when we arrived back in New York, we stayed with them until our apartment was ready. Charles was twenty-six years old, a doctoral student at Columbia. We knew he had lymphosarcoma but not that he would die just two weeks after we moved to East Harlem, on March 23, 1968.

Don and I had experienced death before—all of our grandparents. We'd lived through the assassination of President John Kennedy when we were at Union and the assassination of Prime Minister Hendrik Verwoerd when we were at Lemana. Still, we spoke of Charles as our first death, as he was our peer, younger by two years than we were.

When Charles died, I was in Michigan, visiting college campuses, speaking and preaching, doing radio and TV interviews. Our assignment in South Africa required that we share what we'd learned back in the States. Don called me. *Charles is dead.* I cancelled everything and flew home to Carolyn.

Though I was terrified that I would not know what to do, I went straight to her apartment. She met me in the hall and we embraced, beginning at that moment an uncommon friendship that over the next many months would see her through her deepest sorrow. Her grief was clean and I could help her. I had been well trained, by a woman with a different kind of grief, though Georgia did not acknowledge this and the sadness that burdened her was deeply disguised. I had learned to read her moods and it was my job to take the sadness out of her voice. Carolyn was uncomplicated in comparison. I got from her what I had gotten from Georgia: an intense gratitude for my very presence. For a while it was that simple.

I was back on the campus circuit on April 4, visiting Tulane in New Orleans when Martin Luther King, Jr., was killed in Memphis. I had just finished taping a local TV show when I heard the news. Dr. King had been shot and he died within the hour. Since the March on Washington in 1963, I had followed Dr. King closely, his courageous repudiation of the Vietnam War and his growing emphasis on the need to address the persistence of poverty.

Right after I heard the news of his assassination, I got into a taxi.

"Have you heard?" I said, my voice breaking.

The driver was an older black man, and he turned to look at me, shocked, shaking his head. As he drove me to my next engagement, we talked as if we had known each other all our lives, not wanting to believe it. Believing it.

Back in New York with Don, so soon after Charles died, we experienced Dr. King's death with a similar, personal pain. We joined the myriad throngs across the country and around the world who, in disbelief and rage, tried to imagine our world without Dr. King. Comforting each other, we began to make our apartment feel like home.

"Hand me the hammer," Don said.

He held a reed mat that we'd bought in Johannesburg against the inside wall of the living room with his shoulder and left arm and began to fasten it with tiny nails, dozens of them along the knotted twine that held the mat together at top and bottom. Made in Lesotho, its thin round reeds shifted out of alignment to make a double layer, creating a pattern of solid lines and moiré waves. I had to stand on a stool to hold up the right side, and when the nails were all in place, we stood back to inspect the mat's quiet presence. It would remind us, every day, of our time in South Africa.

The west wall, opposite the mat, held tall, dark green metal shelves, and our books, each with its own shaded spine, added color to the room, as did the spring-green, dawn-yellow, hand-woven Polish rug we'd splurged on.

We made a pact. Don would work at Chambers, earning a regular salary. I would continue our political work on southern Africa. He went to the kitchen to get us a couple beers. I went to my office to get a letter from Georgia. According to the co-op rules, we weren't eligible for two bedrooms, but Mel had convinced the board that we would soon have a child. I had turned the extra room into my office and retrieved the letter from my desk.

Sitting again with Don, I cringed at what Georgia had written about herself: *size 16, lousy sight, sore neck, and a blob of a personality.* This was the woman I loved? Georgia—she'd become a geography, like Lesotho-Lemana-Johannesburg, a state, a country, and maybe I didn't want to live there anymore.

"They have stopped going to their therapist," I said. "Sam screwed up, getting behind on their estimated taxes, so they had to pay them and big fines and there's no money for therapy. But listen to this: *Sam learned from childhood to live in a very narrow band. He doesn't feel joy. He doesn't risk wanting things, and the trouble has come because it means he can't preach. He wants to stop his intellectualizing of everything, to preach out of his own deep self, but he doesn't know how. He lacks a fount of experience.*"

I looked up. Don's expression was uncritically one of sympathy and understanding.

"Do you believe this?" I said.

"Why not? It's confusing how ministers have to do taxes. I can imagine screwing up. And he's not the only one who has to guard against over-intellectualizing!" He grinned. Don's professors at Union wanted him to go on for his doctorate and teach. We both knew that if he'd become an academic, he'd have lived hopelessly in his head, abstracted and unavailable. However uncomfortable it often was for him in the parish, it was the better choice.

"But you're aware of it," I said. "You're getting more and more grounded."

He liked it when I praised him, and the nervous twitching of his left ankle on his right knee stopped. I continued reading. "*For me, the therapy has been liberating. The verdict on me was that I'm not egocentric enough—I sublimate my own needs always thinking his are greater, and I should get on my high horse and insist on being heard, responded to, etc."*

"Not egocentric enough?" I almost shrieked. "Can you believe that? I can't stand it when she blames Sam for their troubles."

"She hasn't told him about you, her relationship with you," Don said, checking.

"No. She never told the therapist either. I know because I asked. He's playing with blinders on. So is Sam."

"What do you think she wants from you, writing this?"

"She wants me to agree with her."

"Or maybe she wants you to help her get honest."

"Tell Sam?"

"Maybe. What you did is a long time ago now."

I shook my head, no. We both knew that our life together, figuring it out, would have been impossible if I hadn't told him about Georgia. I didn't try to understand her choice to be silent. All I could think about was what she might do if I did insist that she tell the truth. Would she thank me? Banish me? Kill herself? I had no idea.

The next killing came in June, Bobby Kennedy shot in Los Angeles. I sat at the kitchen table watching the story play out. His wife, Ethel, went to the cathedral to pray. The newscaster spoke of respecting her privacy, even as she was filmed by a hidden camera while at prayer. I raged on her behalf. What was wrong with this country? We went to Carolyn's for dinner, so she would not have to be alone with another death and we spoke of Bobby. He had come to South Africa while we were there. He gave a speech in Cape Town.

> "There is," said an Italian philosopher, "nothing more difficult to take in hand, more perilous to conduct, or more uncertain in its success than to take the lead in the introduction of a new order of things." Yet this is the measure of the task of your generation, and the road is strewn with many dangers....
>
> But we also know that only those who dare to fail greatly, can ever achieve greatly....
>
> I believe that in this generation those with the courage to enter the moral conflict will find themselves with companions in every corner of the world.

He had been speaking to the young people of South Africa. His words resonated with Carolyn, Don, and me, as they did with the others we had met with in Zambia. We were young Americans with experience in Africa who were now back in the States. We gathered later that summer to strategize how we could pool our resources—vocational and financial—to support the liberation struggles in southern Africa and change U.S. policy in the region. We came to call ourselves the Zambia Group, and we wrote each other quarterly and met annually for more than twenty years.

In the summer of 1968, when the Soviet bloc army marched into Czechoslovakia and the Chicago police assaulted demonstrators at the Democratic National Convention, we couldn't know yet that our experiences in southern Africa would shape our lives for decades to come. What we did know was that we were not alone in our anguish and our passion for change. We had companions. Death made us closer. We never felt more alive.

# 13

# Wipe Away Every Tear

"I want to be a writer," I said, pronouncing my ambition and my calling.

Carolyn and Don were sitting across from me on the couch. I needed them to say, *Yes, do it! You'll be great.* I needed them to do what Georgia did: tell me who I was, affirm enthusiastically what I was trying to assert about myself.

"I thought you already were one," Carolyn said blandly. "Do you mind if I change the subject?"

Yes, I minded, but I nodded for her to continue.

"I want to take a vacation. Gail, would you come with me? It feels too hard to go alone."

My hurt vanished. More than her affirmation of my work, I needed her to want my company, the intimacy we'd shared since Charles died, now a year ago.

We drove to Mystic Seaport in Connecticut, but instead of being on or by the water, we were driven inside by rain. We sat on a big bed in our motel room and we talked. Carolyn worked for the national office of her church which advocated for social justice around the country. I smiled to myself. She had such a fresh, dairymaid expression, one that suggested she would know everything about gardening and home economics, which was not what she was talking about.

"There has to be a concerted effort to get more black faculty members at universities. Not just black students, but faculty as well."

I got up and went to the bathroom to gather my courage. Carolyn trusted me; I could trust her.

I sat back down on the bed. "Can I tell you something?"

"Gail, you have been the most faithful friend imaginable. Of course, you can tell me anything."

"I've never told anyone but Don," I said. "I had this religious teacher.

She's had an incredible influence on my life." I told Carolyn all that I'd learned from Georgia—theology, music, art. "Only the trouble was we … we made love for a time. When I was a teenager. I loved her. I still do. But it's complicated."

Carolyn listened intensely and she smiled at me when I finished. I smiled too. She wasn't going to condemn me.

"Can I tell you something too?"

I hadn't worked out what I wanted from her. Incredibly, I was blind to any connection between my feelings for Georgia and my feelings for Carolyn. But when she changed the subject that fast, I was stunned. Still, I quickly gave her my full attention.

"I've fallen head over heels," she said, blushing, and I heard for the first time about Matthew. "He's kind. He understands my abiding love for Charles."

Her face was radiant the way it is when one's in love. And then her expression paled. "Go on," I said.

She looked away from me and whispered through tight lips, "He's married."

"Oh," I said. "Uh-oh."

They'd met through work, employed as they were by different divisions of their church, he in Washington and she in New York. "His therapist calls what we have an affair. It frightens me, hurts me when he uses that word."

"Why?" I said, gently.

"You know how we grew up. Thou shalt not commit adultery. People like us don't have affairs. We work for the church. He's a minster."

"Why is he seeing a therapist?"

I got the full story: his marriage to a woman he no longer loved, the children he adored, and his wife's unwillingness to set him free. We never spoke another word about Georgia. I didn't try. I didn't say Georgia was married. I didn't say it was "statutory rape." I didn't think like that. I couldn't see that Carolyn spoke only because I had first. I was her confidante. Her affair and so her troubles were right now. Mine were just history, not important, or so I told myself. Driving home in the rain, I wanted to tell her I loved her.

"Never underestimate," I said, "how important you are to me. Never."

Monday morning, after my days away with Carolyn, I took my temperature when I woke. Don and I had been trying to get pregnant for almost a year. Finally, a doctor who specialized in infertility had given us instructions: the charting of my temperature, and intercourse timed to likely ovulation. We couldn't have done this if Don hadn't wanted a child but performing on demand was sometimes impossible for him. Behaving kindly, with so much at stake, was sometimes impossible for me. We learned to cry in each other's arms. We learned to try again and then again, each month a fresh opportunity.

This March morning, I didn't trust the thermometer, but I marked the temperature chart. The line of dots stayed level for the whole week, and then another, and then I skipped a period. I was pregnant.

Don counted on his fingers. "Our first child will be born in November." We hugged each other and danced crazily around the room.

We couldn't quite believe that what everybody else did—make love and conceive a child—had actually happened to us.

"Maybe by November," I said, "I won't be so scared."

Just days later, Carolyn's sister Alice asked us if we would preach her wedding sermon. She didn't know I was pregnant. We had been afraid to talk about it, though of course we told her and Carolyn now.

Alice worked with Don at Chambers Church and I knew her fiancé, Norm, from the Southern Africa Committee. We were in the best state ever to be preaching about love and marriage and we wrote the sermon as a dialogue, our texts selected passages from the second and third chapters of Genesis as well as an E.E. Cummings poem.

The wedding was in June in Alice and Carolyn's hometown. Don stood in the pulpit, I at the lectern, he in his wedding suit, I in a new white dress with a narrow black ribbon running diagonally all the way down my body, like half an X. We spoke in verse, the Cummings poem "i thank you God," and additional stanzas which Don pronounced and I rejoined, and we went back and forth. A man is incomplete without a woman; woman has within her part of man and only by coming together can wholeness come. But we also said that we live together in a time and place of brokenness and disobedience.

> *Woman:*    *Come hold my hand*
>                 *Help me up*
>                 *We'll laugh; we'll cry*
>                 *We'll dry each other's tears.*
> *Man:*       *You are for me and I for you*
>                 *You only I love*
>                 *Yet in that limit*
>                 *The whole world opens.*

We brought to the sermon our deep dependence on each other. We'd survived such struggle and heartache and now had the joy of our new pregnancy. Preaching let us say how we wanted to go through life together. We closed with a Cummings line, one we both loved, saying it in unison: "I thank you God for most this amazing day."

But that night, my pregnancy ended with torrents of clotted blood and invisible flesh falling from my body.

I put on my armor and drove us home. Publicly, to my parents, and even to Georgia, I said I was okay, thank you, would be just fine; women miscarried all the time; we'd try again. Alone in our apartment I wailed, waves of rage and sadness breaking over me. In rational moments, I knew they were out of all proportion. I beat myself up for them. They came anyway. The loss of this child was punishment, like my cyst was punishment, the cyst that destroyed an ovary, gave me a blood clot and made it harder for me to conceive. Deeper than thought, origins inchoate, my anguish was unrelenting.

I stayed in bed for days. I dozed and dreamed bad dreams. Between waking and sleeping, unguarded, there was Georgia, when she was pregnant. Seven months. On her back, her ball of a belly rising enormously.

"Here, put your hand here," she had said, gently placing it for me to feel her baby kick. I wasn't prepared for how hard she felt.

"Maybe you can hear the heartbeat."

I put my ear against her belly button. We slipped into making love, carefully, tenderly, the image of how she looked that afternoon, her naked mountain of a body, burned into my mind. As close as I would ever get to pregnancy?

Was there a connection, one I was unable to entertain, between this awesome memory and what it required me to ignore—that Georgia was a married woman when we made love; seven months pregnant and I'd wanted to make love to her. Was there a connection between all that and my confusion now—nothing bad had happened and I should just get on with it; a terrible thing had happened but I deserved it?

Trying to get on with it, I forced myself up and into the kitchen to make dinner for Don. I tried to tell him it was hormones, and oh how I wanted to believe that my extreme mood swings were just hormones. But I never could. I had to pay for loving Georgia.

Solace came from an unanticipated source. The first Sunday I returned to church, Mary Moore stopped me as I entered the sanctuary. She was a matriarch, mother to four of her own and countless other children, an older, wiser woman revered by everyone in the congregation. She put her arm around my shoulders. "You didn't lose a baby. You created an angel."

If it had been anyone else, I told Don, I would have hit them. From Mary, the words were unexpectedly comforting, because I knew the heart from which they were spoken.

In early 1970, I borrowed a book from Carolyn, *Everything You Always Wanted to Know About Sex: But Were Afraid to Ask.* I began to read on the bus. I got home and kept reading, then I walked back and forth between the bookcases and the woven wall mat on our green and yellow rug, sobbing. Anger took hold of me with more intensity than I could remember though I had been angry all my life, as anger was my magnificent defense against my grief and my despair.

What I would have called the facts in that book are ludicrous now, dated and misogynist. *A mature orgasm is any orgasm that results from penis-vagina intercourse.* My fixation on that sentence was something besides ludicrous. It was testimony to my extreme insecurity about my sexuality. I had not discovered it for myself. Georgia had given it to me. Just as I let her be the authority in all things, I grasped onto that sentence as my new truth. I had never experienced what it called mature.

I paced, my mind locking into right and wrong. We had been married almost six years and I rehearsed them. I had made every single suggestion about how to make sex better, enjoy it more. He was impotent for so long that any kind of intercourse was a triumph. He got better and I asked for more and he agreed but he never initiated anything new. The book not only judged me; it vindicated me. I had wanted what it said. It was Don's fault I had never had it.

I went to the couch and sat down, turned to look across the street to the tenements, the empty brick building with its broken windows like scarred eyes, eyes that would witness our conversation through our curtainless windows. That night I tried to explain why I was so upset. We were in our regular places on the couch, he on the right, I on the left, facing each other. I told Don what a mature orgasm was.

"So you feel gypped," he said, "gypped for six whole years." His voice was flat, and he looked like he was ten years old, guilty and scolded.

"No! Listen. I'm not saying it was all terrible. I'm saying we're stuck, and I don't want to be stuck. I want to have orgasms like normal people do."

Why did it matter such a lot? If he'd had the courage to ask me that, I wonder how I would have answered. Would I have said that I wanted sex with him to be as good as it had been with her? Better? That I wanted him to give me the one thing she couldn't? But he didn't ask so I didn't answer and could blame him for our troubles.

"We got what we deserved," I said. "I'm so goddamned grateful to you for not judging me, and you're so goddamned grateful to me for loving you despite your terrible timidity."

I wish I could say that then we looked at each other and burst out laughing, that we saw how silly all this was, this commotion about orgasm and what was said to be mature. I wish I could say I corrected myself. We hadn't gotten what we *deserved*; we'd gotten what each of us needed, someone to love us just as we were. Better yet, I wish I could say I talked to him about why, because of Georgia, I was desperate for what I thought of as normalcy, that despite my armor of toughness, of humor and of sarcasm, I was damaged by what had happened. I couldn't say that. I didn't understand it yet.

It got worse. I wonder how we had the courage to have sex with so much riding on it, but we loved each other; we wanted a child. More than a child. At least I did. I wanted good sex with Don. I wept that month when my period came. After it was over, we made love again, and I didn't have an orgasm during intercourse. I sat up in bed, and I wailed. "I can't get pregnant and I can't have orgasms." I put my back to the wall and I banged my head hard against it, again and again.

I watched myself doing this, frantically trying to externalize my pain, show Don, show myself just how hurt I was even though a part of me was appalled at my histrionics. But nothing inside me was strong enough to make me stop. Our mattress lay directly on the floor and Don cowered at its foot, each bang of my head screaming his inadequacy. He covered his nakedness with the crumpled sheet. If only he could have seized hold of me, wrapped me in his long arms and held on until I quieted down. He couldn't and then I saw and I couldn't stand the anguish on his face. I scrambled across the bed to take him in my arms.

I can't say that I never did it again, this acting out, or that Don ever found the strength to try to stop me. What I can say is that I apologized to him each time, the next morning. He could hold me then and tell me how

I terrified him. We would get up, eat breakfast and get on with our daily lives, which were demanding and exhilarating. We were tuned into our city where, in addition to actions against the Vietnam War, Black Power was flowing in the streets, gay pride gaining strength and visibility, and a nascent women's movement was telling us to claim our lives. Some complex confluence of these streams, within us and without us, gave me a way to think about Georgia and what I needed. She still insisted on secrecy; I understood at last that whatever else she was to me, she was too important to be kept secret.

I thought of it as a choice I had to make. If I wasn't keeping her secrets, I couldn't be in her life. At breakfast on a day in late March I said to Don, "Listen. I'm going to end it. I'm going to tell Georgia I never want to see her again."

# 14

## Not Unless You Bless Me

I remember the day I met Georgia, April 22, 1956. I don't remember the precise date I said goodbye, only that it was fourteen years later, April 1970. I flew all the way to Chicago, to tell her face to face.

The night before, I rehearsed, even putting on what I would wear—my bright yellow linen dress with its puffed sleeves pulled tight and cuffed just below the elbow, its narrow skirt fitting comfortably on my no longer pleasingly plump body. Georgia had never seen me in this dress. With it I wore long, slim silver earrings and simple black heels, and, with Don, I went over and over why I had to go. I didn't like Georgia anymore. She had started sending us audiotapes, and her recorded voice whined intrusively about how they didn't have enough money, how Sam was stuck professionally and passive beyond belief. She spoke of Sam's emotional absence and once she even threatened suicide, though I didn't believe her; she was just being melodramatic and manipulative. Instead of my extraordinary, adored teacher, she'd become my secret shame, source of my self-pity and self-hatred. I couldn't admit it, not then, not consciously, but how could I have given my life to this pathetic woman?

This I knew: however audacious my request, if I asked to see her, alone and in Chicago, she would find a way to drive the three hours to be with me. So I was unnerved when she pulled into the terminal to pick me up, and I saw through the windshield that someone was sitting next to her. Joel, then eleven years old, was out of the car, running toward me and giving me a big hug just like he had when he was little. I had known him since infancy—earlier—and I now held him at arm's length and looked him over, open face and sparkling eyes beneath his baseball cap. "You are such a handsome chap," I said, punching him playfully on the shoulder. But I resented his presence, which forced me to walk back into Georgia's life. She sat stiffly, her fists clenched white on the steering wheel, her smile guarded, as if to say we had to be careful in front of Joel. Out loud, she said we were taking him to her mother's house where he'd stay while we went to talk. Within the hour, I found myself having apple cider with lovely, gracious Mrs. Patterson in Georgia's immaculate, spacious childhood home where it had all begun with Virginia, when Georgia had been hardly older than Joel was now.

What secrets we had kept from our mothers, Georgia and I. I watched Mrs. Patterson who was her regal self, blonde and blue-eyed like a Danish queen.

"You've flown all the way from New York just to have a conversation with Georgia?" she said to me, her perfect face frowning, mystified.

I turned to Georgia to let her explain. I saw that she would not.

"Yes," I said, trying to sound nonchalant. "I'm flying back this afternoon."

Still frowning in what I could only take as disapproval, she released us. "If you have so little time, you'd better get going."

We left the wide lawns and stately trees of her hometown, and Georgia drove us back toward the airport along a highway lined with warehouses and commercial buildings. Sitting next to her in the front seat of the car, I wondered if she was thinking what I was thinking, about origins and generations, or if she knew how seductive it was for me to be with her in her childhood home, haunted as it was by more than one kind of mother. Hadn't we joked about the sins of the mothers? Now, without asking, she pulled into a restaurant-cocktail-lounge-motel, an anonymous establishment like a thousand others across the country, the details of which I cannot remember but where we could be assured that no one we knew would enter. Still, we sat in a booth for greater privacy.

I looked at Georgia across the table, the soft light kind to her, shadows hiding her heaviness. She had on a creamy blouse and a red jacket that was becoming on her, gave color to her cheeks, a jacket she'd had for a dozen years. The waitress came and Georgia ordered a whiskey sour, I a Bloody Mary. When we were alone again, she studied me as I'd been studying her, taking in not just my dress, my stance, my expression, but trying to discern what she was up against. I saw that we would sit in silence until I spoke. I thanked her for coming.

"The younger kids are jealous," she said, "that Joel gets to see you and they don't."

That's all I needed, all her children. She wasn't going to make this easy. "Let me tell you why I've come."

"Please."

"I need to tell you how I want to live my life," I said, beginning what I'd rehearsed at home. "I've done a lot of reading, thinking, about, like I said, about how I want to live my life. About secrets and the power you've had, the influence you've had in my life. I intend to talk about it. That means I think we can't see each other anymore. I came to tell you that."

It took five seconds to say it. I was astonished. My big speech was over much too soon. I'd said it all, but I'd said nothing, and I couldn't go on until I knew how she'd respond. She pursed her lips and then smiled, as if relieved. She opened her bag, took out her cigarettes, and offered me one. I held the match for her and waited, watched as she prepared to speak, which she did for a long time.

"I tried to imagine why you were coming," Georgia began. "I talked it over with Rose."

Well, of course. Everything she hadn't told her husband, she said to Rose. But Rose helped her keep secrets.

"We spoke about Virginia, my relationship to Virginia, and how different it was from what you and I have. Or should I put that in the past tense?" She gave me a sardonic smile. "Virginia was a fundamentalist. At least you didn't have to contend with that, or with her contempt for what I valued." She looked away for a moment and then directly back at me. "But I'm a liberal. You're radical. Maybe you think the difference is as great."

She spoke in her confident, authoritative voice, changing the subject. This was the Georgia I was prey to, already, and all I could see was that for once she was letting me be different from her, and my heart expanded.

"Of course, the ideological questions are only a tiny part of it," she said, "but they're a shorthand way to speak of difference."

"I had forgotten that she was a fundamentalist. No, I have not had to contend with anything like that." She gave me that we were different. I'd give her that she'd had it tougher, only I didn't believe that. I wanted to say that benign dictators are always the hardest to throw off. I struggled to break free precisely because she gave me attention and affection and more—the music, the art, and the ideas that enriched my world exponentially.

"I'm amazed that you've come to tell me this." Her voice was vulnerable for the first time, with an edge of praise in it. I'd done the right thing, coming. "With Virginia, well, we live far apart now, and we both have growing children. She has four. It all just sort of petered out."

"No way," I said, "could this just peter out. You've been too important, had too much influence. I've already told a friend of mine who you
are. I want to tell my other friends." Telling Carolyn, I'd searched for language, found it hard to put in words, all that I understood about us, and of
course Carolyn had not helped me. "I want to be done with secrets," I said.

"The climate has changed so much between the forties and fifties and
now. Back then hardly anything was even written."

She didn't say written about what, but she meant women loving
women. Since I was whole-heartedly complicit, we didn't question but
celebrated her consummate seduction. I would never know how Georgia
came, in the end, to frame for herself what she did with me. I waited for
her to go on because I could tell that she would, that she was deciding
something. I had said what I had come to say; she had accepted it. I could
go home and tell Don I'd done what I'd promised. Though he had never
questioned my devotion to her, and I'd never asked what it meant to him,
I knew he'd be glad I was ending it. I fell into my familiar role, the one I
always played, audience to her performance.

"I may regret this tomorrow," Georgia said, "but I feel like telling you.
And believe me, I'm not trying to undermine you. But I'm going to see a
divorce lawyer next week."

It was the last thing I expected, though I could hardly be surprised
that once again her more urgent drama would best my own. I settled in
to listen, relieved that the spotlight was removed from me. They were in
therapy together, Sam because he was trying to decide if his marriage
was worth working on, and Georgia for Sam's sake. When she said that,
I flinched. It was always the other guy who needed help, always Georgia,
altruistic Georgia, convincing herself that she acted for the other, that she
needed no help herself. But I lacked the courage to challenge her.

"Sam has withdrawn. He calls me *that woman* in therapy sessions." It
pained her to say this. "It was always a rule in our relationship that I never
hurt him."

"What?" I'd studied their marriage since it began. Sam and the children were her sanity, allowing her, at least sometimes, to let go of her guilt
and shame. I'd witnessed their terrible fights, and listened carefully when
she confided in me, opening a window into adult life. I'd wanted a marriage just like hers, one that wasn't afraid of pyrotechnics. Don and I hurt
each other all the time. It came with the territory. "How can you be close,
have any relationship at all, without hurting each other sometimes?"

"Exactly. I haven't been able to get it into my head, that he really means he wants a divorce. The other day Sam was listing all my faults—domineering, narcissistic, emasculating, manipulative—and after a while I just looked at him and said, 'And you, what have you brought to our relationship?' The therapist broke in and said, 'No, Georgia, you answer that. What has Sam brought?' Something clicked in my head. 'He's brought nothing.' The doctor got up from his chair, came over, took me by the shoulders and said, 'You're right. You're absolutely right.'"

"Georgia, if all that's true, why don't you divorce him?"

She didn't answer but told me instead that Sam's job at the church was over the end of June. He said he couldn't job hunt until he knew if he was going to stay married. It had to do with his integrity. Georgia had gone back to school, just in case she would be the one to get a job, if he couldn't.

"Did you tell the therapist about us?" I asked impulsively. This was their second attempt at therapy. I wanted her to say yes, believing as I did that therapy undertaken without this revelation would be therapy doomed to fail. I was focused on my importance as much as the deception that had accompanied them through all the years of their marriage. If she didn't tell the therapist about us, did that mean I wasn't important to her?

She gave me the same answer. "It isn't relevant." She'd known Sam for three years already when she met me. "If things had been different with him it would never have happened."

She'd never said such a thing. So it was Sam's fault somehow, that she'd made love to me? And not just me, what about the other girls, the ones she gave up when she chose me? What about her declarations of love? She would always honor what was between us even though she would never understand it. God was active in our love.

I didn't question her about these things. I was on a mission not of interrogation but of separation and release. I'd had no way to anticipate what I was getting, and it made me say things I'd never said before.

"For Don and me, it has been incredibly important that he knows. Nothing would be possible for us if he didn't know."

"Sam knows about Virginia," she said calmly, as if that were the equivalent that mattered. "What happened between you and me has nothing to do with us now."

Sam knew about Virginia? Why was I learning this for the first time? The information silenced me. I did not understand how our relationship was irrelevant to her marriage. Maybe I made too much of it, gave it inflated importance. My confidence began to slip.

"Rose didn't want me to come." Georgia smiled at me as she said this. "She thinks I'm dealing with more than I can handle already."

"I needed to say this to you face to face." She'd paid attention to me, not to Rose. Good.

"I dreaded meeting you," she said. "I was afraid you were going to make an impossible demand, that you would insist that we both be open, that I tell Sam. I came prepared to tell you no. I'm afraid of that now. If Sam were to find out, he would use it to take the children, and he'd probably be successful."

So that's why she couldn't talk to her therapist. It wasn't irrelevant; it was too risky.

"I have to ask," she said. "Are you going to write about us?"

"Not for a long time. If I write, it won't be for a long time."

She looked relieved. "It's a stupid legality. But God, I wish you'd been twenty-one."

We were on our second round of drinks when we ordered lunch. The interruption seemed to let Georgia get hold of herself, shift her mood.

"I'm going to take what you say as an affirmation of you," she said, when we were alone again, "not as a rejection. I can't stand any more rejection."

"That's exactly how I want you to take it."

I thought I was asserting my independence, not asking for permission, but the one had slipped into the other. I wanted her approval. No wonder it had taken me years to do this. We were back in that old place I'd believed was safe, where nothing existed but the two of us and our need to be together and tell each other everything.

Georgia stretched in her seat and then looked at me, her face flooded with earnest affection. "Say it again. I need to make sure I understand why you have to do this."

Panicked, I quickly sorted through my reasons, searching for ones she couldn't refute. "It's about power," I said, "not sex. This may sound strange to you, but I discovered I needed to do this when studying colonialism."

Since we returned from South Africa two years before, I'd read Frantz Fanon, *The Wretched of the Earth*, and Albert Memmi, *The Colonizer and the Colonized*. I'd found in these texts the theoretical framework to understand the relationships I'd experienced in the Northern Transvaal. But I also found something far more personal. Of all the devastation visited on colonized peoples, the worst damage was accomplished in the capture of the mind. The colonized person ceased to think for himself, to form his own thoughts out of his own history and experience. Instead, his mind no longer his own, he could see himself only as the colonizer saw him, could imagine his life and possibilities only in the categories dictated to him by those who held power and authority.

"This was a revelation." My voice was firm, and I sat taller. "You colonized my mind. I stopped thinking for myself. I became who I believed you wanted me to be."

This was what I had come to tell her. At home, thinking about it, talking to Don, I felt uneasy. Colonialism was a complex system of control, and opposition to it had launched the Algerian revolution and all the liberation movements we supported in southern Africa. How could I speak in the same language about my little, personal experience? Now, here with Georgia, I found it exhilarating to speak because what I said was true, and something she would never think to say herself.

"Give me an example of how I controlled your mind," she said softly, her eyes troubled and her forehead deeply lined.

I chose an easy one. "You always asked me what I wanted to do. We had this rule that there was complete freedom in our relationship, but it was a standard without meaning because I was so young. You'd ask me what I wanted to do, and I would psych out just as fast as I could what *you* wanted and that was what I wanted."

"Did you ever cross me?" she said, her expression complicated as if she had to know, yet was afraid.

"Yes, I did. I visited right after Joel was born. You spoke increasingly and with anguish about keeping secrets from Sam. My job was to alleviate your guilt, something it got harder and harder to do." I reminded her of my suggestion that we stop having sex. "I told you that our love was not dependent on sex. It wasn't what you wanted to hear; you ostracized me. It was one of the worst days of my life."

She cringed. "I've suppressed all that. It's too painful to remember. But I recall, I do recall, now that you remind me."

"Think of it this way," I said, "if this were a more orthodox relationship, I mean, if one of us were a man, we would never be trying to continue this relationship. Ex-lovers just don't make close friends."

Georgia looked around nervously. "You must speak more quietly."

I took in how deeply frightened she was and felt enormous pity for her.

She lit a cigarette and took command again. "What do you mean that you never want to see me again? Do you mean never?"

I had not expected her to ask; I didn't want to hurt her, and I'd wondered about it myself.

"I'm not trying to write the future, but it has to be a long time. Five years. Ten. After that, who knows? If one or the other of us reaches out, so be it. If not, then not. I only know it has to be a long time."

"Do you want to know if Sam and I divorce?"

"If you want to tell me."

"I won't initiate again."

If they divorced did it change things? Maybe. With Sam out of the picture…

"Why were you, are you, so angry?" she said suddenly. "Tell me what you have been so careful not to say. Maybe it can help me. With Sam, I mean. I don't want it to end with Sam. Despite everything, I believe in him."

I hadn't expected her to ask this either. Where should I start? "It's when you make pronouncements. When you tell me to have a child so you'll know you haven't damaged me." She'd said this countless times.

"I think you misunderstood."

I just looked at her.

"I'm sorry," she said. "Go on."

"Whether I have a child or not has nothing to do with you."

"Of course, but can't I wish it? Can't I want good things for you?"

She didn't want to know why I was angry. She wanted to undermine me with her solicitous vulnerability. "Of course, you can want good things for me."

"You have been very kind," she said. "You could have said all these things in a cruel and hurtful way and you chose not to. Always be radical like that. Maybe I can learn from you."

The remark seemed to embarrass her and she hurried on. "You have become an extraordinarily lovely young woman. Your voice is strong in a way I've never heard it. And you have, like you always have had, expressive eyes. Wonderfully expressive eyes."

Could she see how much I still loved to be embarrassed by her compliments? Is that what made it safe for her to continue? Whatever the reason, she began to speak about herself more honestly than maybe I had ever heard her.

"At home, people seek me out. They bring their troubles to me. And in straight psychological jargon, I play the superior role and they the inferior. It lets me stay in charge and never be vulnerable. But I am, you know. I have no self-confidence. I wrote a paper for this course I'm taking, and I couldn't believe it was any good, didn't even proof it because I knew it was terrible. I got an A+."

She went on quickly, pleading. "Say something nice about me. I've said lovely things about you. Say something nice."

"Georgia, that's exactly the kind of comment that makes me crazy."

"Even in this context?"

I should have said especially in this context. I didn't answer, didn't say that her need for control was so extreme she even had to program in whatever compliments came her way.

"You'll be sad when you get on that plane," she said. "Tomorrow you'll be sorry."

I didn't take her on. Not because her assertion annoyed me, which it did, but because it was true. I didn't resist now how she manipulated me. Instead, I felt closer to her than I had in a very long time.

"I wonder if I'll be sad, if I'll mourn for us."

We ordered coffee.

"Well, what can I tell you," Georgia said. "I'm a Jewish mother. I'm going to go out as a Jewish mother."

She made us laugh. She told me about her professor at McCormick, Hulda, the sister of the great Reinhold Niebuhr, and how, when she died, Georgia vowed to carry on her work.

"It's what I expected for us," she said, "that we would be peers together, that you would carry on my work, even surpass me. It's what every teacher wants, especially for her chosen students. But I won't know now, what you do. My energies will be focused on saving my marriage. Sam's going through adolescence for the first time. I wonder if I have the strength to endure what will come and if we'll still have anything left when he's moved through that. But I believe in him, and the children love him. I worry about Joel. I try to be careful not to get from Joel what I don't get from Sam. My kids are fine. I have been so self-conscious about cutting apron strings. I don't know why I was able to do that with them when I couldn't do it with you. I don't understand why Rose doesn't feel the oppression you feel."

Hearing her say that helped me. I hadn't exaggerated what she'd done to me. Of course, Rose felt differently than I did. They weren't lovers. They had love without sex so love without guilt. I had believed Georgia when she told me that. I still believed it.

Then she tried to make me change my plans. "Get a later flight, come home with us."

"No way," I said.

"Come on. I'll seduce you back." She blanched. "Bad choice of words. I don't mean that. I'm sorry. I mean the children. You could see the children one last time."

I shook my head. We argued about the bill, she finally let me pay half of it, and we got up and left the restaurant.

Then we were back where we'd started, driving in her car like we had when I was a kid and she took me home after our meetings in the church.

"Shall we go out like we came in?" she said. "I want to hold your hand."

To let her do that would have been for me a terrible capitulation, robbing me of my fragile hold on myself. I didn't answer her and stayed safely on my side.

"If you lived nearby," Georgia said, "I wouldn't let you do this. I need all the help I can get now."

What did she mean she wouldn't let me? She never stopped. And then we were at the terminal. She got out of the car and came around to where I stood. Suddenly, I wanted to tell her a thousand things about how much I loved her. But I had already said what I had to say and pretty words would not do it. We clasped hands, locked eyes and held each other for a long moment. We made no more speeches, just said goodbye. I turned, walked to the building, turned back before I entered, and we raised our hands in a kind of salute, a simple gesture that acknowledged the weight of what I'd done. I turned again and went inside.

I had done what I'd set out to do. It had not worked out as I'd imagined. I hadn't expected the old affection to take hold with such intensity. I'd delivered my ultimatum. I'd gotten not her scorn or her dismissal, but her blessing. Wasn't that even better? I did what I said I would. I could tell Don that Georgia understood I would not see her again, not for years, maybe not ever.

# 15

## Tidings

Home from Chicago, from saying goodbye, my life with Don could begin anew, unencumbered. He had thrown himself into work at Chambers Church, preaching, teaching, administering. In addition, he had taken up the housing work Mel Schoonover had begun with community members, renovating tenement houses in the East Harlem Triangle.

At dinner, he told me the latest. "It's already six refrigerators and two stoves that have been stolen out of the buildings. Four members of the community housing board went to see the chief of police today. You will not believe what we were told."

The renovated tenements he spoke of would offer the best housing in East Harlem's poorest neighborhood. Getting this far was a triumph since contractors and suppliers tried to cheat them, missing deadlines and using inferior building materials. Then, before anyone could take up residence, people just walked in, in broad daylight, and carried out the big appliances. The cops did nothing to patrol the block and launched no criminal investigation.

"We reported the situation and demanded action. The chief told us there was nothing he could do, but he'd be glad to issue us licenses for guns if we wanted them."

"Let the vigilantes ride!" I laughed in disbelief. "Forgive me, but it's a little scary. With your brilliant coordination and perfect vision, you'd be great with a gun in your hand."

"We did not take up the offer!"

"So what happens?"

"The problem will disappear once the buildings are occupied. We're working as fast as we can to fill the buildings."

We cleared the table and did the dishes together. I loved seeing Don energized like this and decided to keep still for a while about what troubled me. I brought him up to date on my work on *Southern Africa Magazine* and the fiction class I had enrolled in at The New School. I was writing a novel about our years in South Africa. In time, I would tell him that something had happened these days and weeks after Georgia was out of my life, as we kept no secrets.

For the first time ever, I discovered I had complete control of Georgia because she existed only in my mind. I could erase what I found oppressive—her superiority and her self-denigration, her neediness and manipulative control. That left what I still craved. In my daydreams it was magic, like when I had first come under her spell. One day we'd encounter each other on opposites sides of the barricades, liberal vs. radical. I had tried for years to be and do just what she wanted. Her acknowledgment in Chicago that we did not hold identical positions had felt like salvation. I was free to grow up as my own self. She would see me opposite her in the struggle and still respect me.

That wasn't my favorite fantasy. That one had us walking separately in the city. I'd be down on Second Avenue past the bodegas, or down near The New School where I took my class. Someone approached, caught my eye—a familiar gait or tilt of the head—but it would have been years since we'd seen each other, and the sun could play tricks. We'd each pause, not quite certain, searching for clues and the other's intentions. A smile would break across my face and then across hers. We couldn't help ourselves, our wildly beating hearts, as we hurried forward into an embrace. The power of her seduction, that first incredible falling in love, her appointment of me as her chosen one, making me forever special, these things held me still.

My novel began to take shape. I set it in a fictional "Ukuthula," a place that resembled Elim and Lemana, with Ben as the main male character, a white man I based on Francois, our dear friend and colleague. In my novel, Ben is married to Anna, an American woman. They struggle—as Molly and Francois, Don and I struggled—with how to live a moral life in apartheid South Africa, when the threat of removal hangs over everyone's head, removal which would drive people from their homes, destroy communities and make Ben's life's work impossible. Anna comes to believe that there is nothing they can do and they should move to the States. Ben cannot bear the thought, despite everything, of leaving South Africa.

I wanted to write a tragedy. Ben and Anna love each other deeply. In any sane society, their marriage would survive, no, flourish. Not in South Africa. By early summer, 1971, I had a rough draft and mailed it to Francois and Molly while they were visiting Switzerland, as they told me it was too dangerous to send it to them at home. Self-absorbed, I feared they'd find the manuscript false, naïve, or didactic. I didn't consider that my characters were not very well disguised versions of Francois and me, married to each other, making love, arguing, and finally separating. It was a novel. All I cared about was whether or not its depiction of life in Ukuthula rang true. Don had not objected to what I wrote. Why would they?

July and August came in brutal—record-breaking heat and humidity—and everyone's nerves were on edge. Sonny Boy got beat up by the cops for not having a license for his scooter, and when it got out in the neighborhood, an angry crowd gathered and the cops shot into the river to disperse it. Nobody got hurt. There was a stabbing in Triangle Houses; big brutish Joe with a knife in his chest ran out of the building, and Drake drove him and his wife to the hospital. To everyone's shock, she'd stabbed him and not the other way around. In the car Joe said, "I know she didn't mean it. But I'm a goner." At the hospital, he got out of the car on his own power and walked in, but he pulled the knife out and bled to death.

These things happened the same weekend Ruby's husband Dick beat her up and threatened to kill her. She escaped to our apartment, where Dick wouldn't think to look for her. She couldn't call the police because Dick was on parole. He said he'd kill himself before going back to prison.

Ruby and Dick lived in Triangle Houses and she was an active member of the church, a brilliant, complicated woman who had been involved in radical politics in her youth. Ruby was the one woman from Chambers who was glad to join me for programs of African music and speeches by African political leaders. I welcomed time with her, to hear her stories, about Dick and the children, but also about her political work and time with the Communist Party. After five days, we felt it wasn't safe for Ruby to be with us and we moved her across town. Our friend Hilah was in France, and she'd given me her keys so I could use her place to write. It was a perfect hiding place for Ruby while she figured out what to do.

The letter from Francois and Molly arrived just then. "The story you tell in your novel is terribly compelling and disturbing." I was elated. They got what I was trying to show. Ben is a man trapped. Yes, apartheid is evil, and yes, Ben identifies with the "Sovenga" people with whom he grew up. But he is white. Ukuthula cushions him from this; he marries Anna because she is not a white South African. Still, in his own heart, he is connected inescapably to the system created by his predecessors and, like it or not, the system that he has benefited from promiscuously. He is guilty at his core. Anna wants to leave. He can't. He needs to suffer. Without his guilt, he would be naked and he is terrified of being naked.

Francois wrote that he hated my depiction of him. They encouraged me to finish and to publish. I wrote back immediately, so that they got the letter in Switzerland. "It's a novel. I'm just playing off you." It took me decades to see how I'd given Ben characteristics that were not Francois' but my own. Guilt would remain my subject, warped and misunderstood but standing as a witness until I was finally able to see myself.

That Sunday Ruby risked coming to church and sang the solo. Standing at the edge of the choir, dressed in a midnight blue satin blouse, she was a grave presence, and her contralto wavered as she began, then gained in power, resounding, reverberating throughout the sanctuary. You didn't need to know her story to hear in that voice the depth of her pain and sadness. But I did know some of it. How she had wanted desperately to have children. Dick, not long out of prison, was raising his grandchildren because his daughter had OD'd. Ruby was much better educated than Dick and lived in a much bigger world. But he had the children, and before they married, he was a gentleman, courting her, and the children came to love her like a mother. They married against the advice of Ruby's friends. Dick changed, expecting her to be a subservient traditional wife, and jealousy and rage drove him to beat her when he drank. Ruby's sorrow was all that and deeper still—the terrible fear that she would find no resting place for herself, no place on earth. And so she sang.

> *Come, ye disconsolate, where'er ye languish,*
> *Come to the mercy seat, fervently kneel.*
> *Here bring your wounded hearts, here tell your anguish;*
> *Earth has no sorrow that heaven cannot heal.*

I cried, for Ruby, for myself, in gratitude for her singing as well as in confusion for the still elusive source of my own anxious heartache.

Each Sunday at Chambers Church, Don preached, and I taught junior high kids Sunday school. Only the girls came—Sabrena, Roxie, Annette, Denise, and Rachel, who was older. We sat on folding chairs in a corner of the gym beneath the sanctuary, and I set out this Sunday in October to teach about covenant relationships, beginning with what they knew.

"Why do you live with your parents, your mother?"

Sabrena and Roxie sat next to each other and spoke at the same time. "Because we don't have enough money to move out." They giggled.

"We ran away from home," Sabrena said. "We got to the train station, but there was a cop there and we got scared and went home."

"Why are you afraid of the police?" Easy conversation like this delighted me. I'd rarely been able to have anything like it with students in South Africa.

"The police are pigs," Rachel said. "The Panthers say so."

"Whoa!" I said. "Who are the police supposed to protect?"

"The people!"

"Who are the Panthers working for?"

"The people!"

"So the police and the Panthers are doing the same thing?"

The kids looked at each other in confusion and I looked at them with growing affection. I asked them why the Panthers carried guns.

"For protection!"

"From whom?"

Their answer was less certain. "The police?"

"Why don't you ask them?"

"Who?"

"The Panthers. They're here at the church every morning," I said.

"You mean Huey's here?" Sabrena said, wide-eyed.

"No, Huey Newton is in California." I was surprised they didn't know about the breakfast program, but I didn't answer my question. I wanted them to find out for themselves.

Rachel followed me upstairs and sat with me during worship. She didn't speak in class as often as the younger girls, but when she did it was always precocious, like quoting Freud. I found myself drawn to her and it took me no time at all to see that she was vulnerable. I was relieved at the end of the service when she ran off to be with her friends.

Sitting at our yellow Formica table on one of the mismatched blue plastic chairs, I waited for Don to come home. He'd said on the phone he had something to tell me that had to be said in person. I looked up at the little girl in the framed UNICEF poster that hung to my left on the wall next to the stove. Light from the window opposite me brightened her wind-blown yellow dress, and the same wind pulled strands of jet-black hair across her face. She brought a melancholy playfulness to our table, almost like a third person at meals, the child we didn't have. I twisted a strand of hair that had escaped my long, loose ponytail. It had been two years since my miscarriage. We kept trying, with a kind of courage I would appreciate only later. After the commotion over so-called mature orgasm, it took less time than I expected for me to have them easily. Don still worried about impotence. I tried not to. But I didn't get pregnant. Finally, we began to explore adoption.

I got up and paced to silence myself. Don loved me, whether or not I could conceive. I would banish those bad words—sterile, barren—or ones I wouldn't even say to myself that had to do with sex and Georgia. She'd wanted me to have a child to prove she hadn't damaged me. I couldn't prove it.

Then Don was home and we got beers from the fridge and settled in the living room at opposite ends of the couch. He tried to smile but didn't fool me. I could see in his sweet, familiar face that I wouldn't like whatever was coming.

"Doon summoned me to his office," Don said. "He gave me an ultimatum."

Startled, I watched Don struggle for words. Doon didn't give ultimatums. He was co-pastor at Chambers, rising to that position from his original job as janitor. The congregation had recognized his great rapport with neighborhood kids—he'd been a gang member once—and he was given more and more responsibility. With his slow speech and easy listening, pipe in hand, he would sit back in the chair in his little office as if he had all the time in the world to hear you out. He didn't give advice, almost ever.

"I told Doon last week that we were looking into adoption," Don said. "Today he couldn't have been more direct. 'Don't adopt a black child.' He said every day he takes flak for me in the neighborhood. So does every member of the congregation. If we were to adopt a black child, people would see it as an attempt to be what we can never be, something other than just white. Adopt a black kid? My days at Chambers are done."

"Holy shit!"

"Yeah. He said my motivation, ours, doesn't matter at all. There was only one way people would take it, as an impossible, phony attempt to identify."

"Well, that's clear enough."

Why were we surprised? Race matters were covert or overt but always present. Ever since we returned from South Africa, we'd had white friends tell us that white people couldn't work in black communities anymore. We listened but gave greater weight to what members of the church continued to tell us. They wanted Don to be their minister. We didn't forget for a minute that we were in East Harlem at the pleasure of the congregation. Almost unconsciously, I got to harbor my smug, defensive belief that I was different from other white people, just like I had been in South Africa. If Doon gave us an ultimatum, we would abide by it.

Which meant we never had to grapple, personally, with whether or not we were ready to adopt a child who was black.

# 16

# Your Neighbor as Yourself

"Do you want to give the phone to Don? Since you're not speaking to me?"

Two full years since I'd heard her voice and it shot through me like an electric charge. "I'll talk to you." I hurried to the bedroom, picked up the bedside phone and waited to hear the click, Don hanging up in the kitchen, where we were making dinner with friends.

"Hello," I said.

Georgia launched into what sounded like a prepared speech. "I work for the YWCA. The Y is sponsoring a major, national conference on racism in America. I'm calling Don about it. Racism is the most urgent priority facing the nation, eliminating racism." I couldn't stop her from reading me the program and list of speakers: Harvey Cox, Teresa Hoover, Andy Young, Roy Wilkins…

When she paused at last, I didn't try to keep the sarcasm from my voice. "I know about the conference. Tell me why you're really calling."

"Just what I said."

"Are you coming to New York?"

"Of course. I felt it was my duty to inform Don. That's all I have to say." She hung up.

I leaned against the dresser. I didn't believe for a second that she called just about the conference. She didn't have the guts to say she wanted to see me. I went back to the table and deflected questions about the call though I saw that Don had guessed who it was.

As soon as our friends left, I told Don everything that Georgia had said. He agreed that the conference was just an excuse to be in touch.

"I want to phone her back and call her bluff."

"Go ahead." Don always agreed with me when he saw I wanted something badly.

I waited a few days, infuriated that she thought she had a duty to teach us about racism. I phoned her and asked if we could have a meal.

Georgia granted me an audience; that's what it felt like. I'd learned from Rose that not long after we'd met in Chicago, Sam had divorced Georgia and she had moved to a new state to make a new life with her children.

It wasn't until I sat opposite Georgia at a small table in the crowded bar that I could take her measure. Guarded and argumentative, she ordered a martini and started in. "Eliminating racism is my number one priority now. I have become completely committed to this work. That's the reason I called you."

I smiled at her and shook my head slowly. "I don't believe you." She looked terrible, had gained at least twenty pounds. She was smoking heavily and rested her elbows on the table, as if she couldn't hold herself up without support. I saw with embarrassing relief that she was stunningly unattractive. I had let myself imagine… I dearly loved Don but our sex life was still troubled. When we made love, I was happy with this sweet poet of a man. But I couldn't count on him. His job made him anxious and sometimes impotent. Often, he said he was just too tired.

Georgia stubbed her cigarette out. "You don't believe me? Then don't. If you can't see that your personal obsessions are trivial, that's not my problem. In the face of the mandate to fight racism, we have to put aside personal matters. I'm sorry to say this, but I had no desire to see you. I hardly ever think of you. You don't matter to me anymore."

"I would never, ever use the word *trivial* to describe what went on between us." I was seething. She'd found in racism a mighty shield to hide behind. I'd give her that. Maybe her divorce and all it demanded put me out of her mind for a while. But forget me? Never.

"Don't you get it?" she said. "In the face of the horrors that have been and continue to be inflicted on black people in America *institutionally*, the personal is picayune."

I wanted to laugh. She sounded like the film script of *Dr. Zhivago*. Tom Courtenay's Pasha telling Julie Christie's Lara, "In the time of revolution, the personal life is dead." She was parroting a line, rhetoric to protect herself from what she couldn't face.

"I don't split the personal and the political the way you do. Haven't you heard? The personal *is* political." I found the conversation completely contorted, her energetic exoneration of herself at my expense. "Okay, I was naïve," I said. "I thought we could have a drink and a civil conversation. I admit it. I was curious to know how you are."

I should have gathered my things and left, except my coat was in her room. Why on earth? Because she had insisted, and now she ordered another martini. I ordered a second drink and searched for something less explosive to say.

"Tell me about your job."

She had an administrative position at the YWCA in the suburb where she lived.

"The staff is mixed," she said. "One of the black women took me on. She attacked me for caring more about white people. I was trying to bring white people along with me in this work. I always believe people can change. This woman called me on it, questioning my priorities and exposing my racism. It was excruciating. I went home and wrote my letter of resignation. But I have to earn a living. I didn't resign."

She sighed deeply, as if letting down a barrier. "I miss my teaching and time to write. My poems. I cut to the narrowest focus, limit and hone what's happened in order to survive."

Her anger drained away and left her sounding weary. I couldn't tell if she was just trying to impress me or if I should believe her. "*The New Yorker* wanted five of my poems. I had to finish the last one. But then I didn't send them because they were too personal." She shuddered. "Now I have no time to write poetry."

She did impress me. How could she not send poems to an interested editor at *The New Yorker*? I was about to say as much, but she got out a picture of her children. "That's in front of the house where we live." The kids were smiling, Judy's hair still so blonde it looked almost white, John making devil's horns behind Joel's head. Her eagerness to show them to me was as close to an apology as I would get, and we remarked at how fast they were growing, eight, eleven, and thirteen already. "They're in good shape," she said. "John and Joel asked to go with me on a peace march with the Quakers. It was a good march for them and me too. Someone said God doesn't judge us for being successful. God judges us for being faithful. I can do that. I don't expect to wipe out racism, but I can be faithful to the effort."

I would have said the same, about faithfulness. She was beginning to make sense, to sound like her old self. I didn't see how desperately I was searching for common ground. Tentatively, because I remembered that in Chicago, I had promised not to write about us, I told her I was beginning a novel that would tell our story.

"I don't care what you write," she said impatiently.

"I'm not asking your permission."

"Oh, lay off." She didn't hide her annoyance. "Let go of that trivial personal stuff."

I stared at her. *I don't care what you write?* It's okay to write that you went to bed with teenage girls? Not just me but at least two others? It's all right to say that you were seducing us—it was the only word we knew—the summer you got married? Okay to write about my parents' hospitality? How you made love to me in the guest room just catty corner from their bedroom? Just three months after you married Sam? It's okay if I write a novel about all that?

What would have happened if I could have asked these things? I never did.

"If all you want to do is sit here and insult me, why did we order second drinks?"

"I ordered mine so I can sleep. I assumed you'd have the decency not to make me drink alone." She lit a cigarette. "You may remember you deserted me in my hour of greatest need, when Sam filed for divorce. You utterly abandoned me, disappeared. If you wonder why I'm hostile, that's it. The divorce was more painful than I care to tell you, and I had no one."

I was dumbfounded. I thought she'd understood, respected, even, why I'd said goodbye. Whatever happened, Georgia's needs took precedence. Georgia was wronged. Georgia was never to blame. I waited for her tirade against Sam. To my surprise, she spoke of Virginia.

"My mother told Virginia about the divorce. Virginia sent me a mimeographed letter at Christmas time and then this spring a cookbook she'd put together at her church. She wrote in front, 'To Georgia from Virginia.' That's all she can manage."

Then she railed against Virginia. How she'd only been twelve years old and Virginia had ruled her life. "I did whatever she told me. But she wouldn't talk to me. I wanted her to talk to me about God. We split because of theological and political differences."

Listening to her, I knew the script. Georgia's understanding of Virginia had progressed not an inch in a decade and a half. I would come to understand that her static way of seeing things, her inability to call Virginia what she was, meant that she didn't have to call herself that either. I didn't have this language yet. What I did wonder was: what on earth did she still want from Virginia?

"I'm cold now." She spoke slowly. "I love very few people. Rose is my rock. She's with the children now. She spends as many nights with us as she does at home. She has her PhD, teaches at the university." She smiled weakly. "I'm not the person you saw in Chicago. And I mean it. I don't care what you write. I'm not afraid of your friends, for them to know about us. Homosexuality doesn't frighten me anymore. It used to terrify me. I'm not homosexual."

As if that was the only matter of concern. Still, speaking openly like this, she surprised me. We'd never used the word. At most, she'd mention how much *the climate had changed* since she was involved with Virginia in the forties, as if we were speaking of rainfall and desertification. I was still afraid of the word. During the Stonewall Riots in 1969, when police raided a gay bar in Greenwich Village and the gay community fought back, I knew I should be in the streets because, never mind that I was married, I was connected to that community. But I was afraid to go, and I despised myself for it. I could march against the War in Vietnam and for racial justice, but not for lesbians and gays.

Georgia had said our love was special and I'd believed her. She called it a gift from God. "I don't … I don't like labels," I said.

"Yes, I know, but I would say I'm bisexual. I know this from experience. What about you? Have you had other homosexual relations?"

I shook my head no. It was true. Don was my only love.

I did not like labels. Not just because they were restrictive but because there were things I had no distance from and no name for. Rachel. Rachel in my Sunday school class. Precocious Rachel with her *Oh, that's so Freudian! / You don't have kids. Let me be your kid. / When I'm alone with you, I identify with Bigger in* Native Son, *only just a little bit.* Dear Rachel in her woman's body and fifteen-year-old self. Later I would think about her as the girl I did not seduce. Now she just scared me. It wasn't fair. When I was sixteen with Georgia I was scared. Now I was thirty-two, and I was still scared. The only way I knew to be with Rachel was the way Georgia was with me. The only way Georgia knew to be with me was Virginia's way.

I was too vulnerable, too quick to read innuendos. I wanted to befriend Rachel, to hear what she was crying for, yet it felt too much like the impossibly complicated desire I'd known at her age, and I became my sixteen-year-old tongue-tied self.

Nothing happened. I behaved. I was not moral; I was frightened. Being in Harlem was for me a version of being in South Africa. I was and would always be an outsider. Being an outsider was protection. I would never try to touch Rachel because I had no idea what I would be getting into or what would come down on me if I did. Georgia, when she came to my childhood church, knew exactly where she was, could navigate in her sleep. I would never be at home like that in Harlem, ever. Racism in American? If my behavior was racist, so be it, and lucky Rachel, and lucky me.

Georgia was on her third martini. "You were my last," she said. "Rose and I are not lovers. I'm dead sexually. But I wonder. What would happen if you spent the night with me? You were the aggressive one, you know." She smiled shyly. "I don't mean I wasn't responsible. I mean if you came with me to my room, I'd want to hold you. I'd want you to hold me."

Why wasn't I outraged? This woman whom I'd found completely unattractive and whom I'd managed to disarm now thought she could just walk back into my embrace? Did I so need someone to desire me?

"I thought about it," I said. "Coming to see you, I thought about making love again."

"God, I did love you. But I was terrified that someone would find out about us. If they had, I would have lost everything."

We'd not spoken like this, not for years and never so clearly. I too had been terrified and for the same reason, though I always knew I had less to lose, no husband or children. Despite the terror, she couldn't stop. I'd tried to stop us and she wouldn't let me.

"Remember your first year at seminary?" she said.

It was the year I almost came completely apart. I had that sign in my room. *God be merciful to me a sinner.* I could hardly believe that He might be.

"That year, you called me up. I think it was October. When I realized what shape you were in, I told you to get help. It was more important that you be all right than anything else."

I didn't know that she thought about it like this, that she had been willing to risk for me her reputation, her children, her husband. She had loved me. She did love me. I knew it. "I'm glad it never came to that, exposure, I mean."

"If only you had been of age. Then it wouldn't have been dishonest."

"I never think of it as dishonest."

"I guess," she said, "I confuse illegality with dishonesty."

Sam was the one with whom she had been dishonest, not me. But I didn't say that.

"When I'm fifty-eight and you're fifty, we should make love again to see if we're still good." Her completely unexpected bravado delighted me. She'd never spoken like this before, and the remark made me want to tell her things.

"I can't have children," I said.

"Women don't need children." She said it strongly, like a feminist, but also carefully, as if she was trying very hard not to tell me what to do.

This *was* a different woman. Not the one who had told me again and again until I wanted to strangle her that I had to have a baby so she'd know she hadn't ruined me.

It was time to say goodbye. I had to get my coat, and we entered her room quietly so as not to wake her roommate. I ducked into the bathroom. When I came out, the room was dark, only the light from the bathroom spilling into the hall. Georgia had taken her clothes off, her blouse and skirt. She stood a few feet away from me, barefooted and in her slip. Why on earth?

I had come to see her because I was curious, more than curious. I hadn't thought ahead about what might happen. Now I knew. This display of herself in her flesh-colored slip that didn't cover nearly enough of her flesh for my comfort.... I hugged her goodbye, quickly, because refusing would have been more difficult.

The question crossed my mind—what if she'd had a single room? Intentional or not, her roommate was protection for both of us. It was time to get the hell out of here. I did not need to see her again, ever.

# 17

# The Devotion of Your Youth

Each November, Don and I made our own Christmas cards, sometimes drawing each one individually, and other times typing them up and mimeographing them. It was 1972, and we agreed quickly on the text we wanted, a favorite James Baldwin quote from *Nobody Knows My Name*, though we changed Baldwin's pronouns, eliminating "man" and "he." We read everything Baldwin wrote and quoted him now almost as often as we quoted the Bible. On the front of the card we wrote:

> Any real change implies the breakup of the world as one has always known it, the loss of all that gave one an identity, the end of safety. And at such a moment, unable to see and not daring to imagine what the future will now bring forth, one clings to what one knew, or dreamed that one possessed.

Then, on the inside of the card, the quote continued.

> Yet, it is only when one is able, without bitterness or self-pity, to surrender a dream one has long cherished or a privilege one has long possessed that one is set free—one has set oneself free—for higher dreams, for greater privileges.

Don drew birds in flight on the pale green card stock we chose. I addressed the envelopes, to family and friends, those we'd known in college and seminary, in South Africa, in East Harlem and at Chambers Church.

Don's mother came for Christmas, traveling alone for the first time since Don's father's death in March. We hung our stockings from the bookcases—colorful, handmade Turkish stockings I'd bought in Istanbul on my way home from Beirut. I was grateful for the rituals—the presents, special food and music—as they made it easier to be with my mother-in-law.

I watched Don and his mother untie identical gifts with the same care, not tearing the paper that covered miniature chocolate bars. Don had inherited his height from her, and his religion. Lona was a straight-backed preacher's daughter who grew up in Kansas where her father had been minister of the First Baptist Church in town for forty years. After we wed, she had insisted that I be re-baptized, as the sprinkling I'd received as an infant didn't count. She was prim, shy of overt anger, and her passion for believer's baptism took me completely by surprise. If I was to be a Baptist preacher's wife, she said, within the fold, I must be immersed as an adult and of my own volition. It had not been an auspicious beginning for Lona and me as of course I refused. We were polite with each other but there was little warmth between us.

After we'd opened our stocking presents, Don got up to make breakfast and I put his Baroque Christmas records on, Telemann, and Purcell's "Behold I bring you glad tidings." We cleaned up after breakfast and settled in to open packages. The apartment filled with the aroma of roasting turkey, and by mid-afternoon I got them both to help me in the kitchen, Don mashing potatoes and Lona making gravy. It wasn't until we finished our meal and were enjoying a cup of coffee with our cheese pie that Lona took advantage of a lull in the conversation.

She said, bluntly, "Would you like to have a child?"

Don and I looked at each other, puzzled. We had given up on children since no white infants were available for adoption. The children who were available were older, with difficult histories or special needs, and we agreed quite quickly that we lacked the desire and the ability to care for such a child.

Lona continued. "Mrs. Stewart's assistant has a teenage daughter who got herself pregnant. They want an out-of-state adoption."

Mrs. Stewart, Don explained, had been his Sunday school teacher in fourth grade. She ran the social service agency in the Pennsylvania town where his parents had retired, the town they'd lived in when Don was in grade school.

Don's eyes shone with something more than delight, with longing, and he pressed his lips together as if to contain himself. He wanted a child as much as I did. Maybe more. Only he never said so. When I couldn't get pregnant, he never spoke about his loss. Convinced that my infertility was punishment, I'd gone a little crazy. Had I, with all my Sturm und Drang, made it impossible for him to speak his grief?

I got up and went to his mother, placed my hand on her shoulder. "You're a stork," I said, laughing. She even looked like a stork, tall and angular. "Tell us everything you know about this pregnant girl."

Lona wrote to us shortly after she got home with all the details. The mother was sixteen years old; she had dark hair and hazel eyes. She was the same height I was, five feet, six inches, and a junior in high school. The father was twenty and recently out of the service. A Vietnam vet.

The girl had two sisters. It was a fine family; the parents were very careful with their daughters. The girl hadn't dated but had gone out with a group of friends; she had an eleven o'clock curfew.

We studied the paper as if it were a treasure map, a crystal ball foretelling our future.

They had gone out briefly. Then the careful parents had forbidden their daughter to see the man again. They did not tell him that he got her pregnant. That stopped us.

"He'll never know," Don said, "he fathered a child. Imagine that."

I imagined something else, too. Sixteen years old. I came from a fine family. My parents were careful with their daughters. Yet what I did would never show and could go on and on. Too bad she wasn't infertile like me. I couldn't help but wonder if she'd enjoyed it the way I had. I bet not. I wondered if he forced himself. And such shame must have followed the crushing discovery of her pregnancy. Would her burden be not easier, but simpler than mine? I wondered how often she'd think of her baby. Every day? How long, and at what age, she'd grieve. Even more I wondered who she'd tell. I hoped to God she told the man she later married, the man with whom, I would learn, she had more children. It was none of my business what she said to anyone. I knew that, but I also knew how secrets isolate, turn one into a liar. I felt a kinship with this sixteen-year-old girl that wasn't just about getting her child.

These thoughts came to me at four in the morning, disturbing me enough that I couldn't go back to sleep. I had been the envy of my insomniac friends as I slept soundly all night long. Until now. Now I lay awake with dread and an inexplicable sadness.

Did I dare to take my sadness to my women's group? We'd been meeting every week for ten months, since June 1972. We began by reading feminist texts, beginning with Sheila Rowbotham's *Women, Resistance and Revolution.* Three South Africans—Suzette, Jennifer, and Stephanie—plus Janet, who also worked on *Southern Africa Magazine,* my friend Simone, and others I knew less well. Over the first months, some of the women would drop out and little by little we would begin to speak more personally.

We'd met for the first time in Jennifer's Upper West Side apartment. Sitting in an imperfect circle on worn Persian carpets and second-hand furniture, we spent the first night introducing ourselves. Jen's spacious living room had, in addition to the simple furniture, floor-to-ceiling bookshelves that covered an entire wall and tall curtainless windows opposite that opened out on Riverside Park and the Hudson River. The range of books on the shelves and the art on the walls—tiny pre–Columbian figures, a Rouault print, a silk textile of three Chinese men, and a large abstract oil over the mantel—displayed her serious, eclectic interests.

Jen and her husband were political exiles who had come to New York from South Africa six years before. Mike, who was a lawyer, got out first, and if Jen hadn't joined him, she'd likely have gone to prison, or at least been banned, a kind of house arrest. Jen didn't talk about this, not that first night. Or about how much she'd rather have been back in Johannesburg.

"I think my experience is different from that of most of you," Jen said. "I'm a bit older. I'm thirty-eight." A short woman, she sat among oversized tropical potted plants, in front of the fireplace as if she wanted to be inconspicuous. "Beginning when I was a teenager, I've been part of a small, tight, disciplined group."

Under apartheid, South Africa's people were divided into four groups: Africans, whites, Indians and Coloreds—people of mixed race. Jen's group was made up of all of them, with most of the whites Jews like herself. Since almost everyone lived in radically segregated communities, and political work with people of different groups was difficult and dangerous, Jen's experience was rare.

"I was just fourteen," Jennifer said, "when the Nationalist Party came to power." She spoke intensely and with a strong South African accent. I listened happily because it took me back to Lemana and our years in the Northern Transvaal. Secretly, I loved it that several of my closest friends would not be Americans, would speak English differently than I did.

"My group had an answer for everything," Jennifer said, "and had considerable political punch though it was far too rigid, and I had to fight my way out of that. What I miss is the solidarity I had with comrades back home."

Listening to her speak about what she'd done when she was very young, I couldn't get beyond who she was now, almost as old as Georgia, with a daughter and a son. Though I tended to be outspoken and a leader in the groups I joined, I had a deep habit, hidden even from myself, of abdicating my intellectual independence and subordinating myself to someone else's mind. Jen had none of Georgia's manipulative, commanding charisma. I didn't have to be leery of her, and I came to depend on her hard-earned, finely honed insights and analysis. It was safe to do so because she demanded nothing inappropriate in return.

At that first meeting, I intended to tell the women about Georgia when I introduced myself. It was two years since I'd said goodbye to her and before my charged meeting over drinks with her in New York. I needed these women who would become my most intimate friends to know about her and how she'd shaped my life.

Only at the second meeting did I find the courage to speak. The ceiling in Jennifer's apartment that night seemed enormously high, and I sat isolated at the edge of the carpet. When it was my turn, I hugged my knees. Though I had told a few people about Georgia, I'd never said it in a group before.

"I have to tell you about the best and the worst thing that ever happened to me," I said.

I said it too fast, in a flat voice, as if I were telling them I'd had a Springer Spaniel as a pet when I was a kid.

"Her name was Georgia. She was my religious teacher and we loved each other." I told them a brief version of the whole story and that I had last seen her two years before. To finish, I said, "I will never see her again."

Silence, absolute, awkward silence. No one said a word. No one expressed revulsion or shock, which was a great relief. But couldn't someone say something? I was afraid to look up.

One woman laughed. "Let me tell you about my affair," she said.

Relieved and confused, I couldn't listen well. No one appreciated what I was trying to say. Though it was not their intention, they made me feel that what I said was of no consequence. I lacked the courage to challenge the silence because I didn't know what I wanted from them, though I'd have recognized it if it had been forthcoming. It was New York, 1972, long before churches and universities put in place standards of behavior appropriate between teacher and student. It was a time of feminism rising, when women loving women was hip. Soon after this meeting, Georgia called about the racism conference and I went to have a drink with her. I didn't tell anyone. I didn't talk about Georgia in the women's group again, not for a long time.

If my women's group had not been a safe place to talk about what mattered most, did I dare tell them about the adoption and my dread and sadness? But what good were they if I couldn't?

The women's movement taught us that we didn't have to be mothers and maybe they'd dismiss me like they had before. Except two of us already had children, Jen's kids were eleven and twelve already, and Janet's baby Carla just over a year. We met at Janet's now because it was easier for her with the baby. She lived two blocks from Jen on the Upper West Side in a smaller apartment. As usual we went around the circle and, stoically, I waited my turn, hiding my anxiety by making jokes and comments on what other people said. Just like the first time, when I told them about Georgia, I didn't know what I wanted from them, only that I had to speak. If I didn't, I was keeping a secret. As good as lying. I wanted to be done with lies and secrets.

Then it was my turn. "People are happy for us," I said. "When I say we're going to get a baby, at church or at the magazine, people congratulate me as if I've done something. I haven't done shit. I'm not a mother. They act like I should be in love with this baby. The baby won't be born till May or June. I feel like saying what's so great about sleepless nights and smelly diapers?"

I wasn't saying it right. I saw that they were attentive, all of them.

"What if I can't cope?" I took a deep breath, determined not to cry. "What if the baby is too much for us and we've made a terrible mistake?" I lowered my head, afraid of their judgment, deeply aware of what Jen and Janet had been through with children. Jen had had to uproot hers from their beloved home in South Africa. Janet lost her first pregnancy at five months, horribly and at home, and she dealt with it the way she dealt with everything. She went immediately back to work, monitoring Nigeria's war with Biafra, the war that showed us naked children with distended bellies dying from hunger. Janet carried on. She'd think I was whining.

"It's just like when you're pregnant," Janet said.

The kindness in her voice frightened me. I looked up. She leaned forward, her intensely intelligent face and clear blue eyes full of sympathy.

"It's just like that. Late in the term, when you're so huge and there is no way to turn back, you look at yourself, and you don't know what you've gotten yourself into."

I bit my lip. I wanted her to know how much her words mattered, but if you're pregnant, something begins to happen to your body, and that helps you get ready. This had nothing to do with my body, this fear. It was all in my head.

Then something terrible happened. Suzette got up from her chair and came across the room to me, and there, with everyone watching us, Suzette hugged me. She said something, but I could not hear her.

Suzette couldn't know, and I didn't understand either, but I was exposed in that embrace. It was as terrible as the time I tried to read Radclyffe Hall's *The Well of Loneliness*. I bought it in the train station and the saleswoman gave it to me in a dark green paper sack. I sat down and took it out of the sack. I only remember that I took the book out of the green paper sack and began to read it and then I closed it and put it back in the sack and carried the sack to the trash can and, looking around nervously, I pushed the sack into the trash can.

The book was about a woman who loved women. I could not even hold it in my hands. Anyone walking by would have seen me with it and they would have known what I did with Georgia.

It was the same terror, Suzette embracing me in the middle of the room with Jen and Stephanie, Janet, Simone, Linda, Kay, and Marty standing there looking at us. An irrational terror I understood not at all. I only know I wanted to sink into the floor and, like the Wicked Witch of the West, melt into a puddle and drain away, invisible, gone.

# 18

# A Child Is Born

When our son was born on May 29, 1973, I was at Jen's apartment meeting with representatives from Guinea Bissau's liberation movement, the PAIGC. They brought us up to date on the war against Portugal and developments in the liberated zones. Don was on the phone with his mother when I got home.

"We have a baby boy," he said.

We hugged in disbelief.

"I'm so happy. I'm so scared. I'll be right back."

I ran out and bought a bottle of champagne and we started making calls.

First, my parents, as this was an occasion when it was simple to be a dutiful daughter. They were thrilled. Then, starting on the East Coast and moving through the time zones, we spread the news to our siblings and friends. It was the strangest, most confusing joy I'd ever experienced. We had a baby. Or so Don's mother said.

Finally, we called my old roommate and her husband, Pat and Bill, in Berkeley. "Guess what?" I said.

"You're parents!"

Don filled them in. "A baby boy. Seven pounds, eight ounces. Twenty inches long. We're going to call him Alex. We're flying out tomorrow to get him."

Pat and Bill had three-year-old twins. Their enthusiasm was contagious. I was incredibly excited until, on the plane the next day, I panicked.

"We haven't signed anything yet. Can't we change our minds?" Neither of us was any good when we were overtired and babies made you overtired all the time. I thought of baby shit and the smell of ammonia. I understood my terror was bigger than that even if I couldn't say what it was. Strapped into the seat by the little window, I looked out at a gray sky and cried. Don put his arm around me, and I guessed it calmed his fears to comfort me. He was scared too.

Then a bureaucratic miscommunication gave us a twenty-four-hour reprieve. The baby had to be left overnight in the hospital after his mother was discharged. Then, technically, he was abandoned and available for adoption. We could not receive him until the next day. Feeling sorry for us, Don's mother took us out to dinner.

"Tell us," I said, after we'd ordered, "about your conversation with the baby's grandmother when she came to talk to you about the adoption." I had tried to picture this encounter between the biological grandmother— what a term—and the adoptive grandmother. Neither woman would have had any experience to prepare for such a conversation. Who would speak first? How euphemistically would they talk? Very.

Don's mother put her knife and fork down, as if she understood the importance of the question and wanted to give it her full consideration. She looked at Don, not at me, as she spoke, hardly able to contain her happiness in finding her son the baby he wanted. "Well, she was very pleased to learn that you're a minister. She saw that as a very good sign. She explained about the lawyer drawing up papers that she and her daughter would sign. Then the two of you have to sign. It didn't take long to agree on the arrangements. She's the only one who will know who you are. She is not telling her husband, and her daughter doesn't want to know."

"Thank you!" Don said, raising a glass to his mother.

"To the stork!" I said, and we all laughed.

Don's mother undoubtedly thought we were celebrating the baby's birth and our imminent parenthood. Don and I also toasted the delay. I could get totally intrigued by everything about this adoption—the parents, the grandparents, the war, the high school, the law, the stigma—except the outcome, that I would be a mother. The word wasn't me. The meaning of *mother* was being scrutinized by the women's movement, which only reinforced my own reservations. *Mother* meant domestic and tethered, someone subsuming her own desires for those of her family. Even if I couldn't articulate this notion, I felt the threat of it, that I would lose myself before I'd recovered from what had happened to me and had found my own way.

On June 2 at ten o'clock in the morning, Mrs. Stewart walked up the sidewalk with a bundle in her arms. She came through the front door and into the living room. Mrs. Stewart put the bundle into my arms.

With fear and trembling I received him. But he wasn't fragile, and I didn't need to be afraid. His face looked like a little nut, an acorn, compact and perfectly shaped. He had hair, brown with a touch of rust, that made him look like a little person, and he had slate blue eyes. I looked into his eyes. He stared blindly back and I saw myself, my face reflected and distorted in his pupils. I saw, right then, that if we could come to love each other we'd be all right.

We flew home with a six-day-old baby who slept the entire way, to our colossal relief. Janet met us at LaGuardia in her father's car with eighteen-month-old Carla in the front seat, and she drove us home. Then we had to do everything ourselves, and we learned how to change diapers and bathe Alex and fill plastic disposable bottle liners with formula. The liners came rolled up in a box and the box was empty.

"You used the last one and didn't tell me, didn't get more?" It was a preventable problem, and I had no tolerance for preventable problems. "Go!" I yelled at Don while I held a hungry, crying baby. I paced the hall and talked to Alex. "Daddy will be right back. I'll feed you really really soon."

It made me frantic if I couldn't stop his crying. If I fed him, changed him, rocked and walked with him, and he still cried, my heart hurt so much I wanted to take his little head and bash it against the refrigerator to silence him. I read a book that helped me. Something about the normal craziness of mothering, but the urge to hurt him terrified me.

By the end of the first month, I would have said I loved him, but I didn't have a life. I still worked for *Southern Africa*, but the baby and the housework and cooking took all my energy. I hadn't gotten near the novel I was writing since he'd been born. I was thirty-three years old but I behaved like a child in adolescence—perfectly grown up one minute and a raving two-year-old the next. Never mind that my rational mind tried to tell me otherwise, I absolutely could not believe that this time of exhaustion would ever end.

Yet it was also sweet. I settled into the rocking chair to give Alex a bottle. He sucked happily, oblivious to my struggles, or so I told myself. That day, when he was one month old, looking at his little face, I thought for the first time about boys and girls. What made him look like a boy? He just did. Don and I had insisted that we did not care about the sex of the baby. Now I saw that wasn't true. What if we'd gotten a girl, one into all the girly things I'd fought against? What if she wanted dolls, to paint her fingernails? I had been the best little boy a girl could be, fighting for myself my whole childhood. Rocking gently, listening to the sucking sounds, the noise from the street, I felt the rebellion still raging inside me. I understood that I could let a boy be a boy, and I gave thanks that my little baby was Alex.

Two months after Alex was born, we flew to Colorado for a family reunion at Snow Mountain Ranch in the Rockies. I'd been eight or nine when my family took its first trip west. We'd gone horseback riding, and I'd found the deer antler that had hung in my bedroom. The wild landscape—immense meadow surrounded by dark lodgepole pine forests with snow-capped peaks beyond—was breathing space for me back then. Now it wasn't the landscape I needed but the many hands eager to help with the baby.

Don put a sleeping Alex into the white painted crib in the bedroom of our cabin and went to fix him a bottle while I unpacked, putting our things into the simple wooden dresser. I was almost done when my brother-in-law Bruce appeared in the doorway, grinning. He looked almost menacing with his long sideburns and dark, unshaven jaw.

"I see you've got him completely domesticated!"

"What?"

"Don's in the kitchen," he said in a singsong voice. "Don's making formula!"

"And why not?" I punched him good-naturedly. Don and I inhabited a different universe than the one Bruce and Carmen lived in. I found it outrageous that she did everything—cook and clean and take care of their kids, Russell and Cindy.

"I can't wait to see how you guys raise your kid," Bruce said.

When I told Don about the conversation, he shook his head dismissively. "It's a ritual he has to go through to confirm his manhood."

"Mother's offered to get up in the night with Alex," I said.

Maybe the myths were true. Maybe a child did make mothers and daughters close. We were always missing each other emotionally, Mother and I. After my first full night of sleep in what felt like ages, I was convinced that the only sane way to raise a child was with a crowd of people—grandparents, great aunts, aunts, uncles, and cousins who were fascinated by the baby and loved to watch us feed, bathe, and change him.

I could say yes when Carmen and Bruce proposed an all-day hike because Mother offered, happily, to take care of Alex, and she'd have lots of help from Aunt Carmen and Bruce's mother. I hadn't been away from Alex a whole day since he was born. I couldn't wait. Though Cindy didn't feel good and stayed with the grandparents, thirteen-year-old Russell came with us and we drove and then climbed to 12,000 feet, hiked a high ridge above timberline, and picnicked on a carpet of wildflowers. Russell—articulate, compact, and as nimble as a mountain goat—helped us imagine what Alex might become. Whatever Carmen and Bruce were doing as parents, however conventional their roles, I had to admit they had a super kid.

We didn't get back to the cabin until four-thirty in the afternoon, later than we'd said, and I was anxious by the time we arrived. I found Alex sound asleep in his little crib. I went out to thank Mother.

She was a wreck. "I gave him his bottle at ten, like you instructed," she said. "But he started to whimper while we were having lunch. I couldn't get him to quiet down. He just cried and cried." She looked as if she was about to cry, not for Alex but because she felt guilty. "I took him and put him in the other room and closed the door, so I wouldn't hear him."

"Why didn't you feed him?" I said as neutrally as I could muster.

"It wasn't time."

I stared at the ceiling. I had given her very careful instructions: yes, feed him every four hours, but sooner if he's hungry. Mother could not break the rules. She would feed Alex the very same way she'd fed Carmen and me more than thirty years before. Every four hours on schedule. I saw her reading the disapproval on my face.

"I meant to do the right thing," she said. "I should have paid better attention to your instructions. I should have fed him. I should—"

"Let it go," I said coldly. Her *shoulds* made me nuts. We had no kind way to deal with this. She'd made me feel guilty for years. How could she expect me to absolve her? She'd never absolved me.

Now I regret my intolerance. I couldn't see that an inconsolable child hurt her the same way it hurt me. Who knows, probably for the same reasons. I can't help but imagine what if Mother could have said to me, right then, *You're a wonderful mother.* What if she had said that instead of wallowing in guilt? *I have such respect for how you and Don care for your baby.* That's what I needed from her, though I didn't know it then.

The next morning Mother was her usual cheerful self as if nothing had happened. But she took Don aside. He came immediately to tell me.

I was sitting outside on a log, part of a circle that surrounded a campfire, giving Alex a bottle. Don sat down next to me.

"Listen to what your mother said. She said that your father and she could never imagine you being a mother, though of course she would never say that to you. They had discussed this and they think it will be all right because you married me."

I handed the baby to Don and stood up, agitated. I wasn't angry that he told me; I'd have been angry if he hadn't.

They thought he was a better mother than I was. No surprise there. They had no idea what I was capable of. I didn't cry. I straightened. I'd show them what a mother I was. I'd show them.

# 19

# Talk Leads Only To...

In 1974, Don's seventh year at Chambers Church, he got the whole summer off. The sabbatical came just in time. We were exhausted and it wasn't just Alex. Because of the women's movement, nothing about relationships or women's and men's roles could be taken for granted; everything had to be negotiated, even the value of marriage and, within it, monogamy. We discussed these things in my women's group. Some of us had conventional marriages; others, though partnered, refused on principal to marry, and affairs were not uncommon.

Don and I agreed that we were equal partners, but what would that mean in practice? Who would cook, who would take care of the baby, and whose work would take precedence? How could it be equal, if he had the paycheck and demands on his time we couldn't control? I was trying to keep *Southern Africa* solvent and write a second novel and I earned virtually no money as the occasional article I published paid loose change. In the face of all this I was often angry; Don was passive. What made me most unhappy—intimate matters—stayed with us like an uninvited guest content to disrupt our hard-fought, fragile equilibrium.

We kept trying, talking.

"With my mother," Don said, "you have to pay close attention to her first reaction. She says she's so proud of her minister son. But when I first told her I wanted to go to seminary, she burst out crying. Her perfect life as the good little minister's daughter, her saint of a father. She will never say a word against any of it. That outburst showed me what she really felt about life inside the parish."

"My mother," I said, "*really* loves that you're a minister. She really loves that we were *missionaries*. I can't stand how she tries to live through me."

"And my dad," Don said. "I was five years old. I went to him for a hug.

He pushed me back and held out his hand. 'Men shake hands.' We never hugged again." We talked about our families. We talked about Georgia. We didn't see that over time our talk had become interminable. We faced what troubled us with words, words that reinforced our shared illusions and defenses instead of exposing them because exposure, illumination, would have required us to change. All this was exhausting.

Drained and depleted, we flew to California for the summer. Pat and Bill in Berkeley had invited us to share their home. When they offered, we'd waited five seconds to accept. It would be like the family reunion with more hands to do the work, four adults and just three children—one-year-old Alex, and Madelia and Hilary who were four-year-old twins. We quickly made a schedule—one parent on duty with the children in the morning, another in the afternoon, each of us on duty just once every other day. We took outings to the ocean and up the coast, all seven of us in their little blue VW bug. The routine began to work a kind of magic, giving Don and me breathing space, Pat and Bill's presence providing rich new content to our daily lives and the kids adding simple pleasures and delight.

Evenings, after we put the children to bed, the four of us began to gather in the living room, a space encircled high on the walls by a red, blue, and black Central Asian woven tent band, like the interior of a yurt. Bill brought the whiskey bottle, which he set down on the large round engraved Turkish tray that served as their coffee table. We settled ourselves around it on cushions or couch as if we were in some Ottoman salon, and we talked. We talked about childhood and travel, politics and pacifism— Bill was a Quaker. It was Don's idea to give each of us an entire evening to explain why we were doing what we were doing and where we wanted to be in five years' time.

Because it was his idea, we made Don go first. He'd come to Berkeley with a writing project but bought a flute and began to learn to play instead. Now he sat straight-backed and cross-legged on the floor, his pale blue short-sleeved shirt tucked neatly into black cotton pants, and he poured himself a drink.

"Why am I doing what I'm doing?" he said. "Because Chambers is the first church I've found that *is* the church, a community of forgiven sinners." He paused to light a cigarette, relaxed. By now we had learned each other's proclivities and procrastinations, each other's quirks, and we had found them tolerable, compatible. I could see that Don was happy to have a captive audience.

"What I hadn't realized when I started at Chambers," Don said, "was how much I'd be involved in housing work. We had such big dreams. We were going to establish, well, the beloved community in the East Harlem Triangle. It would be an economically integrated community, with role models for kids and visible success stories. That's not what happened."

The city's rent structures sabotaged the dream. The gap between the subsidies low income people got and the full rent that more affluent people had to pay was too great. Families doing better couldn't afford to stay and didn't and the Triangle was condemned to be a permanent slum. It broke his heart.

He sighed. "There's so much trouble. Even in the church." He began to cite examples: women who played vital leadership roles but who had children out of control. People he'd helped who'd then turned against him. Sure, he'd made mistakes. Sure, it was sometimes a problem that he was white and he tried to explain what he meant.

I'd heard it all before and watched the ash on his cigarette get longer and longer. This habit of his annoyed me. Why didn't he knock it off? And then it fell off onto the metal table where it did no harm.

His voice dropped. "I'm ashamed to say this, but I'm anxious all the time."

Bill sat directly opposite Don and he stroked his beard, a habitual gesture, before he spoke. "Are you aware that you've talked more than an hour about your life and you've never once mentioned Gail or Alex?"

"Bill's right, you know," Pat said kindly when Don started to object.

I hugged my knees. Why hadn't I noticed? Good for them, to point it out.

Caught, Don cringed. "Can't get away with anything here." Then he said out loud what I knew to be true, but I loved hearing him say it. "Without Gail, I couldn't be Chambers' pastor. She's my smart sounding board, my savvy critic, my ally and comforter." He gave me a guilty smile. "But I didn't finish. Let me finish. I haven't talked about what's next. Maybe it's time that I let myself imagine something else, somewhere else, some other congregation."

It was the first I'd heard of it. I let Pat and Bill talk to him. They didn't judge. He imagined a white working-class church, one that wouldn't be so hard. Then, as if to return Don's status to him, his expertise, Bill changed the subject and asked for advice.

"I don't know how to talk to children about God," he said. "Quakers don't talk about God."

"Presbyterians do," Pat said, "but it was all hypocritical in my church. Love everybody. Except the Mexicans on the other side of the tracks. I don't want my kids to learn that."

Don brightened. "Kids know about God," he said eagerly. "They know without being taught, until we kill it in them. I was feeding Alex a banana yesterday, and he was really hungry, but he wanted to feed me too. Something more basic than hunger is going on. It's love responding to love."

"Maybe if we talked about God as a Shared Banana," I said.

Pat smiled. "Our Shared Banana that art in heaven…"

We laughed and the laughter made us close. Don would return to New York and begin to look for a new job. In a year's time, we would leave East Harlem for Brooklyn. We had that summer with Pat and Bill to thank for the beginning of the rest of our lives.

The night it was Pat's turn to talk, as I put Alex to bed, I thought about how we had done very little together, just the two of us. She wasn't political like my New York friends, though we'd all gathered around their tiny black and white TV to watch the buildup to impeachment, and we'd celebrated when President Nixon resigned. Pat was engaged in a drawing class and preparation for her first art degree, at the master's level, which she'd begin in the fall. She had time for very little else.

"You know," I said, laughing, as we took our places around the copper tray, "you're not as nice as you used to be, not as pliable. And you have much narrower taste."

We teased her all summer because she vetoed films she thought would waste her time.

"Because I know at last what I want to do," Pat said fiercely. "I'm thirty-three already. I have to make up for lost time." She sat where Don had sat, in the same cross-legged position, her dark hair, tan face with its slightly crooked nose, peasant blouse and baggy pants making her look almost Turkish or maybe just quintessential Berkeley. "My high school art teacher was the coach. He gave me a C. It's the only C I ever got and it sent me off on the wrong path for years." It wasn't until she was teaching English in Turkey that she began to see—turbans on tombstones, embroidered headscarves, carpets. "I had little money but, in the bazaar, I got friendly with the rug merchants and they let me bring rugs home to live with, for weeks. I began to learn to weave."

Pat talked about her daughters, their imaginative play, Hilary's health challenges, Madelia's dominance, and how she and Bill took care of them, had lunch dates, kept figuring it out. Though of course we couldn't know it then, of the four of us, she was on the clearest track. She would get her degree and then she would teach, first as an adjunct at whatever college would have her, and finally as a full professor in a university art department. She would make fiber art that over time would become sculptural and include installations. Though she was admirably unpretentious, she would become a leader in her field.

We took a break from talk to attend a festival of erotic films. I was preoccupied that summer, wondering about my sexuality and intent on going to the festival, and pleased that the others were interested too. Better than any film with body parts was one showing—very close up—the bright, sunlit peeling of an orange, segments separated in slow motion, allowing the imagination to expose and pull open luscious bits. We all chose it as the winner.

We were close enough by this time to tell our dreams, even the one I had after the festival, an erotic dream about Bill. I didn't say I'd wished it was Don or that he and I still struggled to please each other. The summer was supposed to help us. It had in every other way.

Bill was a bit embarrassed and I thought flattered by my discreet telling of my dream, and then, when it was his night to talk, he told us his dream, only it was a daytime one.

"I'd rather be a postman." He laughed, making it a joke. "The Near Eastern Languages and Literature Department is like the region itself, fractured and full of hostilities. The moderns don't talk to the ancients, the Arabs don't talk to the Jews, and I have no one to talk to about my research." He nodded to Don and me. "You have no idea what a pleasure it is that you're interested in my old Sufi poet."

We didn't take him seriously because he had yet to take himself seriously. But fifteen years later, he would walk away from his tenured position as a teacher of Turkish language and literature, shocking his colleagues and saving his sanity and soul though not his marriage.

My night, I brought a copy of *People* magazine which had just begun publishing and I'd read my first issue, curious after the promotional hype. "Serious political reporting is dying in America," I announced. "This is the beginning of the end. It's not going to be about issues anymore but about personalities. Watch. Before long, it will degenerate into gossip and scandal."

My summer project was to write but I didn't want to talk about that. The agent who circulated my first novel, the one set in South Africa, had not been able to place it. I was writing now out of my relationship with Georgia, a novel based on our experience. Every day at the little desk set up on the tiny back porch, I put words on paper, groping. I would, with sadness and despair, shred all of it when I got home.

Besides writing I had ventured out into Berkeley because Berkeley offered safe ways to explore what I was tentatively, obliquely, beginning to wonder about myself. I took in a gathering of lesbians: young, lively, stunning women who could have been the senior class of any women's college. I was struck by how ordinary they looked, how impossible to stereotype. Just regular women, women who loved women. Nothing frightening. Yet I was frightened and talked to no one.

The bisexual group I investigated was attended by slightly older, dowdier women, one of whom asked me out for coffee. I pleaded childcare and fled. I was looking for something that summer but didn't yet know what. Not giving up Don but maybe finding someone to give me what he didn't. Except I was not ready to accept even a cup of coffee.

I prepared very carefully for my night to speak. Alex and motherhood in this time of heightened feminist consciousness. Activism on southern Africa. I did not talk about the meetings I'd been attending, though they all knew I went. No one asked about them or challenged me the way Don was challenged. Why didn't Bill and Pat ask Don what it was like for him when I went out? Did it not occur to them? Did they feel it was not their business? Or was the subject simply too uncomfortable for everyone?

Looking at old photos now, I see again how much fun we had that summer, playing in a way Don and I no longer played at home. Yet, despite that, the hope I'd brought to Berkeley dissipated, the dilemmas I'd come with didn't disappear. Nothing—not Don's time to play the flute or mine to write, not the meetings I attended, not the open conversation—changed our intimate ineptness. We even went to San Francisco, just the two of us, stayed overnight in a hotel, a second honeymoon. It didn't help.

The week before Don and I returned to New York, the four of us were at the table in the middle of the day, the kids down for naps. We hadn't cleared the dishes but sat as if there was unfinished business. I could not hide that I was sad.

"I thought things would change," I said, "over the summer, since we had time."

Don grimaced, his *here we go again* look. But he didn't speak.

"Maybe we need help," I said.

"It's your problem," he said. "Not mine."

"It's a good idea," Bill said. "Talk to someone."

Pat nodded energetically.

"I'm fine," Don said. "But do it if you need to."

And so I did.

That's what the summer gave us. Don would move on professionally and I would find myself a therapist. Both decisions were exactly right and both would open doors and change us in ways far more complex and far-reaching than anything we might have imagined as we boarded the plane, held Alex on our laps, and headed home.

# 20

## Nothing on My Own

"Tell me about yourself before you met Georgia."

Dr. Mila Aizenberg sat opposite me in what felt like a living room. My chair made me sit up straight. Hers was larger and could recline. Taking in her short, solid stature, her sturdy composure, I thought she looked like an Eastern European peasant, though it was an odd association as she was nicely dressed in a gray suit and stylish, low-heeled gray shoes. I guessed she was near fifty, fifteen years beyond me.

Yes, I had made the right decision, choosing her. I'd interviewed someone else first. I had no idea what I should be looking for, no more idea what to expect than I'd had when my father introduced me to Georgia. I went to see Leslie Cunningham first because she advertised herself as a feminist. About my age, she had big compassionate eyes, and she prompted me encouragingly when I hesitated in my Georgia story. I could see that Georgia aroused her interest. That made me uneasy. Maybe she was too eager. Maybe she'd never worked with somebody like me before.

I'd dressed for both therapists in my best jeans, my Mao jacket freshly ironed and my all-purpose ankle-high boots. I saw quickly that Dr. Aizenberg would not prompt me. She would wait as long as it took for me to speak and, haltingly, I told her why I'd come. First my anger and how it frightened me, that I might hurt Alex. Then, what was even harder. Georgia and all that. I loved Don. He was my best friend. Sex with him … I was afraid I was … maybe our troubles were my fault … maybe I needed a woman lover.

Her calm attentive expression didn't change; she'd heard these things before. She said, "Tell me about yourself before Georgia."

As if what happened with Georgia came from somewhere. When the session ended, she said that she would work with me but I needed to come two times a week.

Which meant she thought I was really sick. I didn't know how I would pay her but I did not hesitate and said yes to her conditions. Then, before I rose from that upright chair, naively and blindly from my heart, I blurted out, "I know what will happen here. I'm going to fight with you and I'm going to fall in love with you."

Before Georgia. No one raised their voice in my family except me. My sister Carmen stood across the room from me, our twin beds between us, and she said I *shouldn't*, which pissed me off. I grabbed a wooden yo-yo and, with my strong arm and my good eye, I got her right in the mouth. She wore braces. It was a bloody mess.

I felt awful. I loved my big sister, though in the savvy way of youngsters, I sensed I could not be like her and set out to be as unlike her as possible, having absorbed already simplistic opposites, the currency in our parents' universe, the only one we knew.

I was the best little boy a girl could be, but only in my own eyes. Maybe I was ten and Carmen twelve when our family acted out Carmen's school assignment. We pretended we were a pioneer family, 100 years before. At first it was fun. Carmen and I sat on the floor, and Dad and Mother turned their chairs to the hearth. By the light of the fire, we ate our meal and we each got to say what our lives would be like. I would chop wood and hunt and have my own horse.

"No, you wouldn't," Dad said immediately, "you're a girl."

He might as well have ordered me to leave the room. He wouldn't let me be, even in make believe. That night I kept my hurt and rage inside. Other times I couldn't.

Dad's chair by the fireplace held center stage in our carefully laid out living room. I planted myself in front of it, in front of him, arms crossed, fists clenched, the red cover of *Time Magazine* a barrier between us. Determined not to speak until he looked up, I stared at the cover picture, Israel's Ben-Gurion with his bushy eyebrows. His mouth was turned down at the corners, his eyes not sharply focused, as if he was oblivious to his surroundings, oblivious as my father was oblivious to me. He had told me I couldn't go to meet Georgia. I studied the cover to hold my ground. *Twenty Cents. March 11, 1957.*

I had loved that big red chair, where Dad sat pretending to read. I would jump into his lap and he'd scratch my back. I purred. Then he cheated and sneaked his fingers around under my arms, tickling, and I shrieked, "Stop!" His fingers retreated, and then he cheated again and I shrieked again and leapt away.

A place of play no longer, Dad's red leather chair with its brass studs had become his bunker. Trapped by my need for his attention, I was losing the battle of wills. I hated him for putting me in this position, annihilating my presence by his silence.

"When are you going to stop treating me like a child?" I demanded, tears streaming down my face.

He raised his eyes. "I will stop treating you like a child when you stop acting like one."

He would listen to me, but only if I became what he wanted, an obedient little girl.

It would take me longer to tell Dr. Aizenberg about me and my mother. She was conscientious and fair. Each morning, first Carmen and then I would sit on a little chair holding a book in our lap, and as Mother braided our hair, she read to us before school, the neighborhood kids coming in to sit with us and hear the stories. When I was little, I wanted to be near her and sat on the floor in the kitchen, playing with my puppy while she cooked. We fought over language, even adjectives. I said my shirt was *dirty*. She said no, *soiled*. She would never accept that I was a tomboy because to her the word meant crude and boisterous. She had grown up a Methodist, abhorred drink, and lived in a black and white world of absolutes. When the little restaurant in town began to let people play cards for money, Mother marched into the store to lay down the law. "There is no gambling in our town."

And so, there wasn't.

She was a good citizen, president of the PTA and very active in our church. I was proud of her for these things. She took pride in my accomplishments, bragged about them to her friends, and welcomed my friends to our home. We were such a model family that we were chosen to host the first foreign student our high school ever had and Ingegerd came from Sweden to live with us my senior year.

All this—her rectitude, her diligence, her high standards for her children and herself—made what happened all the more bewildering.

I was a teen already when it started, and it continued irregularly and unpredictably until Ingegerd came. I would be in the bath, warm and secure behind a closed door. In our family, only one person was in the bathroom at a time.

"May I come in?" Mother entered and shut the door behind her. "You won't mind if I use the sink here." She spoke in her regular, modulated voice.

She stood at the sink which was to the right of the toilet opposite the tub, and I looked up as she bent down to step out of her white underpants. She placed them on the toilet seat top. She took her pink washcloth, soaped it and, hitching up her skirt to keep it dry, she began to wash herself between her legs. She wanted me to see her. She wanted an excuse to see me. I watched just long enough to take it in then hugged my knees to my body to hide myself. We didn't have a shower; there was no curtain to pull.

"Cleanliness is next to Godliness," Mother said too brightly, hiding her behavior behind a platitude.

I wanted to scream. I wanted to die. I didn't understand her compulsion, her terribly specific washing. It was perverse. It was more perverse than anything I ever did with Georgia. I wanted what I got from Georgia. I did not want my mother to make me see her. I did not want my mother to see me.

I wasn't wrong that first day with Dr. Aizenberg. I did argue with her, tentatively at first, because I was afraid. Six months later I was still afraid, but I had to know.

"Tell me your theoretical position on homosexuality."

"What matters is how relationships work for you," she said.

"Yes," I said, anxiously. "But if you operate within a framework that understands homosexuality as sick then the game is fixed from the start."

"Can you see how you're trying to get me to tell you what to do?"

She meant about Simone, my old friend Simone. She was an artist, a painter, and she was married, though she and her husband now lived separately. For months, I had been aware of my desire. I had told Mila, as I called Dr. Aizenberg now, that I fantasized about making love to her.

"I am not trying to get you to tell me what to do."

Mila began again. "Can you see that your attraction to Simone might be burdened by what you are trying to work out about Georgia?"

She didn't approve of homosexuality. If she did, she would say so. I would not let her reduce what I had with Georgia to simple sickness or perversion. But it frightened me to argue with her. I couldn't stand it if she rejected me like Georgia had when I said the wrong thing.

Mila understood me like no one since Georgia. Not even Don. That she'd accomplished this over many weeks and months showed itself in a single sentence. She said to me, "Georgia made you feel special."

That simple acknowledgment left me speechless, touching as it did even what came before Georgia, what made me vulnerable to Georgia.

Mila said, "Georgia made you feel special."

I managed to say, "Yes." I felt as if I had been blessed.

Georgia made me feel special.

Georgia made me special.

Georgia made me.

The shorter the sentence, the more danger there was in it. Mila said it just right, keeping the danger at bay.

We were quiet for a long time.

Mila made it possible for me to trust her. Now I was terrified that I'd displease her. But I had to know what she believed, theoretically, about homosexuality, and she would not tell me.

One of the simplest things the women's movement gave us was permission to go out without our husbands. The Yorkville bar where I met Simone on a Saturday night in early June was empty when I arrived. I sat where I could watch the door and ordered a beer. My reflection in the big window pleased me—a woman in a deep blue tunic-like shirt, tight-fitting flowered jeans, and my sturdy boots. A handsome woman, hair pulled back tight in a French roll, dimples when she smiled but someone not to mess with. Even more than how I looked, I liked that I had an easy conscience. Don would put Alex to bed. Don would finish his sermon. Though being his reader and critic was important to me, I didn't have to help him every single week.

I lit a cigarette and watched the smoke rise in a thick spiral like spun glass. Simone was uncharacteristically late. The waiters played darts and left me alone. Watching them, I was happy, anonymous, autonomous. Then the door to the bar opened, and there she was. I got up and hugged her shyly. With her extravagantly long hair, her black shirt and hip-hugging black pants, she looked like a New York artist, and the picture we made, sitting together at a little table, excited me.

"I got stuck on the phone with Frank," she said apologetically.

I did not want to talk about her husband. "Never mind," I said quickly.

She ordered a Coke. Her round, guileless face was vulnerable, as if she'd been crying, and beautiful to me.

"Oh, Gail," she said the instant we were alone, "don't desert me."

Sometimes her pleas seemed melodramatic and her neediness frightening. Not tonight. More than any other woman in the women's group, Simone made me feel safe, though I didn't understand yet that it was because we were both troubled and she was not afraid to show it. Secretly, I believed I was more together than she was, had a better husband.

"I'm not going anywhere," I said.

I could see it bothered Simone that I smoked, and I stubbed out my cigarette.

"I know what you think." She looked at me intently. "You think what Ann thinks. But I'm not going to leave Frank."

Ann was her therapist. We talked about our therapists and we talked about our husbands. And she was right. I did think she should leave him. They were both brilliant and had a rich intellectual life, but they came from different planets. Frank was a blustering agnostic Jew from Detroit. Simone was from West Texas and grew up in the Church of Christ with its rigid fundamentalisms and literal heaven and hell. Simone had graduated from Union Seminary the year before we arrived, and it was there that she had begun her journey away from religious extremes, but she was still a deeply devoted believer. Not only that. Frank had affairs. The pain they caused her was extreme enough that the previous summer she'd moved out to her own apartment. What kind of marriage was that?

"Fine," I said, quietly. "Don't leave him. If that's what you want."

She leaned forward. "I watch what other people do when they divorce. They make *bastards* out of their husbands, demonizing them to have the strength to kick them out. I will not do that."

How could she kick him out? They hadn't lived together for a year. I wanted to tell Simone that she was wedded to her pain as much as to Frank.

I flagged the waiter and ordered another drink. Something in Simone's unwavering stubbornness registered with me, her declaration that only she would choose what was good for her. Mila tried to show me that I wanted her to tell me what to do. Georgia had. I wanted there to be a simple right and wrong. I couldn't find one. Simone couldn't imagine her life without Frank, no matter the limitations or how much he hurt her. I couldn't imagine my life without Don either.

I changed the subject. "I think we really are going to move."

Don had been job hunting. He told the denominational personnel counselor assisting him that he wanted a white working-class congregation. The counselor laughed at him. Don was, he said, everything wrong for such a congregation—intellectual, bookish, without an ounce of interest in sports or trucks.

"Don plays the flute, for God's sake," I said. "There's an opening in Brooklyn, Park Slope. Middle-class, mixed black and white, some professionals and some business people. Don's interviewing next week."

"Isn't it a bit bizarre," Simone said, "that Don could work in East Harlem for years but this counselor thinks he'd be a complete misfit in a white working-class church?"

"Very astute," I said. Chambers accepted us despite the obvious differences in race and class. We had knowledge and skills to offer and a willingness to learn. The church in South Africa had wanted us to stay on and the differences there were even more extreme. I could hear Don's voice, *There is no Jew, no Greek...* He really believed such distinctions could be superseded among the faithful. Did I believe this? Anymore? What about the need to be conscious, always, of race and class and gender in human institutions and interactions?

We stopped talking about our men. I told Simone about my writing. She told me how much she hated the art world, how it had been bollixed by the art market and how it had been complicit in the system that had perpetrated the Vietnam War. It was time to go. We walked on 86th Street over to First Avenue. The bus up First Avenue would drop me right across the street from my door.

The night was warm and gentle. Taller than Simone, I put my arm around her shoulders; she put her arm around my waist, and we walked up the street in step. People looked at us. Defiant, I kept my arm where it was though I felt naked and incensed. Waiting for the bus, we stood tight against each other in the entranceway to a darkened store, and when we saw the bus coming, we held each other close and we kissed each other. Though I was not thinking of Georgia, I kissed Simone like Georgia had first kissed me, that secret, special kiss in her car that changed me forever. That's what it felt like, a kiss I could never retreat from. And didn't want to.

# 21

# Thou Shalt Not

That kiss frightened me. Three days later, Alex in tow, I went to Janet and Carl's house in Connecticut to take care of their children. Janet, representing *Southern Africa Magazine*, was traveling to Mozambique to attend its June 25, 1975, independence celebration.

Mozambique was important to everyone at the magazine and in my women's group. Many of us had worked with the liberation movement Frelimo, and all of us were devastated when President Eduardo Mondlane was assassinated by letter bomb in Dar es Salaam in 1969.

Now, at last, Frelimo would become the Government of Mozambique. Yes, absolutely, Janet needed to make this journey for all of us. The first of the women's group to leave New York City for good, she remained deeply involved. Stephanie and I would take care of her girls: Carla, three and a half, and ten-month-old Britton. We planned to take turns with the kids and to write. Stephanie had traveled in the liberated zones of Guinea-Bissau with the guerrilla army of the PAIGC. She was writing what would become *Fighting Two Colonialisms: Women in Guinea-Bissau*. I was working on my novel about Georgia and me.

But this morning, we sat together on the lawn with the kids. I had to tell her my dream. I was with Agostinho Neto, head of the Angolan liberation movement, the MPLA. "We were in a cathedral-like structure," I said. "We were both reading from the Book of Isaiah. It gave us something in common when we met later in an elevator."

Stephanie was sitting on the ground next to me, playing with blonde baby Britton.

"Then we started to make out, Neto and I, as we were having an affair. You knew about this, and we talked about how dangerous and exciting it is to have affairs with political people like Neto; one can learn things it's not safe to know."

Stephanie laughed, stretching her long, slender body to retrieve a rattle that Britton had tossed away. "Why are you dreaming about Neto?"

"I'm reading his poems." With two colleagues, I was compiling a booklet to help readers understand more about the region: *If You Want to Know Me: A New Collection of Poetry, Art and Photography from Southern Africa.* "Neto's a soldier and a poet. Power and imagination joined. No liberation without power to banish the Portuguese and take control of the land. But no liberation either without a vision of human society expressed by the creative imagination that is taught but not bound by the past."

Stephanie raised her eyebrows and nodded in agreement. "You dream amazing dreams. I'll give you that. I don't remember mine."

"Go into therapy," I said. "It's great training for dream retention."

She grinned. "You know what your real problem is?"

"What?"

"You think too much."

"Meaning?"

"You dream about having an affair. You talk to me about having an affair. Just do it. And see what happens."

"You make it sound so easy."

"It is if you want it badly enough."

I got up and occupied myself pulling Alex and Carla in her little red wagon because Stephanie scared me. She knew I fantasized a woman lover. I hadn't told her I'd kissed Simone.

When Carl came home from work that night, before we had dinner, we put the children to bed. Carl sat at the head of the table, Stephanie on his right, and I on his left. I watched him as he served the curried chicken that Stephanie had prepared. I'd always thought Carl was gorgeous, now exaggeratedly so in the low light from the chandelier over the old, narrow table. His skin was golden brown and his eyes mottled brown and blue. This man had no narrow ancestral line, that was for sure, and the labels seemed ridiculous. He was black. Janet was white. Their daughters would always be taken for white. Watching him, I wondered what it meant to him that this was true. I wanted to talk to him about it, about the strange word *passing*. I didn't know him well. I was afraid of offending.

"You know everybody's not like the two of you," Carl said, filling the silence.

"Yes," I said. "We are rather exceptional." It was easy to joke with him.

"Why do you say that?" Stephanie said.

"You encouraged Janet to go. Other people objected, but not for the reason I would have thought. I thought people would be worried about her safety."

"She'll be fine," Stephanie said.

Stephanie had been in war zones and knew what she was talking about. I wasn't worried about Janet either.

Carl poured more wine. "What people asked me wasn't about safety. They wanted to know how I could let my wife go away for such a long time."

"You're failing the patriarchy," I said, laughing.

"Exactly," he said. "It's funny and insulting. I can't get along for a few weeks without my wife?"

"Who said that?" Stephanie wanted to know. "Men or women?"

"Both. And the other big question was whispered to Janet. How can you leave Carl with two women?"

"Safety in numbers," I said.

"You're such a conservative," he said, a wicked smile on his face.

"No, you're so conventional. What if I'm more interested in women?" I could hardly believe myself, that I'd said it. Maybe it was the wine, but being with Stephanie and Carl, I wanted to sound sophisticated, not hung up the way I really was. I told Carl about Georgia, the novel I was writing, and that I'd gone into therapy to sort out what she'd meant to me.

"Good for you," he said. His approval seemed genuine and without judgment.

Sitting at the table in the dining room of the gracious, comfortable home, the oldest part of which was early nineteenth century, my apartment in East Harlem seemed a world away, making it easy to talk, like it had been in Berkeley, even about sex.

Carl surprised me when he spoke again. "You have to do what you have to do. Make your own choices and then be responsible for them. I lived a long time by other people's standards, doing what I thought I was supposed to. I try not to anymore. Janet helps me."

How on earth had he stopped, changed? But he continued before I could figure out how to ask.

"If you really are bisexual, then it means you have to have both kinds of lovers. Right? That you'll want to?"

His word choice, *bisexual*, startled me. I'd tried it on, of course, attended that gathering of women in Berkeley. But the word carried little power, none of the appeal or the terror of the word *lesbian.* "I don't know how to answer you," I said. "I don't see how I can. I think it would kill Don."

Then I listened intently as Carl and Stephanie talked about husbands and wives, the affairs one could have that needn't threaten a marriage. Carl spoke generally about discretion, Stephanie specifically about being away from home. This was not the morality I was taught in childhood but something freer, riskier. Were they naïve, or was I? Could there actually be affairs in which no one got hurt? I was grateful that they didn't ask what I thought, if I agreed with them. I wouldn't have known how to answer.

Greenwood Baptist Church called Don to be their new minister. He'd preached powerfully at his trial sermon, on Psalm 98, *Oh sing to the Lord a new song, for he has done marvelous things.* But it wasn't marvelous when Don learned from the Methodist minister's wife that it had been the talk of Park Slope that I'd worn pants to church. Yes, but dressy ones with a colorful green Indian top. We groaned. We would indeed have to teach a new song or two.

We rented an apartment within walking distance of the church; we'd move on September 1. In East Harlem until then, I didn't think much about the Brooklyn congregation. I'd never been a conventional minister's wife. Chambers hadn't minded. The standards of behavior I cared about were the ones my women's group provided me and what I grappled with in therapy, except it was August now and Mila was on vacation.

A hot Sunday afternoon late in the month, Simone came to see me. I made lemonade and we sat at our yellow table with the little girl in the poster, in her bright yellow dress, keeping us company. I told Simone about Don's new job, that I hadn't been sure he'd get it. He smoked, and some in the church were so conservative that I feared it might disqualify him.

"God help you!" Simone laughed. "It sounds like my church in Texas. No drinking, no smoking, no music, no dance. Oh, you are going to miss Chambers Church."

"It gets worse. After they hired him, the chair of the search committee told Don that she'd wanted to ask if he believed in the virgin birth. She hadn't asked because she was afraid of how he would answer. She didn't want to have to vote against him."

"What you don't know can't hurt you." Simone said this as if she wanted to joke but couldn't. "No, I don't believe that. It's worse not to know."

It had driven her crazy not to know when Frank was with another woman. Not knowing gave her imagination free rein and she'd imagined the worst. Now it had come to pass. Frank told her that although he knew he was a fool to leave her, he wanted a divorce.

"In a strange way," she said, "it's a relief to have the matter settled."

"You look like a widow," I said. She was like Carolyn after Charles died.

"Yes. It's how I feel."

Don came in the living room, interrupting my thoughts. Thoughts about grief. I had subtly, happily subordinated myself to Carolyn, becoming indispensable, and then increasingly frustrated as she began to emerge from her deepest sadness and no longer needed my unbridled devotion. I was good at devotion.

"Alex is down for his nap," Don said. "I'm going to take one too."

"Sweet dreams." I was glad he wasn't going to join us at the table.

I went to sit by the windows and Simone followed. I put my hand on her outstretched leg, rubbed it lightly. Later, I would worry that I had taken advantage of her, as I'd been taken advantage of, though she was not a child and would deny that I had used her in any way. I moved closer, put my arm around her shoulders and kissed her, reckless, ravenous. We kept our clothes on, only opening shirts to touch, unzipping pants. She was not shy and I came quickly, stifling a cry, and then I reciprocated. It was much too quick. Don was right on the other side of the wall. That didn't inhibit me any more than having my parents right across the hall had inhibited Georgia.

Though we were fully clothed and sitting apart, how could Don not see in our faces what we'd just done, when, shortly, he came in from his nap?

# 22

## Through a Glass Darkly

I dusted the frame and cleaned the glass protecting the little girl in the poster, and her hair became blacker, her yellow dress brighter. Don and I loved her for the same reasons—her vibrant presence and enigmatic expression, some days melancholy but other days serene. Wrapping her in thick layers of newspaper for the move to Brooklyn, I thought of Don and of Simone and what we'd done the day before.

I kept at it, going from room to room in the apartment, cleaning mirrors and pictures, taking them down and packing them up. Loving Simone, I would love Don no less. I wanted it to be like me and Georgia and Sam. I was no threat to Sam. Simone was no threat to Don. It was too early for me to appreciate how mad this thinking was.

That afternoon, I only knew that to be true to myself, I had to do what I had done. And I had to tell Don. Why? I would have said it was because of the danger of secrets. I needed him to accept me, absolutely, just as I was.

I walked over to the next building to pick up Alex from his babysitter. I had told Alana the previous week that we were moving to Brooklyn. She wept. Her husband Marcos, her mother, and her children, five-year-old Sonia and six-year-old Pablo, had all gotten involved taking care of Alex.

"No. No," Alana had said. "You can't take Alex. We love little Alex."

"Don has a new job. We're going the first of September."

"We'll keep him. Let us keep him."

We hugged. How had I been so fortunate to find this family to watch Alex while I wrote?

Alex and I loitered on the way home. "Mommy, watch!" His chubby little legs carried him straight to the low playground wall, which he struggled to scale. He stood up. He jumped down. He beamed and turned to do it again. The phone was ringing when we got home. Don was calling to say he'd be late and for once I was grateful. I fed Alex and put him to bed.

"Someone's missing from our table," Don said when we sat down for dinner, nodding to the bare wall.

"She's carefully wrapped," I said. I told him about my conversation with Alana. "She still can't believe that we are taking Alex away."

"How could she ask for him? People don't give their children away!"

"Well, he is adopted."

"Hmm. Maybe she thinks we don't love him as much because he's adopted." He shook his head in dismay and disbelief.

"I have to tell you something." Eating dinner, talking, carrying on as before, I felt profoundly dishonest. "I have to tell you something. Yesterday, when you took a nap. Simone and I ... Simone and I made love."

Don looked at me with unexpected calm, and then his face slipped into the deeply sober expression of an older man. His pale eyes behind his big glasses were distant, guarded, as if he were removing himself to a safer place. He took a while to speak and he put his hands on the table, palms down and fingers extended, as if to steady himself. "Well, I'm hardly thrilled, though not, of course, completely surprised." He sighed, the wind going out of him.

"I don't know if you can understand this," I said urgently. "This isn't about you. It's about me. Something I need to find out about myself."

He looked at me darkly, skeptically, but his mouth was free of its worst expression, a pinched, impenetrable tightness. He wanted to believe me. He didn't believe me for a second.

I pushed my chair back and went to him. His reaction was nowhere near as terrible as I'd feared and, relieved, I hugged him, awkwardly, as he remained seated.

If he'd crumbled, like he had when I hurt myself, bashing my head, if he'd let himself be angry... I'd have been shocked if he'd been angry and overwhelmed with guilt if he'd collapsed. We finished eating and cleaned up the dishes in a silence less dangerous than anything either of us might have been tempted to say, and we didn't speak about it again, not directly, not for some days.

There was an old saying in my family. An aunt of mine said it and so did my mother. *Silence means consent.* It meant that one must speak up in the face of injustice or moral wrong. I put the saying to use. Don's silence meant I could do what I needed to do. He didn't say he was upset.

He didn't put his foot down and forbid me. "No. Stop. You mustn't." Only later would I be able to wonder why.

Brooklyn and Simone existed for me in liminal space between what had been and what would come. Don and I still lived in East Harlem but each morning now I took the long subway ride to Park Slope to get our new apartment ready. Simone met me there, and the first time she came, she was barely inside the door before we were in each other's arms. I threw an old sheet down, and unmindful of the hard kitchen floor, we lay together. Not like our hurried silent joining, with Don on the other side of the wall, but alone and safe, where no one could see or hear how we came together, and we did so exuberantly. I cried out in the vacant apartment, a long resounding cry of pleasure sharp as pain.

Then, just as urgently, I had to get away from her. On weak legs, I fled into the next room and slid to the floor with my back against the wall, as far from her as I could get. Though I wasn't conscious of it, indeed this had to do with Georgia. I was terrified that Simone, with her boundless intensity and vulnerability, would smother me. I watched her. Sitting against the opposite wall, she smiled at me. I waited for her irrevocable demands, her clinging conditions. No such things came. I had my first inkling that I didn't have to be afraid of her, of losing myself if I loved her.

We scrubbed the kitchen. She came every day to help me, and then one night we stayed together in Brooklyn. Friends were away and had given me their keys because a repairman was coming early and it made no sense for me to go all the way back to East Harlem.

"I feel like a novice," Simone said. "I've never made love to a woman before. I don't know how."

Sitting on the bed, I began to undo the round, hard buttons of her pale blue cotton pajamas. "I'll be more than happy to teach you everything you need to know," I said with delight, cupping her breasts in my hands. Firm and warm, they ignited a desire fueled not just by this moment, but by memory, transgression embraced and maybe, just maybe, disarmed.

Simone reciprocated.

"I always knew you were a fast learner."

We laughed, happy and unafraid as we began to discover each other's bodies.

We already knew each other's stories. Mine about Georgia. Hers about Clyde, her high school boyfriend. I knew that she'd grown up in a troubled home, each parent claiming her as an ally against the other. Clyde was her escape, and she loved and needed him enough to have sex with him for several years, secretly, in his car, before they were to wed. Until the night he told her that he was getting married the next day to someone else. Fraught first loves for both of us.

That night we talked about loving each other. What felt good and what didn't and what we did with our husbands, how they hurt us. Hers by always wanting more. Mine by never wanting enough. And then we slept.

September 1, 1975, we moved to Brooklyn—Don, two-year-old Alex, and I. It helped us that we had so many things to do—unpack, buy a table and chairs to fill the dining room. In the living room, which had a stalactite ceiling and small windows, I hung Simone's collage. I asked Don if he minded; he said no, it was a good piece. Three feet by two feet, it was stitched fragments of different textures and colors of cloth, a layered abstract landscape, irregular with a broken path of white cordage running through it, a slim corridor. Though I wanted it in our living room, I kept expecting Don to tell me to take it down. He never did.

Simone was our old friend. Simone was my lover. I wanted both to still be true. Don didn't say I couldn't invite her over. Don didn't say I couldn't go out at night with her or sleep over at her place.

Her place was commercial space, a store on the eastern edge of SoHo, the front room where she had her studio separated from the back by an enclosed section that held her sleeping loft. Dark already with the front windows half-shuttered and the back one high and small, she made it cave-like by painting the huge north wall a deep shade of velvet brown. When I came to see her, we'd sit in the cavernous back room on a mattress on the floor, cushions against the wall making it a couch. We sat amidst her books and her music, the long-necked, alien totemic heads she'd made watching us from the back window.

It was in this room that Simone asked me not to smoke, and I quit for good, just like that, obedient, as if she were Georgia. It was her only urgent request and my only act of utter compliance. I expected her to make demands, like Georgia had. *Tell me when I will see you again.* I couldn't plan ahead like that; I didn't know Don's schedule. Then I saw that she didn't expect me to.

We went out to hear jazz, at Rashid Ali's or Sam River's Studio Rivbea—Leroy Jenkins on the violin, Abdullah Ibrahim's piano. I was be-

side myself, with my lover, a woman, in public, as if it were the most normal thing in the whole wide world.

After the music, we walked to the subway arm in arm. A car with
Jersey plates cruised slowly by, and after it passed, a teenage boy leaned
out the window and yelled back at us, "Hey, are you guys dykes?"

"Damn straight!" I yelled back at him. Trying it on. We were not guys
or dykes, but in that outlaw moment, those kids named me and I exalted.
Simone admonished me, but I didn't think she really minded.

The subway ride home gave me time to take it in. Simone wasn't like
Georgia; there were no power games. I didn't have to buckle to her will.
Georgia had railed against Virginia, *her* religious teacher, because Virginia made Georgia *buckle.* She vowed she would never do that to me. I
could see at last that she couldn't help herself. It was all she knew.

At Simone's table, over a simple meal and full of gratitude, I explained
this to Simone.

"It's not Georgia's will you're talking about," she said. "I don't believe
in will. It's her need, her own damaged self, struggling to make sense out
of what Virginia did to her by doing the same to you."

Had Georgia framed it wrong all these years? Calling it *will* made it
intentional and rational. And then I couldn't think about this anymore
because Simone had come up behind me and begun to rub my shoulders.

Standing where I couldn't see her face, she sounded troubled. "You're
doing everything right. I have to tell you. It doesn't work so well for me. I
miss the penetration, the connection."

"Maybe you're just heterosexual," I said, trying to sound as if it were
a small matter.

She took me by the hand to sit with her on the mattress. She seemed
genuinely disturbed, as if it were a failure that she couldn't get what I got,
not as fully. "It's all right," I said, even though it wasn't. I kissed her and she
didn't try to stop me and by the time we finished her body had belied any
assertion that I couldn't give her some serious pleasure.

It was no accident that I'd done what I'd done with Simone while
Mila was on vacation. She refused to tell me what she believed about homosexual relationships, which meant I believed she disapproved of them.
Frightened and defiant, I went for a showdown. There she was, standing
in the doorway to her office, a short, solid Jewish Buddha, smiling as if she
was genuinely pleased to see me no matter what. I entered a bit disarmed

already. I told her, slowly, haltingly, as I gathered courage, what I'd done while she was gone.

"I make love with Simone," I said, "and it's what I want. Like what I had with Georgia." I was extremely tense. "I think it means I'm a lesbian."

"I think it means," Mila said in a strong, level voice, "that at last you have a sexual partner who wants you as much as you want her. It has to do with being wanted more than with the gender of your partner."

I didn't know what I'd expected from Mila, but certainly not what I got. I was quiet, but my mind raced. Didn't this prove that she was against gay relationships, that she'd always try to explain them away? I didn't ask. Taking in what she said, I was flooded with such relief. Maybe it was only a reprieve. I didn't care. I couldn't see that this abhorrence of homosexuality didn't belong to Mila but to me. What I could see was that I'd been wrong, wrong when I said Simone had nothing to do with Don.

"It's not all my fault," I said. "My disappointment with him. What I want isn't sick or wrong. Is that what you mean?"

"Yes, that's part of it," she said quietly, an affirmation that was for me a deliverance. I wasn't, maybe, as terrible as I had known myself to be.

I couldn't wait to tell this to Simone. Then, one by one, I let the women's group members know what we were doing. Their casual acceptance of our affair unnerved me. Since they didn't understand the depth of my self-loathing, they couldn't appreciate what I was going through, publicly admitting I loved a woman. It left me feeling terribly alone.

In October, we all went to Jen's country house for a weekend. Janet and Stephanie decided quickly that Simone and I would sleep in the only double bed. None of them treated me any differently for being with her. I learned to hug them without wanting to disappear through the floor.

Don didn't object when I told him I was going away for that weekend but he didn't want to hear about it when I returned. Two days later, Alex was at his babysitter and I was reading in the living room when Don came home from work early. He was six feet, three inches tall, and barging into the apartment, he grew another foot, morphed into a giant puppet, Big Bird in distress, wing-like arms flapping, long, stilt-legs marching him back and forth between living and dining rooms, every inch of his body shrieking, "I can't stand it anymore."

I'd never seen him in such a state, enlarged in his anguish, and unreachable—he pushed me away when I tried to go to him. Retreating to the couch, I waited, watched as his pacing slowed. He hesitated, taking in that he had no one to turn to but me. He crossed to where I sat, sank down and wept in my arms.

"Talk to me," I said gently, shifting myself to see his face. He'd collapsed on the floor, his head in my lap like a little boy.

"It feels terrible when you're with her." His voice was muffled and he didn't look up.

It was what I'd been expecting. Not wanting but waiting to hear. Ever since I told him that first day, he had avoided anything that might have caused trouble between us. Consumed by his new job, he went about his business as if nothing unusual was going on, as if he didn't care where I went or what I did. I welcomed his silence because it made what I needed to do easier. But it hurt that he didn't seem to care what I did. Now we could stop pretending.

I stroked his head, very close to crying myself. "I'm not doing this to hurt you."

He started to cry again. "You're all I have. You and Alex." He'd taken his glasses off and looked up at me with naked, wounded eyes.

"We need help," I said without hesitation. "Will you come with me to get help?"

He sat up and put his glasses on. "You mean Mila?"

"Yes. The problems we face are not just mine."

"Will it make a difference with Simone?"

"It isn't just Simone, what's wrong between us."

He struggled to his feet, left the room and I heard him close the bathroom door. Why did therapy frighten him so? He'd liked Jim, the therapist he talked to about his impotency when we were students at Union. He'd been intrigued by what he'd begun to learn about himself. Jim gave him a puzzle. He'd told me how proud he was when he could see immediately that the scattered pieces would make a hand. Then, he'd been perplexed and chagrined that he could not put the pieces together, even though he knew what he was trying to make. I never forgot that therapist. He told me we'd been married such a short time that I was not implicated in Don's impotence.

Well, I was implicated now, in everything.

Instead of coming back to me on the couch, Don sat, pale and distraught, upright in the recliner and lit a cigarette, his hands trembling. His left ankle on his right knee, his foot, enclosed in a shiny brown shoe, twitched nervously.

"I know what I want," he said. "I want you and Alex. What do I need therapy for?"

"You think it's all my fault, everything that's wrong between us?"

"You're the one having the affair."

"But why?" I heard my voice go shrill and clamped my mouth shut. I wanted to scream at him to stop twitching his fucking foot. Only that would make it worse and I did not want, this time, to make it worse. I held my hands up protectively as if to quiet us both. "Let's not do this to each other," I said softly.

I got up and went to the kitchen to calm down, took two cans of beer from the refrigerator. I heard Don as he came to join me—slow, heavy steps. He lowered himself into the chair opposite me.

"All right," he said. "If you want me to. If it will help you. I'll do it."

*It-doesn't-matter-why-he'll-do-it-don't-yell-at him.* "Good." *All-that-matters-is-that-he-agree.* I kept talking to myself. Because I didn't yell at him, he started to talk in his normal voice—when to see Mila and then what was happening at church. I hadn't been going because of Simone. It was impossible for me to come home from her at one or two in the morning and then with too little sleep transform myself into a minister's wife, the conventional kind the congregation wanted.

"It hurts me that you don't come to church. You came to Chambers. People ask where you are. I keep telling them Alex doesn't feel good."

I laughed quietly. "That's terrible, putting it on Alex."

"What do you suggest I say?" But he smiled at me. For the first time, we could both see the impossibility of continuing as we were. We kept talking, as if we were afraid we wouldn't know how to start again if we stopped.

We needn't have worried about talking as we began what I came to think of as our therapy triathlon. Before we were done, we would do individual therapy and we'd do couples therapy and then we'd do sex therapy. As if that weren't enough, Don would do group therapy. We did it all because, in the end, we wanted to stay together, whatever it took, though it would be awhile before I was ready unequivocally to affirm this.

# 23

# Only in Part

When I remember that apartment on Twelfth Street, where we lived for a single, troubled year, I can't get the layout of the whole of it, only individual rooms. The kitchen where Simone and I made love that first day. The dining and living rooms where Don became a battered Big Bird. I had an office, a room of my own, with a long narrow bulletin board made from a window shade, unrolled to full length and attached to the wall. In the center of it, a drawing of a woman warrior, an Amazon. Photos of writers who gave me courage cut from the pages of *Ms. Magazine*—Gertrude Stein, Virginia Woolf, Toni Morrison—were juxtaposed with fliers from the latest demonstrations, Dr. Mila Aizenberg's business card, matches from the jazz joints I went to with Simone. In this room, I worked on my novel.

Though I have a clear picture of Alex's little room, I can't see where it is. I remember our bedroom with its windows looking out on an inside courtyard, clotheslines on pulleys stretching across to the opposite building, sheets and brightly colored clothes drying in the wind. But I can't get how this bedroom was connected to the rest of the apartment.

I was in the bedroom, reading, when Don came home Friday night. His mother had been visiting, and he'd taken her to Port Authority to catch the bus back to Pennsylvania. We'd had back-to-back appointments with Mila in the morning. I wanted to tell him about mine so asked about his.

Untying his tie, he hung it on the rack, smoothing it with his long graceful fingers. "My session was hard," he said. He looked like a kid who'd gotten caught playing hooky or stealing his parents' booze. "Hard at my instigation. I have to tell you something, but maybe not until morning."

I set my book down carefully so as not to appear too eager. What on earth? He took off his sports coat and hung it carefully on a hanger.

He faced me. "Remember what Mila said last week about honest marriage?"

Did I remember! I had accused her of being biased against my relationship with Simone, biased in favor of marriage and Don. Mila corrected me. She said she was biased in favor of *honest* marriage. Such a marriage requires love and sex and a lot of hard work. If we didn't do the work, we'd carry the baggage we brought into our marriage into any subsequent relationship.

I had agreed to stop having sex with Simone. Not because having it was wrong. I wanted something else even more. I wanted Don to give me what I got from her.

He sat in the armchair by the bed. "What the hell. I might as well tell you and get it over with. Monday, after we had therapy, I stopped at a newsstand. I bought a magazine. A gay one." He took a long drag on his cigarette and stared out into the room. "I bought a gay magazine to masturbate with. I do it compulsively. To get back at Mother, and you too. I've done it for years." He looked at me. "When I feel like a victim, like I did Monday. You were so vague about our life together."

Too stunned to defend myself, I knew what he meant. I had agreed to give up Simone and work with him. "We'll have to see what happens," I'd said about the future.

He ran his tongue over his lower lip and then bit down on it. "I know it's really sick. When I'm hurt, like I was Monday, I can't help it. Doing it." He held his cigarette in his left hand, gripped the arm of the chair in his right one, and continued. "Then, of course, I despise myself. It means I don't need anybody. I can take care of myself." He searched my face, unable to continue until I reacted.

Astonished, speechless, enthralled, I would never have guessed. I thought I knew him. How could I not have known this? Since I wasn't visibly upset, he continued almost as a boast. "I have a connoisseur's knowledge of the porn scene, over the last decade, longer." Then, as if chastising himself for bragging, he said, "I know. I should have told you ages ago."

"Why didn't you?" I asked reflexively, not expecting him to be able to tell me. The reasons must be complex, like my need for Simone. He surprised me again.

"I didn't tell you because it goes way back to when you first told me about Georgia. I told you about my one homosexual experience, when I was a kid. You said they weren't the same. You made me feel it was like comparing a deep wound with a scratch. You let me off the hook by saying that. What I did was nothing. Nothing to tell. Except I knew I should. I didn't trust you enough to tell you."

He couldn't have hurt me more if he'd slapped me. Trust was us, the ground I stood on. Had I belittled him, that long-ago summer? That had hardly been my intention. I needed to have no guilty secrets. What had happened to me was profoundly different from his single adolescent episode. Which he wouldn't even have spoken of, if I hadn't told him about Georgia. I looked at his familiar, anguished face. What he'd done bewildered me.

I reached for him. "You know what you look like? The time you finally told your parents you smoked. It's what you look like now. Come to bed." He was twenty-three years old when he'd told them. I was with him on my first visit to his parents' home. He used me for protection. I'd thought the way he told them—a bad little boy—was pitiful.

He sighed and stubbed out his cigarette. "Yeah. I used to think I was fine except for two things. I smoked and I masturbated."

I lay awake for a long time, sadness at first smothering every other emotion. Sadness for him. Sadness for us. He'd kept his sorry secret to himself all these years. No wonder he didn't care much about making love to me. He got his kicks knocking off in the men's room with a porno magazine. No wonder he didn't judge me about Georgia. He could hide behind my big guilt and gratitude, from what he couldn't face about himself.

The word *ammunition* came to me. He had given me such ammunition. All our troubles had been my fault. He was the good guy. I was the one unsatisfied, unfaithful, screwed up because of Georgia. That one-sided blame had just blown up. How was I going to contain what would surely come as righteous rage? I had leveled with him, from the beginning, always. How was I going to keep from punishing him for sabotaging us all these years?

I took my anger to Mila. "Why did it take Don thirteen years to tell me the truth?"

"Why do you think?"

I spoke after a long silence and with great reluctance, hating to admit it. "He was more frightened than I was."

"You could blame Georgia for what you did," she said. "He had no one to blame but himself."

"But he didn't do anything."

"That's how you see it."

How was it possible to equate what Georgia did—to, with, for me—over years, with masturbatory fantasies that involved no one but himself? I had great difficulty accepting that, for Don, his sexual shame was as terrible as mine, maybe more terrible.

When I kept insisting that he didn't do anything, Mila surprised me. "Don did do something. He convinced you that you were wrong to want what you wanted from him."

I cried. Because she meant that what I wanted was not obsessive and depraved.

When we were twenty-three years old, I told Don my secret and he told me his. The *what ifs* came to mind irresistibly. What if I'd been able to ask him what it meant to him, that twelve-year-old sexual encounter, instead of dismissing it? What if I'd asked why he did it only once and what did it have to do with his mother? What if, when I told Don about Georgia, he'd been able to see her clearly? What if he'd not gotten swept away, just as I had, by Georgia's complicated charisma?

For me, it all kept coming back to Georgia.

At my next session with Mila, I confronted her with my old question. "When you told us that you were biased in favor of honest marriage, you meant you are biased in favor of marriage. Over homosexual relationships. Why wouldn't you say that before?"

Mila looked at me intently. "All right. I am biased. But what matters, as I said before, is how relationships work for you."

I looked at her in anger and dismay. "I knew it," I said.

"When you came to see me," Mila said forcefully but kindly, "you didn't say you were a lesbian. You said you were confused. I would have approached things differently if you came in saying you were a lesbian. I would never, ever have tried to change you."

"Why wouldn't you tell me your position on homosexuality when I first asked?"

"I didn't tell you because if I had, I was afraid that you would get up and walk out of here and never come back."

"I had a right to know."

"Yes," Mila said, "but you were asking more than one thing. What you verbalized and what you couldn't yet verbalize."

"I would not have gotten up and left for good." I pointed my finger at her. "Only one thing would have made me get up and walk out of here and never come back." I hesitated and my voice dropped. "If you had been seductive, in any way, that's when I would have fled."

Alex got sick in April 1976 with what the doctor feared was spinal meningitis. After a miserable first night in an upright chair, and ignoring objections from the nursing staff, I brought an air mattress and sleeping bag and slept on the floor. This was my first, fierce labor for Alex. I'd been taking care of him from the beginning, of course, and I did what mothers do—feeding, clothing, sheltering, playing with him and finding playmates, most recently in a nearby daycare program where the teacher adored him. "You have a very special child," Joanna said.

"All kids are special," I said quickly, dogmatically. I had been working with Mila on how Georgia's *special* had colonized my mind and stranded me in a universe of two. I was also disingenuous. I loved what Joanna said. She was right, and it was not my doing—not my genes and not my mothering.

The second morning in the hospital, I stood watch as Alex slept, curled on his side, fists clenched. Not quite three, he looked older, fragile, his robust, energetic little self stolen by his sickness. I tried without much success to feed him. I read to him. I made up stories. At night, my fingers on his hot cheek, I listened to his labored breathing in the dark and let myself think, "What if his breathing stopped altogether?" I sat, blindly, in the chair beside him. I couldn't live without him. I hadn't known that. The realization settled me down. I was Alex's mother, fully, forever, and for real.

Alex had a bacterial infection, not meningitis, and after he came home, he wasn't allowed to play with other children for some time. I took a picture of him then. His light brown hair has lost its baby curls and looks as if I'm still cutting it, as it's adorably uneven. He's wearing a navy turtleneck and bright red corduroy overalls with a denim jacket on top, and his almost heart-shaped face is looking up at me, his mouth turned slightly down. It's as if he can't take his eyes off me, as if he is unsure what might be coming next. That expression, so unlike the I-can-take-on-anything look of his earlier photos, still makes me want to take him in my arms and reassure him that everything is going to be all right. He is unconscionably beautiful.

I came across a photo in a magazine of a mother rhinoceros standing protectively next to her calf. Me and Alex. From that day on an image of a rhino mother and calf has hung near my desk. Sometimes a black rhino. Sometimes a white one. Always that incredibly powerful beast with her cupped ears, square jaw, her stubby and pointed tusks, standing protectively beside her offspring. She might not see well. It might take a lot to provoke her. But watch out. Head for cover if you ever do anything that endangers her son.

# 24

## Then Face to Face

We moved a block away to a classic brownstone on Thirteenth Street. Bequeathed to Greenwood Baptist Church, the house had been tied up in legalities for the first year of Don's pastorate. Moving was starting over. The house had three floors, the top one rented out. The middle floor held the parlor with bay windows and a high ceiling, elegant. We put up a plush, patterned maroon velvet curtain to separate the parlor from a middle space traditionally used as a music room or library. This would be our bedroom, and the master bedroom, with its fireplace and windows looking out on the back garden, would be my study.

That small, cozy middle room with its dark woodwork, sliding door to the back, and theatrical curtain shutting out the living room, was where I recuperated after I had a myomectomy. My menstrual periods had come to involve such pain and bleeding that I lost days of work each month and was impossible to live with. My new doctor talked me out of a hysterectomy. He wasn't convinced I couldn't conceive and argued to remove fibroids instead of my whole uterus. Don was delighted that I would entertain the possibility of a child.

A year later, I was in bed with flu, drifting in and out of sleep. What had Don said about passivity? Things came to him. I had said I loved him. Chambers had asked him to apply. He never had to initiate.

The phone jarred me out of my musings.

"This is Lisa Colliers."

Who the hell was Lisa Colliers?

"How are you?" she said.

"Pretty miserable. I have the flu."

"I read your book."

Holy shit. She was the agent. I came quickly completely awake. "Yes?"

"What is going against it, in my opinion," she said, "is that it's an interior book without much plot. But lesbian books are selling."

She thought I was a lesbian.

She went on about my manuscript. Like Erica Jong's work, what I had done hadn't been done before. She would start by sending it to William Morrow. The editor there was divorced, knew nothing about women, and was fascinated by things that tell him about women.

"Does it matter to you," she said, "if I send it to men editors or women?"

Did she think I was some kind of radical feminist who would not want men involved? "I don't care," I said.

"*The Joy of Lesbian Sex* outsold *The Joy of Gay Sex* by five to one. That's why I'll take it. It's the right moment. I wonder about your title, *Four in the Morning*, but I don't dislike it."

The more we talked, the more I wasn't sure she understood my book. But then she was explaining how the process worked and telling me about film options and translation rights.

"It needs a bit of cutting," she said at last, "but we don't need to worry about that now."

She promised to keep me posted; she hung up.

I sat up. I had an agent. I didn't care if she got my book if she could sell it, except I would fight for my title. Four in the morning is deep in the night. Four in the morning is morning. Both/and. Not either/or. I loved Don but that didn't keep me from loving Simone, though we were chaste with each other now.

My congenital optimism leapt into action. Just like it did when sex with Don was good. I assumed we were out of the woods once and for all, which was madness. But I had an agent. My novel would be published, maybe made into a movie and translated into twenty languages. I could die happy. I lay down and curled into a ball. Yes, I could die now. I had done something real. I had found a way to write my story. My secrets and my self-hatred, my struggles to figure out who the hell I was, they were not for nothing.

Not only would my book be published. I would have a baby. The possibility my doctor gave me began to grow into a desire. Don and I had such a lot to talk about.

"I have read the first chapters of Genesis dozens of times," I told Don.

"In English and in Hebrew. The first great, overwhelming art I ever saw was in Rome, on my way to Beirut, the Sistine Chapel. Just now I get it. In that magnificent painting of creation, the male artist has the male God creating the man. In the Genesis story, the woman is taken out of the man. The exact opposite of how it actually happens."

We were sitting with a glass of wine before dinner, waiting for Alex to come home from Heath's house around the corner.

Don looked surprised. "I've never thought about it like that."

"Phyllis Chesler and Adrienne Rich. We are only beginning to appreciate how patriarchal society still is. I don't want to have a baby because women are supposed to. I have to do it for my own real reasons. It's what I'm talking to Mila about now."

"It's a bigger loss for you not to have a child that it is for me," Don said. "For a man, there's not that much difference between adopting and begetting."

His remark puzzled me but I didn't challenge him. "Alex is why I want another child," I said. "He sits with me on the floor in the living room with that pressure-color toy. When he makes the color change, he says, 'Mommy, see how beautiful it is.' Pure joy. A second child, in her own way, would also bring joy."

I was still scared, and I did not get pregnant quickly. Then, to my delight, Don got himself another job, not in a parish church but in Manhattan, with his denomination's Metropolitan New York office. For four years, Don had been the only staff person at Greenwood, along with a janitor. He hadn't realized how lonely he'd been. Now he had colleagues, men to talk to about politics, theology, and the church.

"I haven't been this excited about work since the good years at Chambers," he said. Alex was overnight at Heath's and Don and I were enjoying a Saturday night when he did not have to write a sermon.

"There's something I need to tell you," he said, "about having a baby. I don't need another child. I have a job I love. It's enough. If you want to have a child, I won't stop you. But you will have to be the major parent."

It was a sign of how far we'd come, that I took this in without anger. I never wanted to be a parent only, or alone. Now I kept imagining a new baby, a daughter. Spending time with Alex, he was sufficient—the way he sang, the time he took to carefully pick a bonsai plant for his daddy's birthday. We went to the Botanical Garden shop to find it. He took forever to choose the exact right little tree. Walking along Eastern Parkway past the library to catch the bus home, joy and sadness kept tripping over each other. If Alex gave me such pleasure, another child would do the same, in a different way. People we passed, with more than one child, made me sad. One is too thin. It is too near to none. I wanted another child. Alex was more than I could ever want. All day long. The sadness cut the joy which then spilled over to cut the sadness.

She was not to be, this second child. I couldn't get pregnant. We did the fertility work up, beginning with sperm tests. But after an endometrial biopsy, a cervical hostility test, Don's growing reluctance, and finally the necessity of surgery with only a 50/50 chance of success, I said no. It was time to give it up.

It was 1979. We had moved in December out of our brownstone and into a fourth-floor walk-up on Eighth Street. Lisa Colliers returned my manuscript. She had sent it to twelve publishers, found no takers, and was discouraged with the project. I was well into writing another novel by this time. Rereading *Four in the Morning*, I could see how to make it stronger and vowed to do that after my current writing project was finished.

No published novel. No second child. I took my sadness with me when Alex and I went out to do errands in the pouring rain. We stomped in all the puddles and he snuggled against me to keep dry. I could handle this. I'd be all right. I was better off than so many people, like Simone, who had no child at all.

Until I went to see Mila, where I could not pretend I was fine. How do you grieve for a child you don't have? What do you do with a body that can't grow anything but cysts and fibroids? What good had it ever done me to be a woman? When I was a kid, I wanted to be a boy. I should have been a boy.

"I see pregnant women everywhere now. But I have Don. I have Alex. It's crazy to be upset like this."

Mila just looked at me, as if to say, "You are too much."

As I struggled closer to my own real and frightening emotions, Mila did something she'd never done.

"Gail, there is something I have wanted to tell you for a long time. I had three miscarriages. For years I dreamed that a real mother has five children."

Her sadness was still there. Maybe there were tears in her eyes. She had told me almost nothing about herself, though I knew she had two sons. She had waited all these months to tell me. Maybe some of her sadness was for me too.

Gratitude that she had waited, and kinship, accompanied the words that came to me immediately. I had given up knowing what I thought of God, but I would never give up the language.

"Acquainted with grief," I said. "Sorrow and acquainted with grief." I had to pause because I was crying, and crying was what I needed to do. Grief and gratitude, that Mila had told me. I could stop pretending that I was just fine and let myself experience my own lonely and im-measurable loss, one that Don did not share. He hadn't wanted a second child.

October. Stephanie's book, *Fighting Two Colonialisms: Women in Guinea-Bissau*, was published. The party to celebrate was in Jen's spacious apartment on 86th and Riverside. I was standing with a group of women at the north corner of the living room, which had been cleared for danc-ing, when Don came late to the party. He'd been at meetings in Washing-ton, D.C., and the first sight of him filled me with pleasure. I watched as he greeted people, reaching out to shake hands and then withdrawing his body at the same time, a gesture I knew well, one that suggested he was ill at ease, and that annoyed me.

Later I watched Don talking to a group of men in Jen's bedroom, where copies of Stephanie's book had been laid out on a table. Towering over the others, he made a familiar pointing gesture, and that's when it struck me. There would always be things about Don that annoyed me and they didn't matter. Tapping my foot to Miriam Makeba's "Pata Pata," I had to laugh at myself. I wanted to dance with Don, only I wouldn't because the way he danced—stiff and self-conscious—took the fun out of it. And that didn't matter either. We had been through such a lot. We had Alex. We had each other. That was plenty.

At nine-fifteen the next morning, Don picked Alex up from Adam's where he'd spent the night, and I did laundry. As soon as I finished, I did what Alex asked: I took him and Jude, a new boy next door, to the park. From time to time they'd come to where I sat, to make sure I was watching the feat they'd mastered on the jungle gym. My tiredness, I realized, was different this morning. Since we'd moved to Brooklyn, I had been in this park in many moods—angry, lost in confusion over my sexuality, or sad, sad about Don or my novel or not bearing a child. Today I was just tired for lack of sleep. The day was unusually warm and bright with low clouds that cast fantastic shadows onto the playground. I couldn't get over the simple pleasure of watching the boys climb and call to each other, watching without something else intruding, some festering unhappiness.

Alex went to Jude's for lunch and I came home. Don and I had to catch up with each other because he'd been gone all week, getting back just in time for Stephanie's party. The next weekend a national gay liberation march was scheduled in Washington. I needed to go because the Christian right was rising up against it. They made me furious. I wanted moral values removed from sexual identity. It would have been so much easier to sort out what had happened to me if being a lesbian held the same value and status in society as being with a man did. Happy with my husband now, this struggle for gay rights was still, also, mine. Don had said earlier he might go to the march with me, and either way we needed to plan.

He sat at the end of the table, in the chair nearest the kitchen; I sat on his left. The dining room was a second-rate imitation of the paneled rooms we'd left behind in our brownstone, mirrors set in dark frames that were painted. I watched him in the mirror. He had on an old red flannel shirt that made him look huggable, though he seemed sleepy and distracted. At the strange pitch of his voice, high and thin, I turned to look at him directly.

"I have to tell you something," he said. "I was going to wait till I saw Mila. I'd better tell you. When I was in Washington, I had … a … sexual encounter … with a man." He started to smile, a guilty, irrepressible smile. "It was wonderful. I feel in touch with myself like I never did." He said the last almost belligerently, conflicted, as if he didn't know whether he spoke something wonderful or something awful. Then, in a steady, deliberate voice, he said, "I'm gay." He folded his arms across his chest and waited.

Tenderness and terror.

How could he do this to us now, after all we'd been through?

If anyone could understand why he needed to do what he'd done, I could.

I finally got my voice. "You matter too much to me," I said, leaning toward him. "You and Alex. We have to figure this out." I meant nothing as temporary as confusion about sexual identity would be allowed to tear us apart.

He started to tell me what had happened. I did and did not want to know. He'd just had the best sex of his life and with a stranger. I climbed into his lap, tears streaming down my face. He held me close.

"We never should have married," Don said gently.

"That's why I'm crying."

Then Alex came home. "Let's go to Coney Island," he said, always raring to go.

We agreed with relief. It was something to do. We got on the F train and rode all the way out to the end of the line. The atmosphere was charged, strange, almost yellow sand, de Chirico empty, the sky wild with black clouds out to sea. Alex went on ride after ride, getting what he wanted, happy. And why not, I thought. He would be what made us find our way through this because we both loved him, because we couldn't let his family abandon him again. At last he rode the Tilt-A-Whirl and he was the only one on it, spinning around and around all by himself. Don and I looked at each other, gripped by the same fear, this image of what his life might become.

Alex came off the ride with the world's biggest grin on his face. "Look," he said, holding out his fists and opening them for us. They were filled with quarters, nickels and dimes. He'd found them where he sat, and then he'd gone from compartment to compartment checking all the seats and filling his pockets with lost change. It had been raining out to sea and the first drops began to reach us as we hurried for the subway. I paused to watch the sky a moment longer. The light was electric, thick yellow and cobalt blue that stayed distinct, and I thought to myself, this is the color that the sky will turn when the world comes to an end.

# 25

# Your Flight Be Not in Winter

We entered the winter of the waters, Don and I. For him the baths—New York City's famous gay baths—where he went, he said, to make himself a man. For me the swimming pool—in a YMCA on Ninth Street, down the slope our neighborhood was named after—where I went to find my strength. I had given up Simone to see if we could make our marriage work. Don had what he said he wanted, me and Alex. Only now he said that he was gay.

The last Tuesday afternoon in November, in my old turquoise suit and white cap, I pushed open the door to the steamy, chlorine-pungent pool room, slipped into the cloudy warmth, pulled goggles over my eyes and swam, forcing myself forward with my awkward crawl. I was breaking up inside, the water I knew we are all made of—50, 60 percent?—was melting my hard parts, blood and lymph liquefying bone and muscle. Leaving nothing solid. Nothing to keep me from dissolving away.

I had to have Simone to find myself.

Don had to have men to find himself.

He had to do what he had to do.

I gave him my weary blessing.

The end of the lane came up faster than I expected and I banged my hand on the pool's edge, winced, cursed, turned, and pushed off hard to go another lap.

Why didn't I just admit he was gay?

Loving a woman, I came to love myself.

He would do the equivalent, return renewed to our marriage bed.

It's what he said he wanted.

Mila said it could happen.

I had no money.

Alex.

December came in unusually cold. I sat huddled in a blanket at my desk in the little room at the back of our apartment. Once the maid's room, it had no radiator, but it had my stuff, my books and filing cabinets, my rhino picture. I stayed put while Don got Alex to bed. He was going to the baths. I was his best friend; he could tell me anything. I was his wife; he couldn't say a word.

Then he was there in the doorway. Tall. No, *taller*, as if he were at last filling his own frame. I followed him through the kitchen, the dining room, and down the hall past Alex's bedroom, the bath, our room, and into the living room. He went to switch on the lamp, a white oval globe that rested on a slender stem, like a large, graceful, glowing egg. It was one of the first things we bought when we returned from South Africa, and I was amazed that we hadn't broken it, though once I'd caught the globe just inches from the floor, when Alex had put his little fist around the stem and pulled.

Don remained standing yet strangely at ease in his pressed khakis and his maroon turtleneck. I curled up at the end of the couch leaving space for him; he took the rocking chair.

"My therapy group says I've changed," Don said, smiling sheepishly. "They told me today that I'm more masculine. Sexier."

"You are," I said lightly. "I like your faggy haircut." It was cropped close to expose the power of his great skull.

His eyes behind his big glasses got bigger. "It's incredible. Men find me desirable."

"That's why you're so gorgeous?"

He blushed. "I need to be with men now. I wasn't allowed, even as a kid. I've never been with guys. I told Mila I was thirty-nine going on seventeen. She said no, going on seven. I'm tired of saying I'm sorry."

"I didn't ask you to apologize."

"I remember what it was like when you were with Simone."

"And for weeks you said nothing. You've never understood that what hurts me most is being shut out."

"I'm not doing this to hurt you."

"I know. But you are."

"I am sorry," he said. "I have to do this now."

"What do I get?" I said quietly.

"Maybe I'll be a better fucker."

He spoke as if he might believe it, claiming something for himself.

I was not used to such directness. I didn't tell him what I'd done the last time he went to the baths. I lay right here on the couch and had sex with myself. *Fuck me, Don. Fuck me*, horny and angry and sad.

I went to the pool the next afternoon. Why were the lanes crowded? I had to look carefully to find a place to swim at my slow, steady pace. Water seeped into my goggles, stinging my eyes. I finished a lap, stood, took them off and shook the water out, spat into them to clear them. Two swimmers went by before I could reenter the lane.

I was going to be somebody.

I had published one short story. Both novels rejected.

I had no job.

I had no money.

Where was my big life? The one Georgia told me I would have.

I slapped the water with my arm, stinging it, switched to my back and slammed my arms hard as I swam, trying to exorcise my rage and self-pity.

Get thee behind me, Georgia.

Though now it's hard to remember, I did do more than talk to Don and swim those winter weeks. I went to see Mila. I went to my women's group. We got ready for Christmas, and just before it, six-year-old Alex announced that he did not believe in Santa anymore, and he was proud that he'd figured it out for himself. He didn't stop with Santa.

"I don't believe in G-O-D," he said, spelling it out. "Do you?"

I was chopping garlic for salad dressing, my eyes on the big knife. "Not the way your daddy does," I said, hoping this would silence him. I wasn't in a mood for big questions.

"How does Daddy believe?"

"You'll have to ask him."

"Do you believe?"

I set the knife down and turned to him, his bright expectant face. I would not satisfy him if I tried to answer. I'd started learning about God in church when I was his age—the songs we sang, the story of the Good Samaritan. The church had shaped me, included Georgia, and I had to get rid of that part. How could I explain all that? "I think of God as a way of saying something," I said. "About how people should treat each other, about love."

"Then you don't believe?"

"Do you?"

"No, because God would be dead by now."

In the silence left by his departure, I tried to think of how I might have answered better. The strong garlic odor filled my nostrils. On the sixth day God created garlic and it was good. I chastised myself for not having a simple way to talk to Alex about these things. He had disliked Sunday school at Greenwood. We didn't make him go. He wasn't learning the stories, singing the songs, experiencing what Don and I had experienced as little children, that sense of being part of something so much larger than ourselves. It was Don's fault. Mine.

That night Don and I talked in our big bed, which occupied most of the small room. Backed against the wall opposite the foot of the bed, our dresser, my dresser from my childhood, had barely enough space for the drawers to pull out. The mirror above it was the one my father had painted and hung for me. I'd left my antlers and my cowboy hat behind.

"I set limits," Don said, facing me, his elbow bent, his big hand with his long fingers supporting his tilted head. "Guys want my contact information. I don't give it. The last one said, 'Sounds like you have a wife and four kids.' 'Something like that,' I told him."

I smoothed out the sheet between us, but I didn't speak my complicated reaction. Good for Don, I thought. And what was the matter with me? Just because I knew exactly how this nameless man felt, wanting more of Don than he could have, didn't mean I had to pity him.

"I have to make you understand," he said, "how good it is that you give me space. I don't have to worry about my marriage falling apart. It takes the pressure off."

"This isn't easy for me," I said. I did not tell him I had thought of divorce. Because all I was doing was *thinking*.

"I know."

Talking made us closer. He wanted to make love and so did I and he was, in fact, a better fucker. If we could just do it like this, uninhibited, regularly.

"You're amazing," he said at the end.

"It's all I want."

"No, that you'll love me like this, when I'm going to the baths."

Walking Ninth Street down the slope from Eighth to Seventh Avenue, I wrapped my scarf around my face and bent against the late-December wind, Don's note burning in my mind. He'd written it late at night after being away for a few days, on a scrap of paper, and like everything he wrote, it was with his Rapidograph pen in India ink, permanent, his script clear but cramped. "I did not have a good time," it began.

I was supposed to feel sorry for him? I was supposed to be glad? I waited for the light to change by the pizzeria. Don had gone to Washington just after Christmas to be with someone he'd met. Don liked this man. Don had been impotent.

I couldn't get to the Y fast enough. Usually modest, today I didn't care if anyone saw me, and I stuffed my clothes into the little locker instead of folding them carefully. My towel around my shoulders, my feet bare, I pushed into the pool room, set my towel on a bench, and claimed space in the third lane.

Don was impotent with men.

Like he'd been with me.

Good.

It wasn't just about homosexuality.

I swam faster than usual, agitated, then consciously slowed down, determined to increase my laps. I was up to thirty-four and I wanted to see if I could get to thirty-six, forty. He was never impotent with strangers. He was still incredulous that men found him desirable. He let them do what they would, passive, receiving. Just like he'd been with me at the beginning of our sex therapy. Absolutely nothing like my first time with Georgia, every single time with Georgia. Our lovemaking was reciprocal, always.

What was this supposed to mean, that he was never impotent with strangers? I reached the end of the lane, turned, sank down, placed my feet firmly against the wall and pushed off, using my breaststroke to take me ahead underwater.

He was afraid of losing control.

Except with strangers.

This was nothing to be glad about.

I drew the shade on the tall window more for privacy than to block out the pale light of New Year's Day. We'd gotten in late from a party and Alex was at Heath's for the afternoon. I wanted to make love and sleep, but Don was tired so we slept first.

Two hours later and filled with sadness, I held him in my arms. We would have been better off staying asleep. Though we'd started out fine, wanting each other, he lost it and we were back in our old pit. Except we were more scared now.

"I get into my head. I'm despondent now, day after day. I've lost so much time." He swallowed, fighting tears. "What if I can't get pleasure from anyone? Not from men and not from you?"

"I want you," I said fiercely. I did not say I was afraid too, afraid that I'd leave him and three weeks later he'd get it together, free himself, and be the man I knew he was.

"I know." He was completely unguarded now. "It's astonishing you talk to me when we make love. It's really good. You say what you want. I think a lot of women couldn't do that. I mean what *you* do. Now. I don't know what to do with your generosity."

Don never spoke to me like this. It made me want him even more. If I told him, would it send him running?

I went to the pool the next afternoon to get hold of myself. I swam. Don had, as we sat at supper the night before, told me about the baths and what went on there. How could I not be curious? The baths were for men, for me forbidden. Since I was Alex's age, younger, my tomboy-self went after what wasn't allowed to little girls.

Showers where you look at people.

The sauna where sex happened.

And men watched.

The pools.

The orgy room.

The private bedrooms.

Though he had given me no visual details, it was not hard to imagine. He said there was no coercion. No one pressures anyone to do anything he doesn't want to do.

Listening to him had turned me on. Listening to him had troubled me. What was this voyeurism—watching strangers sucking off? Ass fucking? I pictured it all.

Except what Don did, had done to him.

I put on a black turtleneck and good black pants as we were going out later. Looking in the mirror, I squared my shoulders and smiled until my dimples showed, which made me smile more. *Chubby, blonde, blue-eyed and dimpled.* The image of myself I'd been given by my parents. Only I'd not been chubby, blonde or even clearly blue-eyed for ages. Only dimpled. Smiling, I saw that I was not unattractive. That was not the problem. I went into the kitchen, got the onion dip from the refrigerator, potato chips, and put them on a tray with a bottle of wine, two glasses and carried the tray to the living room. Alex was at Heath's; we were going there for dinner. Because we had time on our hands, and because we didn't know what to say to each other if we weren't talking about *it*, we hunted for something safe to do. We were going to look at slides. Our friend Pat had completed her master's at Berkeley just the year before, the degree she was preparing for when we lived with her and Bill that long-ago summer. Because we'd asked, she'd sent images of her latest work.

I put the projector up on a card table, slipped the small square slide into it, and the first image filled the screen. It was a seal-gut parka from Alaska. The note Pat had included explained that she found these translucent skins, which were tough and waterproof and used by the Yu'pik Eskimos to protect themselves from the elements, deeply suggestive. After studying them, she'd begun to work with a new material—hog gut, ordinarily used for sausage casings.

We were both intrigued. Her first piece was called *Waiting for the Calligrapher*. Out of gut she had made a sheet that looked rather like parchment—a large, empty manuscript page—and she had stitched parallel horizontal lines with thin pale thread, lines the scribe would use to write in flowing Arabic script. She had stitched diagonal lines for the artist's embellishments. We looked at all the slides but kept coming back to *Calligrapher*. We both found it hauntingly suggestive, this inner skin transformed.

Looking at the slides took us back to Berkeley. The texture of that summer—the fun we'd had and the rich conversation—seeped into the afternoon, reminding us why we were trying so hard. We put the screen and projector away, put on our jackets and went downstairs. It would be good to be with Rick and Muriel, Heath's parents, who were becoming our best Brooklyn friends. We'd told them nothing. We both understood that our private struggle made us not just fragile and scared but sometimes, like now, incredibly close. We walked along the sidewalk opposite the park.

"You know," I said lightly, flirting, "my whole childhood, I wanted to be a boy. If I were just a boy…"

I could still make him smile. He took my hand. We walked to the corner and turned down Twelfth Street, pushing our conundrum aside for the evening. We were like Don's old hand puzzle. We saw what we wanted, but we hadn't yet found a way to fit the pieces together to make it whole.

Late January, just before the start of the spring term, I went to see Alex's first grade teacher, and I could hardly wait to report to Don what I'd been told. He sat in the big recliner, upright, with a cigarette in one hand, a book by Edmund White in the other.

"It is such a good thing you weren't with me," I said. "We would have laughed. Miss Pope started out by telling me that Alex is perfect." An experienced, warm, and plump woman, she meant it as the highest of compliments. "She told me he was doing well in everything, that he worked hard and cleaned up. He was imaginative and smart and he learns and is just perfect."

Don had put his book down and smiled, no longer annoyed that I was interrupting him.

"I tried to tell her that no kid is perfect, that Alex has anxieties. Maybe about being adopted. You won't believe what she told me." I mimicked her high, childish voice. "Oh, don't worry. I don't teach the family. I used to teach the family but in Alex's class there's a couple splitting and there are lesbian families. It's too hard to teach the family."

Don shook his head. "And this is what they call one of the really good teachers?"

I patted the cushion. "Come, sit close." We hadn't talked seriously for days, except about Alex. We hadn't made love, or even tried to, since New Year's Day. But Don stayed put and went back to his book.

I slipped into the water, my mind troubled and unfocused. I saw the lights in the water. I'd never paid attention before. I swam a whole length, just watching how the light played on the surface and underneath. My mind cleared. Why did I think in such absolute, such opposing terms? Well, because Don said it himself. He didn't know if he was just discovering his sexuality or if he was gay.

He went to the baths.

He's gay.

No, he's afraid of intimacy.

He went to the baths.

Not to a prostitute.

He's fantasized about boys since he was six.

He is gay.

He is terrified of himself, of letting go.

Both, not either/or.

Maybe it was time for us to let each other go. It was not what I wanted. Maybe it would not be so terrible. If I could see myself going and see myself staying, then I could choose. And then I thought of Alex. He was having trouble falling asleep at night. Nightmares.

I'd failed at my writing.

I'd failed at my marriage.

But I was a good mother.

I didn't feel guilty about Alex.

That guilt would kill me.

February 29. A day that doesn't usually exist. In 1980, it seemed strangely right that it began an anniversary I did not want, marking the day our little family sat at the dining room table and Don told Alex that he was moving out. Decades later when I asked Alex what he remembered, he said that his father told him we were getting a divorce. In fact, Don had been tentative and not used the word. More startling, Alex set the scene in the wrong house. Six and a half years old at the time, he had us in our brownstone on Thirteenth Street. Placing us there, he eliminated Don from the apartment where the three of us lived for a full year, and though he was too little to know it, where his parents tried as hard as they could to solve the puzzle of their lives, one that in the end didn't have the pieces it needed to make it whole.

# By Their Fruits

# 26

## Spirit and Soul and Body

"I'm forty years old and my husband left me for another man."

It was October already and I stood on the crowded Broadway-Nassau subway platform with my colleague from work, Dumisani Kumalo. Years later, he would remind me of this, our first personal conversation and how, as I told him, I seemed to be trying to convince myself. Don was gone. Despite everything—my mind knew it was the right decision—I could hardly believe it; I hated it.

I said yes when Dumisani asked me out. We both worked at the American Committee on Africa. ACOA had been founded in the early 1950s by black and white civil rights activists, and it had quickly developed into a center of American solidarity with independence movements on the African continent. Because of my work on *Southern Africa Magazine* and my years at Lemana, I was, to my great relief, offered a job soon after Don left. Just weeks later, in March, Dumisani, a journalist and political exile from South Africa, had also joined the staff.

We both lived in Brooklyn on the F-line. He came to my apartment on Eighth Street on a Saturday night in early November, and he left his coat on the end of the couch when we went out to dinner. We weren't going far, just to Ninth Street to eat at Raintrees. The corner establishment across from Prospect Park had been until recently an old-fashioned ice cream parlor, and now it was a pricey restaurant I couldn't afford. I made an exception. The food was excellent, the ambiance intimate. His left-behind-coat showed me at the beginning of the evening what he had in mind for the end of it.

In the restaurant's soft light, Dumisani's face was dark and animated. He wore glasses and his eyes were lively. Sitting across from him, I was struck by his big smile. It helped me relax. We were both accustomed to being in the company of black people and white, Americans and Africans. Still, I was aware that he was the only black person in the room and that at home, his home, we couldn't have sat like this, publicly having a meal. Conversation with him was easy, easy in a way it had never been at Lemana. He told me how he had managed to get out of South Africa in 1977, just before the organization he worked with was declared illegal and he would have been arrested. His job at ACOA was to travel the country, speaking, organizing, and energizing the divestment movement that would eventually succeed in getting the U.S. Congress to impose economic sanctions on South Africa.

We didn't know each other well and talked first about our work. My job was to do research and create resource materials for the divestment movement. What ACOA published was used to persuade universities, trade unions, religious bodies, and state and city governments to take their investments out of banks and corporations that operated in South Africa and Namibia.

"You have to take the Moral Majority seriously," Dumisani said, when I objected to the organization's offensive positions. His big hands dwarfed the cup of coffee he'd ordered as soon as we sat down. "I like the people in the Moral Majority. I like getting them to listen to me."

He would engage with anyone if he saw that they might be allies in the fight against apartheid, including those I would dismiss outright. His speech, his accent and intonation, were seductive, taking me back to my time in his country, connecting me to my own memories and experience. In the office he was gregarious, a storyteller with an easy laugh. Now his geniality, his refusal to stereotype or judge people appealed to me and I began to let down my guard. Defended against being hurt again, I found him more and more interesting as he began to talk about South Africa. He'd been to Robben Island to visit Nelson Mandela. Not many people got to do that. This man had connections. He told me of other visits, to men in solitary confinement.

"Some of the guards are sadistic. They take the food I bring, the fresh fruit. They eat it in front of the prisoners."

What struck me as much as the sheer nastiness was the calm with which he spoke of it. He was telling me about his regular experience. Good. If he would do that, so could I. I told him the story behind my announcement on the subway platform. Don had someone already, a man named Tim.

"Before I met Tim, my son, Alex, told me that he looks like Prince Barin in the movie *Flash Gordon*. I expected him to be handsome. What I didn't expect is that he is in no way Don's equal. He's lots younger and not nearly as well educated. I admit it. It hurts me that Don has replaced me so fast, and with someone I don't think is worthy of him."

Dumisani hesitated, as if censoring himself. "I've just ended a relationship too," he said. "We were together in South Africa. I came first and then got her and the children out, hers and mine. Only my son's mother is still there. We separated when he was very young."

We discovered that our sons were exactly the same age, seven and a half. I explained co-parenting. Alex was a week with me, a week with Don. Dumisani explained that he lived alone; his son lived with the other children and their mother.

"You have just one child?" I said to be sure.

"My first child was a daughter. She died when she was five months old. I don't know why. They made a law in the 1960s that all Africans die of natural causes so we were not allowed an autopsy."

We sat quietly for a few minutes. He'd ordered veal. I'd ordered fish. When I asked if we should get a bottle of wine, he'd said he didn't drink. Later, I would wonder about how bold I was, about how quickly and uncharacteristically we got personal that first night. Sitting across from him, sipping a glass of wine, I felt he wouldn't abuse my vulnerability, that we were like old friends, that I could ask him anything.

"How have you managed?" I said. "How have you managed to survive all you've had to endure?"

He frowned, looked at me carefully, unsure I'd asked a serious question. His face relaxed. "The thing to do is be very realistic. This is what is. What are you going to do about it?"

"Yes," I said earnestly. "But don't we also have to face, take in, the things that happen? The loss. Not pretend about loss. Otherwise it just comes back to haunt you."

"Yes, but it takes time." His voice was solemn, melodious. "One needs to talk. I have friends in California I can call any hour of the night or day and that saves me."

"Funny," I said. "So do I." I had talked to Bill and Pat for an hour just the day before.

He had to come back to my apartment to get his coat. I hung mine in the closet and turned to him. I liked it that he was only slightly taller than I was and I didn't have to look up to him the way I did with Don, but I held him off as he moved closer.

"My friends say never get involved with someone you work with." I was quoting my women's group. Jen also worked at ACOA and Janet had worked there before. They had warned me that if I took his side in a discussion or opposed him, our colleagues would read our personal relationship into it.

Dumisani was dismissive. "It is not a problem."

By then I wanted a way around my friends' advice. "The office is too small. I don't want people in the office to know we're seeing each other."

"Fine," he said.

Mila had told me that only in B-grade movies does one get what one wants immediately with a new lover. Instead of ending therapy as I'd planned, after Don left, I badly needed to keep seeing her. But she was wrong this time. What I got that first night with Dumisani was more than I'd ever gotten from Don. He was at ease, taking to me as if I were irresistible, and with infinite patience and attentiveness giving me, as I suppose I gave him, the simple pleasures our bodies are designed for. At last, I thought. What a dreadful lover Don had been. And then I cried. I got what I wanted and all it did was make me wish the body in the bed was Don's.

In early December, Dumisani spent the whole night in my bed for the first time. We had slept after we made love, and it was one o'clock when we woke. I asked if he wanted to stay. He reached for me and we made love again, and slept, keeping each other warm in my bed that was so cold I needed long underwear and long socks when I slept alone. In the morning, waking next to him, I ran my fingers down his back, his skin smooth, lustrous. I breathed him in, the lingering hint of his cologne a bit too sweet for me and strange then. I took a shower. We had breakfast at the little table in the kitchen.

"I want your opinion," I said. "Something Don just told me about Tim."

"Did you say they live together?" he said.

"Of course."

"Couldn't they live next door to each other or something?"

I laughed, poured him more coffee. I'd never seen him uncomfortable like this. I changed the subject. Then he was gone and I had to mull over to myself what I'd wanted to talk about.

Tuesday night Tim was putting Alex to bed because Don had a meeting. Tim said to Alex, "Into the bath in five minutes or I'll put you there."

I knew exactly what Tim was up to. Alex had constructed an elaborate bedtime routine with his dad that could go on for half an hour. Tim was one of eight children and such nonsense at bedtime made no sense to him or to me either. Alex kept procrastinating; Tim picked him up, clothes and all, and tossed him into the tub. Alex was furious. Tim told Don, expecting to be commended. Don was furious.

Don related the story over the phone, "I told Tim, 'Don't you ever manhandle my son again.'"

Disturbed by Don's choice of words, I began to rethink my opinion of Tim.

The next Friday afternoon, Dumisani got me to sneak out of the office early. He had to see a film, *Resurrection*, with Ellen Burstyn dying and coming back to life with healing powers. I'd never have guessed that he'd choose such a film and realized how little I knew him. We ate in a small Italian restaurant halfway home, and I wondered how much he was ready to know me. Don's abandonment felt absolute. I wanted to hurt myself, like I had when I banged my head against the wall. Don didn't just leave me, he left women. If I wasn't careful, my self-hatred consumed me in the night. Gay men, I'd read somewhere, had a hierarchy, with the passive role, like that of a woman in a traditional marriage, at the bottom of the heap. An actual woman, that made me the lowest of the low. I couldn't say that to Dumisani, but if I could tell him about Georgia, even the barest facts, he could begin to know me better.

He listened attentively and then smiled mischievously. "You know, it's a turn on for men. To imagine women doing it with each other."

"Remember how young I was."

"The age difference. Hmm. About that between you and me. I've always been attracted to older women."

His teasing surprised me, not because he wouldn't be serious but because I had never thought of him as younger. Born into and growing up under apartheid, and politically active, he'd seen in his thirty-three years far more than I had. "Okay, so tell me. How come you're such an extraordinary lover?"

He grinned. "Not just me. All Zulu boys."

"But why?" I was amused and curious.

"We are taught not by our parents but by our peers." With a mix of impishness and pride, he explained how men are taught to treat women with respect, to stay fit and not to come too quickly. He lifted an eyebrow. "There is no reason for a man to have to come before a woman is satisfied."

I laughed in disbelief. "Is it really in the culture? All boys?"

Girls and boys, he told me. They did what was natural, and they did not practice abstinence. When I asked about pregnancy, he said they did it lying on their sides, so there was clitoral stimulation but no penetration. The semen just ran down the girl's leg. No one got pregnant.

I looked at him skeptically.

"All right. There are stories, stories handed down, of girls who could not control themselves and got themselves pregnant."

"And the stories are told by the men?"

"Yes."

"Perhaps, in just one or maybe two cases, there might have been a boy, not a girl, but a boy, who could not control himself?"

Dumisani laughed hard. "I never thought of that."

I couldn't resist going on. "What about boys with boys?" I said, provocatively. "Girls with girls."

"We don't have it in our culture."

"Oh, come on."

"The church agrees with me on this one," he said, clearly uncomfortable. He changed the subject. "The impact of the church only goes so far. The labor laws. You know. They keep men away from home for long periods of time. It is understood that husbands and wives will take lovers. There are conventions, safeguards. For example, when the husband returns home, he does not come quietly. Walking up the road, he sings, loudly, a particular song, one that identifies him. He whistles. The family dogs begin to bark. All to give the wife time, if need be, to get her lover off the property."

We fell into our own rhythm, Dumisani and I. On weekends when Alex was with Don, or overnight at Heath's house, when Dumisani wasn't on the road, we went for dinner, saw a film, came home to each other's roaring needs and slept. After Don, this was just what I needed, a relationship centered on what we did in bed—in bed, on the couch, the big recliner, the braided rug. We had work in common, liked each other, told each other stories, and I found his moving and instructive. But underneath, and in ways I wasn't even conscious of yet, his prowess—meeting desire boldly, unscripted—made sex simply good. Made me and my desire good too.

We were eating at Gaylord's when Dumisani told me he'd grown up poor. "I didn't have money for school books and had to borrow from the other kids. I hated it. I determined that I would always be first in my class."

"Were you?"

He smiled his bright, open smile. "Oh, yes." He became serious again. "When I first went to school, the night before I began, my father said to me, 'Go and learn the white man's language so that you can tell me what they are up to.' He did not tell me to study to be a doctor or to make money or anything like that because he knew that was impossible. But go, learn the language of the enemy so that you can survive and tell me what's going on."

"You did that, didn't you?"

He nodded.

"You know what's remarkable about you?" I said. "You seem so free of bitterness."

He smiled gravely. "Whatever happens, it has happened to somebody else before. There is no such thing as uniqueness."

I stared at him across the table, this man now beautiful to me, who had become my lover. He had no idea how apropos, how funny I found his big assertion, how wise. An antidote to specialness. Though I wanted him to know why I needed what he said, it was too soon, too complicated to try to explain.

The following Monday, Dumisani put a note on my desk at the office, printed in big letters on a folded sheet of paper. *Just wanted to tell you that I love you very much. You are a terrific person.* And then his illegible signature. Flattered, touched, I shook my head. How could he say he loved me? He hardly knew me. I was not in love with him. I had been in love with Georgia. I'd been in love with Don and with Simone. I knew what love was and this wasn't it, not for me. He was the one who said it was important to be realistic. What was real was this: he was an ordinary person and so was I, and we were both lonely and gave each other such pleasure. Quite enough for now.

# 27

## The Dust from Your Feet

April 1982, more than two years after Don left, Mother wrote me about our divorce. She wrote what I'd always feared she'd say. *Don's behavior was deviant and repulsive.* I'd never told her and Dad why Don left because I knew they'd say something like this. When they did, I would have to defend Don. I couldn't defend him, not yet, not when he'd hurt me so. Mother wouldn't have understood. I wasn't hurt because he was gay but because he left me. Mother didn't know about Georgia. Mother didn't know about Simone. Mother didn't know I'd also done what she considered deviant and repulsive.

Mother had learned the truth from my sister. What her letter said next surprised me. *Sixteen years was a long time to suffer, even a part of it—for suffer you both must have since I feel quite sure there was real affection and love between you.* She had assumed I must have been equally to blame for the divorce. *I thought it takes two to tango. How wrong I was.*

I went to the window, looked out over the housetops to the Verrazano-Narrows Bridge far in the distance. Mother could never just be my mother, on my side, giving me the benefit of the doubt. She had to be fair. She was still assigning blame, though this time she *was* on my side and I loved her for it. Standing there, I read the letter again and cried. Why did there always have to be just two sides, wrong in order for there to be right? Our divorce—beginning with why we married in the first place—was immensely more complicated than that. Never knowing the full story, my mother would never know me.

It was time to talk to Dumisani about us. He didn't know my boy and I didn't know his. Our sons were almost nine, lived in different worlds and this didn't work for me anymore. After a year and a half together, I didn't know Dumisani that much better than I had at the beginning. When I pushed for more—vulnerability and real intimacy—he disappeared for a while. Though he was wonderful company, I couldn't get close to him except physically, which wasn't enough anymore.

I don't remember the film we saw or the name of the restaurant where we had dinner, only that they left us alone to talk. First about South Africa, our shared preoccupation, the talk that sucked me in with its moral clarity and political complexity. Did he agree with yesterday's briefing at ACOA's office on the Black Consciousness Movement? Were my ideas on South Africa's destabilization of Mozambique, Angola, and Zimbabwe clear enough? I had to speak on destabilization the following week at Brown University.

Then, with my usual straightforwardness, I said, "I have to talk to you. About us. It's not working for me anymore."

Saying that, we had the best conversation about ourselves we'd ever had, acknowledging that it was no accident we'd never integrated our sons into our relationship.

"After work," I said, "I pick up Alex and we go to the park to play baseball on that long narrow stretch of grass just over the wall at Eighth Street. We take turns, pitching to ourselves, hitting grounders and flies. Back and forth. I think it's the happiest time of day for both of us. Except recently, he's started calling me Mommy again. Which he hasn't in years. Never mind that there's a note of mockery in his voice, he shouldn't be calling me 'Mommy Dear,' 'Mommy Darling,' as if he is my sweetheart and not just my son."

Dumisani listened intently, his expression hard to read. Because he was quiet, I continued. "I'm too dependent on Alex. I need an adult to share my intimate emotional life. I don't get that from you. I think I'm not going to."

He frowned, then slowly nodded. "I do not like what you say, but I am not surprised. I do know what you mean. I cannot give you what you need although I know that you need it."

His directness startled and seduced me. He never promised more than he could deliver. Don had tried hard to say what he thought I wanted to hear, then didn't follow through because he hadn't really meant what he said. I didn't want to think of Don. Dumisani was, again, just realistic. I loved him for it.

"It's not just you." His voice resonated with a sadness I'd not heard before. "I don't know how to be a father." His son still stayed with the other kids and their mother, the woman who'd been caring for him since they all lived in South Africa. "My therapist asked me why I didn't spend more time with my son. No one's ever asked me that. If someone needs me, I do not know how to act." He crossed his arms against his chest and rocked in his chair. "I am completely self-sufficient. I have lived this way for years. It is not good. I see that. You are right about us."

Seeing a therapist was a profoundly unlikely commitment for a man like him. I didn't know what had prompted him to begin. I couldn't ask. Now, sitting across the table from me, his grave expression lightening with his generous smile, he said, "We can still be friends."

I smiled back, wary, his handsome, honest face familiar, comfortable. He was in therapy. Maybe he'd change. I shook my head. I wanted to find someone else, now. Not wait for some possible new Dumisani in some indefinite future.

Walking to the subway, to distance myself I chatted about Alex. "I overheard him the other day," I said. "He told his friend Nathan, 'You know what's good about shoes? They never turn inside out.'"

Dumisani laughed. "That's deep. You can count on shoes." He came to a full stop. "I almost forgot to tell you. You have to read this wonderful book by James Baldwin. *Just Above My Head.* I get it now. Two men loving each other is just ordinary. I have gotten that from you and reading this book. You have to read this book."

We descended into the subway. "The final word on what you've gotten from going out with me is that gay relationships are okay. I just love it."

He was in front of me on the stairs going down. I wasn't sure he'd heard me. Never mind.

Because Dumisani and I never told anyone at work except Jennifer that we were seeing each other, no one but she knew of the change in our relationship, and we managed fine in the office. By this time, Jen had become executive director and I had been promoted to her position as research director. Late spring, she asked me to lead a workshop on divestment at the YWCA national conference in Washington, D.C. We wanted Ys around the country to join in isolating South Africa.

That evening going home from work I got on the first car of the A train to Brooklyn and stood at the front window isolated from the rush hour crowd. Alex and I used to stand up front like this, peering into the dark tunnel, watching the lights emerge as the next station came into view.

When I'd last seen Georgia, she worked for the YWCA. That was a decade ago. What if she still did? What if she was at this conference?

Did I want to see her? Now, after ten years? After I had tried and failed to write our story? Not once but twice. I had worked on weekends, when Alex was at Don's, and my second agent was better than my first, engaging with the text and recommending changes. After I had done the rewrite I thought she'd asked for, she returned the manuscript with a curt note. "You've done what I suggested. Unfortunately, your main character is deeply unlikeable. I can't gather the enthusiasm I would need to represent this novel."

My main character was me. I wrote to tell the truth. The truth was that I was deeply unlikeable? When I said what really happened, the things my friends didn't even know, I was awful? I put the note in the manuscript box and thrust the box on a high closet shelf where I couldn't see it.

Georgia. Would it have been better if I'd never met her? I couldn't say a simple *yes*. Still, she was a dirty secret. Just the other day the interns at the office were talking casually about when they first had sex. They asked me. I lied. It wasn't intercourse so it didn't count. How could I say Georgia didn't count? I had no name for what had happened. Yes, something in me hoped I'd see her.

I changed to the F train at Jay Street, got a seat where I could see out to the harbor between apartment buildings as the subway came out of the tunnel to become for a few stations an elevated train. Why would I want to see her? To show her that my work had nothing to do with her, or that it was more important that hers? Because I wanted her approval? To prove she hadn't damaged me? I wasn't sure. Probably all those things, though she had damaged me. Did I want an apology?

One thousand six hundred women came to the June YWCA conference. The registration desk couldn't give me a list of attendees. Maybe just as well. I entered the large auditorium for the opening plenary and found a seat for myself in the center, three-quarters of the way back. Looking over the assembled women, my eyes caught on a familiar shape. No, it wasn't Georgia, but now I was keyed up. The woman sat with a group of colleagues who talked up and down the row, laughing and whispering to each other. I studied her back. Was it her back? How could I be certain if I couldn't see her face? She was heavier than Georgia had ever been and her short brown hair was, from behind, generic and unrevealing. With disappointment and relief, I convinced myself she was not Georgia.

Until the woman put her arm on the back of the seat next to her, her left arm on the back of the pew in the church of my childhood. Georgia had often sat at the front of the sanctuary, where I could watch her stretching out her arm on the pew. Relaxed, yes, but her bare arm exposed. I wanted her to be more dignified, covered up. Here she was, with the same gesture, the same posture. Everything disappeared except her, six rows down. She didn't know I was behind her; I could slip away without seeing her.

When the plenary ended, I had fifteen minutes until my workshop. I left the auditorium. I came right back. Almost gleefully, as if we were as important to each other as we'd once been and because I had the upper hand, I planted myself at the top of the aisle she would have to ascend. I couldn't wait to see her expression.

Georgia recognized me instantly and blanched. I couldn't hear what she said, as she turned away from me to her friends, gesturing them to go on without her. She did not want to have to introduce us.

"What on earth are you doing here?"

"I can't talk now. I have to lead a workshop."

"Just tell me when," she said, in an unfamiliar tone that was almost obsequious. "I'll meet you anywhere. Anytime."

"Tomorrow," I said. "Breakfast."

The next morning, we both arrived promptly. I looked at her across the small table, her heaviness unattractive, but her eyes as penetrating as ever.

Georgia waited to speak until we had ordered. "Why haven't you been in touch with me? I've been to New York. I've tried to find you."

My dismay must have shown on my face. "You don't know?"

"I would like to be in touch," she said boldly. "You're forty-two. I'm fifty. We're old enough to be friends, peers as adults. What I always hoped for."

I picked up my coffee and sipped the hot liquid slowly to keep from burning my mouth. "I don't know," I said cautiously, "if that's possible."

Georgia hurried on. "I've never stopped caring for you. I recently came up to New York and spent a long afternoon at the Met." She spoke earnestly, her hands pressed together as if she were praying. "I imagined being there with you. Looking at paintings together."

Renoir in Chicago. Picasso's *Guernica*. These paintings had to be added to the music—*La Bohème*, Rachmaninoff, too many hymns—that I could never see or hear without Georgia coming to mind. No, I would not let her possess the paintings at the Met.

"I wondered if you'd be here," I said carefully. "I saw you first and could have avoided you. I realized I wanted to know how you are." I held her gaze, the one that had intimidated me for years. "I've been in therapy. I needed to understand what happened between us. I don't know how you understand it. I'm not asking for that conversation. But without it, I don't see any way for us to be friends, as if nothing happened."

She spoke matter-of-factly. "There comes a time when you have to let go of the past."

She was telling me I should too. Part of me wanted to believe her. She had loved me. I had wanted what I got. She made me special.

"Look," I said. "I'm not here to open old wounds or lay blame. But because of you, I've had to deal with things in my life I would rather not have had to deal with."

"It hurts me to hear you say that," she said quietly. "It makes me feel guilty."

I could see the guilt in her eyes. It was my job to take it away. All I had to do was reassure her that I wanted what I got. I had, and not just the sex. I got that power to vanquish her pain, which made her happy. Nothing mattered more, but it was a vicious circle. Sex and our secrets made her guilty. I wanted them. No need for guilt. Only I had to keep saying exactly what she wanted to hear in order to have the power over her that I relished. I hadn't anticipated that we'd return to this conversation. I hadn't thought clearly what it would mean to sit down with her. I should have known.

She broke the awkward silence. "May I ask about your divorce?"

Mother must have told her. "It was Don's doing. I wanted to stay married." I could see her surprise but I was not going to explain. "So tell me what you're doing now."

"I've taken a new job." She said it proudly, relaxing. "Executive director of the city's Y." It was a multi-million-dollar program with two hundred staff members, though several of the branches were in trouble. "I was warned not to touch it. But I still have this feeling that I can get along with anyone, do anything. Besides, I felt called. God thought me up for the challenge. Or maybe," she said, smiling, "he just wants to teach me my limitations at last."

Still a believer, on familiar terms with her deity. Her job impressed me. ACOA at its largest never had more than twelve employees and as many interns.

I asked about her children.

"Well, irony of ironies, my mother has come to live with us. Just as the kids are out from under, Mother arrives." She made a face to show her displeasure.

We fell into an easy conversation, as if we were just old friends who hadn't seen each other for a long while. I could still be seduced by the details of her life. She was living with Rose, steadfast Rose, who'd known Georgia almost as long as I had. Rose, the only person, as far as I knew, besides me and the other girls, who knew what Georgia had done. Rose was teaching at the university; they'd bought a house together. Georgia's older son was doing a Ph.D. in clinical psychology. Her younger son was trying to make it as an actor. Her daughter was still an undergraduate.

She'd never known me as a mother. She didn't ask about Alex. Good. Let me keep him absolutely away from her.

"Don't let me sugar coat," Georgia said. "I had to go into therapy myself. I stayed angry at Sam as a way of not letting go. But I worked it through, painfully. In the end, I felt a great release." She spoke with the authority that had made her irrefutable. Then her voice turned sad. "Sam could not stand for me to be strong and locked me in with babies."

Before I could ask the one thing I had to know—had she told her therapist about us?—she signaled the waitress for more coffee. When she spoke again her voice was full of affection.

"It's odd we're here, terribly odd. I've been thinking about you a lot the last couple of months—" she had had to search for the word—"prayerfully."

"You pray and I appear?" I said, joking.

"God has a sense of humor." The lightness with which she said this was contradicted by the serious way she looked at me. "But now, are you going out? Dating?"

I saw no reason not to answer. "I just ended a lovely relationship, a man from my office." That's all she needed to know. "I'm still in shock, I guess, stunned that I'm single."

"Oh yes, I understand perfectly. It's why I let myself get heavy like this. Armor against involvement. Only I know it's not healthy." She smiled at me. "You're very attractive. You'll find someone else when you're ready."

I was glad that she saw me looking good. I wanted to tell her I'd break the pattern, the replication I chose not to recite—that I had gone to her university, followed her into seminary, married a minister, and now had divorced one. I would find someone new even if she didn't. And I had not taken any vulnerable young girl to bed. Maybe the two things were linked. However debilitating my guilt had been, it couldn't have been as bad as hers. We should not have been surprised that our marriages failed, given the conditions under which they began, given what we needed when we choose the men we married.

"When you were in therapy," I said, "did you tell the therapist about us?"

She shook her head no.

"Well, I did. My therapy was long and you were a big part of it. I have only one regret. I should have done it ten years earlier."

"My therapist has become my friend," she said. "She's thirty-two."

I froze. I had nothing more to say to her. I did not trust that she was friends with her therapist or that the therapist was young. Mila worked with clear boundaries, wanting nothing from me that a friend would legitimately require. How could I have projected all my stuff on to her, if I'd known her as friend? Violating boundaries was Georgia's forte. Had she just found one more young woman she could control?

Georgia had figured out a life for herself by leaving out what had happened to her when she was twelve. Leaving out how she had repeated with me what had been done to her. How could I trust anything she told me about herself, burying as she did such early, wrongful acts committed on her and by her? It was time to go. All I needed was to say goodbye at last. And then she wanted to give me her business card.

"I'm glad I saw you," I said. "I'm glad to know what you're doing. I'm glad to tell you I'm all right. Maybe we've just done all that's necessary—possible—between us."

She insisted. I took her business card. I gave her mine. Her card was printed in blue, not black ink. I kept it for a long time.

# 28

# Unless I See

In 1984, I went to work for the journal *Christianity and Crisis*, or *C&C*, as it was commonly called. Its founder, the renowned theologian and ethicist Reinhold Niebuhr, taught at Union Theological Seminary for more than three decades, retiring just two years before I had entered the seminary. His ideas still permeated the institution and were subject to intense scrutiny by those of us who hadn't had the privilege of working with him. Instead of our classroom teacher, he'd become a stooped, slow-moving presence to be glimpsed occasionally, making his way down a cloistered hall like an embodied spirit.

> O God, give us the serenity to accept what cannot be changed, the courage to change what can be changed, and the wisdom to know the difference.
>
> The tendency to claim God as the ally for our partisan value and ends is the source of all religious fanaticism.
>
> Man's capacity for justice makes democracy possible; but man's inclination to injustice makes democracy necessary.
>
> If we can find God only as He is revealed in nature, we have no moral God.

As a student, I found what he said about democracy and religious fanaticism extremely useful. I puzzled over what he said about nature and a moral God. I was startled when a classmate asked in seminar, "Who gets to decide what can and can't be changed?"

Nineteen years after I graduated from seminary, *C&C* had an editorial job open. Niebuhr had founded the journal in 1941 to argue for Christian involvement in the war against fascism and against perfectionism and utopianism. In the decades since, it had continued to bring a faithful, ethical eye to world events, publishing, for example, in 1963, Martin Luther King, Jr.'s "Letter from a Birmingham Jail," and, in 1979, articles calling for the churches to rethink their condemnation of homosexuality.

That issue on sexuality had made me extremely agitated. Joan Clark reported on how she was fired by the United Methodist Church, after seven years of employment, when she came out as a lesbian. Episcopal priest Carter Heyward wrote, even as she was coming out as a lesbian, that the labels—heterosexual, bisexual, homosexual—limit and distort. I had desperately wanted to be part of that conversation, but since I was married to Don, my intense affinity with these women seemed inexpressible, maybe even disingenuous.

Now, I needed a new job. I wasn't making enough money to support myself and Alex. Even *C&C's* modest salary was more than ACOA could pay. And I had to find a job I wouldn't feel guilty about, one unconnected to the larger, commercial, consumer culture. This wasn't just good politics and moral courage. I was still fending off a vague, anticipated attack that would come when I least expected it and expose me. Don had left me for a man. Georgia had chosen me. These things were somehow my fault. Underneath my reason and intelligence, there still lay an invisible sinkhole of self-hatred, one I could slip into if I wasn't careful.

As managing editor of *C&C*, I could write editorials, and solicit reports, analysis, and book reviews about the struggle to end apartheid, getting my friends to write. I also had to get up to speed fast on a whole range of subjects: Central America, abortion rights, gay rights, nuclear disarmament, economic justice, the Middle East. Leading thinkers wrote for us about liberation theology, feminist and womanist theology, and I got to manage a grant to cover Native American concerns. I was aware that *C&C's* subscriber list was small and its influence less than it had once been, but that didn't diminish its value for me and I was grateful when I was hired.

With this job, I walked back into the world of faith I grew up in, Georgia's world. She had first introduced me to the Niebuhrs. She had studied with Reinhold's sister Ursula. At seminary, Don and I had shared our deepening knowledge of theology, church history, and the Bible. Yet I'd come to wonder if for years I'd been a kind of intellectual and spiritual parasite, living in the shadow of true believers, feeding first off Georgia's faith and then off Don's.

As a young child, I embraced the Good Samaritan as a primal story. When I was ten and had my epiphany on Good Friday, that Jesus died for our sins, that was mine. The thrill I experienced when I first heard the words in Old Testament class, *A wandering Aramean was my father*, that was mine too; I claimed that lineage. *C&C* didn't demand a personal statement of faith or require that one belong to a local church. I could give them what they asked: professional excellence and respect for the journal's history and tradition. Maybe the journal would be next in line after Georgia and Don, letting me dwell in a community of faith without resolving my dilemmas about affirmation. Maybe any personal affirmation of mine could never be completely unraveled from Georgia. Maybe I'd find faith. Or maybe I'd walk away at last from this still-familiar, appealing, complex place.

It was Dumisani who took me back to church. I can't remember exactly when we began to see each other again after we parted in 1982. My efforts to date other men never found me anyone as interesting, and the memory of his body in my bed was strong persuasion to resume. More than once I would say I was through with him and then change my mind.

Dumisani was a seeker, and though he claimed he would never join anything, he joined the United Methodist Church in my neighborhood. When he asked me to come with him, I said yes. I had the hypercritical eye of an insider, and I approved of the church he'd chosen. Sunday mornings we would walk from my apartment down to the eleven o'clock service, under the old trees whose roots sometimes buckled the sidewalks, past tiny gardens in front of solid stone houses. I had more on my mind than worship. Walking to church with Dumisani, after we'd been out on Saturday night, after we'd slept together, I began to imagine that we could be more than lovers, could, maybe, make a life together.

When Dumisani called to pick up where we'd left off, I insisted on a new condition. We had to include our sons, now twelve years old, in our life together. It was his idea to go to a Yankees game. He found my need to tie things down ahead of time impossibly controlling. I found his need for flexibility, to let things happen as they would, controlling in a different way. We managed to get to the ballpark on a Saturday afternoon. Dumisani overruled me and bought more expensive seats than I thought necessary, and I told him so, annoyed. We sat along the third base line, at first mother-son, son-father, but pretty soon the boys were horsing around and climbing on Dumisani, and then they went off together to get hot dogs.

I wanted to tell Dumisani how it touched me to see the boys all over him. He'd be good for Alex. Don was a pushover. I was tired of being the sole disciplinarian. Before I could speak, he leaned over to me across the boys' chairs. "I just found out," he said in a low voice, "my son's mother has been arrested."

The news had come from an absolutely credible source. She was not wanted by the police but had simply been at the wrong place at the wrong time when the police raided.

"I haven't told him yet."

I moved to sit next to him, thought about us being a family, the complications and multiple loyalties involved. When the boys returned, we changed the subject and watched the Yankees beat the Angels, ten to four.

Afterward, we went to my apartment for dinner. I hadn't known if they would come. I'd shopped and made spaghetti sauce ahead of time just in case, and the three guys watched the Mets game in the living room while I worked in the kitchen, heating things up, making a salad, my heart happy.

When they were finished eating, the boys huddled and then informed us that they wanted to go out to the little store and play video games, this being long before such things were household items.

"We'll go," Alex said magnanimously, "to be out of your way."

"You see what I'm up against," I said, laughing, when they were gone. "He knows too well how to get what he wants." He was becoming increasingly obstinate and doing less well in school. But I didn't want to talk about Alex. Dumisani and I were at opposite ends of the dining room table, the boys had been on either side, and the distance between us made it easier somehow to talk things through, which was new for us.

"It hurts me," I said, "when you say I'm controlling."

"Okay. If you hadn't thought ahead there would have been no food on the table." He granted that I had to negotiate with Don and Tim to make plans with Alex. He shook his head slowly. "Nobody tells me how to spend money." He meant the tickets to the ball game.

"It's a question of values," I said as calmly as I could. "You tell me you can't afford things but then pay more than necessary." I didn't know how much he made; he didn't know how much I made. We split whatever it cost when we went out.

"It's not values," he said. "It's choices."

He thought values were about more important matters. I thought the way one spent one's money reflected one's values. But he looked like he belonged at the other end of the table, as if he were the father and this were our home.

Troubled about his son and his son's mother, he changed the subject. "I've never said this to anyone. I feel guilty, being away such a lot." His son lived with him now and he was on the road a great deal.

"How could you not? I would too. Any parent would."

Dumisani called home every night at 6:30, no matter where he was. It was the best he could do, he said. "He's alone too much, but I have to travel."

"Yes, you do." I didn't say what I was thinking. If we lived together, the four of us, I would be with the boys; the boys would be like brothers.

Lying in bed that night, I was sorry I'd been such a prude about money. Why couldn't I have remembered? Earlier, when I'd wondered if I might fall in love with him, I needed to know how he felt about me. I wanted reciprocity before I committed myself. He had sat on the floor in the living room, struggling to speak. I'd wanted him to say he loved me. I thought he would, and because he struggled, I almost said it for him.

"I can't stand being poor."

Startled and disappointed, I was glad I'd kept my mouth shut.

What pleasure it must give him to buy from time to time something that cost top dollar. We were a cliché, a couple arguing about money. Small as my salaries always were, I'd grown up with modest plenty and I did not worry, not deeply, about money. Why did I jeopardize what I wanted with a silly, pompous argument about money? I saw how vulnerable I was, wanting this man to love me and love my kid. I fell asleep figuring out how to rearrange the space for all of us to live in my apartment.

A large wooden desk filled my small square office at _C&C_, the journal's production schedule under its glass top, my electric typewriter on a separate table to the left, and hanging on the wall in the corner where I could see it when I worked, a poster of Lillian Ngoyi. She had been a leader of the South African Federation of Women and the image was from 1956 when some 20,000 women marched on government buildings in Pretoria, protesting new repressive laws. Ngoyi's fist is raised and the caption beneath her proclaims: _You have touched the women. You have struck a rock. You have dislodged a boulder. You will be crushed._ It gave me courage, that poster.

_C&C_ was proving to be an even better place to work than I had expected. The rhythm of our biweekly publication meant that we had routines to follow, ones that repeated themselves and gave me a sense of security. My colleagues commended me for my editing. _Bob makes every writer sound like Bob. You make the writer sound like himself, only with greater clarity._

Now I sat staring at my poster without seeing it. What did it mean to say that no one is in authority except if God wills it? Ronald Reagan? P.W. Botha? But the assertion came from Alan Boesak, the black South African activist theologian who was president of the World Alliance of Reformed Churches. I'd just finished editing his piece. Most of our readers would not question the assertion. Maybe they understood something that escaped me. I left the text alone.

I'd met Boesak, respected him, but my literal, rational mind resisted what he said, and I argued with him in my head. I got myself tangled in matters like this frequently, ones the church had grappled with since the beginning, and often about faith and works and how they were or were not bound together.

I took myself to church right before Christmas. Dumisani was out of town and Alex was at Don's, though I knew Alex wouldn't want to come with me to church. Don had joined a congregation in the Village which had long welcomed gays and lesbians. At work, his immediate colleagues knew he was gay, didn't care, and it was no one else's business. It was not my business either that Don didn't share his church community with Alex. But it angered me because Alex got to be a little prince, only doing what he wanted. Don was a believer. How could he not care that his son was growing up outside the church?

I was too ambivalent myself to insist that Alex come with me, and I went this third Sunday in Advent alone. I wanted to see what it might mean to attend again, regularly, of my own volition. It felt like flirting with faith. It felt isolating, separating me from my women, as none of them were believers. Sprigs of evergreens were tied to the end of each pew, filling the air with the clean scent of the forest. My voice joined with the voices of dozens of others, singing the familiar carol. "Long lay the world in sin and error pining / 'Till he appeared and the soul felt its worth." It was as if I was singing for the first time, *the soul felt its worth.* Yes, the world was weary but I felt that worth, worth that would counter a bit more of my useless guilt.

Spring 1986. Dumisani and his son had not moved in with us, but he gave me his travel schedule now, letting me know where he was and when he'd be back. We talked about our sons all the time now. He would send his to a boarding school. He had to travel and it wasn't good for his son to be alone such a lot. I sent my son to a therapist. Mila confirmed my fear that a boy as bright as Alex had to have something serious going on to perform so badly in school.

Sometimes Dumisani's son came with us when we went to church. I liked sitting in church with them. Maybe I'd always like being special, different, sucking up status by association. Let people think we were family. I listened carefully to the language of the service, all the words. The hymns, like that Christmas carol, stirred me. "See the streams of living waters / springing from eternal love / well supply thy sons and daughters / and all fear of want remove." I loved the singing. I loved the stories, this morning, Jesus calling his disciples. It stunned me every time. He'd say, "Come, follow me." And they did, just like that, leaving their fathers and their fishing boats behind. Talk about charisma. *Charisma* was a word I'd learned from Georgia. It wasn't that she owned it anymore, only that it always brought her to my mind.

This Sunday, the church was taking in new members, a young couple and an older man. I didn't know them. I didn't participate in the life of the congregation. I'd become the kind of worshipper Don and I had disdained. The kind who only came occasionally, gave nothing back, and criticized how things were done. The three new members stood with their backs to the congregation, but their unison "I do" was clearly audible when the minister asked them, "Do you accept Jesus Christ as your Savior and Lord?"

There it was. I could not make that affirmation, and I respected the tradition far too much to merely mouth the words. Strange how at home I could be in this sanctuary, bringing with me as I did my childhood church, those services at Union that saved my life, the chapel at Lemana, Chambers Church. And then I'd stopped. I affirmed many things about the faith—it had to be communal, not just individual; it demanded justice, offered grace. The music, the stories and teachings had penetrated so deeply they would always be part of me. But I did not know anymore what it meant to accept a savior or a lord. I wanted neither.

When the service was over, Dumisani suggested we go to brunch at the big deli at Cadman Plaza. Perfect, I thought. Get me out of here. I had no heart, no desire, none at all, to resolve the contradictions made visible by the service, by the job I held and my lack of faith affirmations. Let me have bagels, lox and bagels and a good cup of coffee.

# 29

## The Third and
## Fourth Generation

It's an old joke: if babies knew in the womb what lay before them, they'd never head down that birth canal. What about parents? If we knew what was coming?

Some parents are lucky. What we have to give is what our kids need. We bring our experience to the task, try to be the moms and dads we needed, give our kids what we didn't get, doing it better this time.

Georgia said she was trying to do just that. Give me what she didn't get from Virginia, as if that would make it right. We even joked about it; the sins of the mothers visited…

"I don't care what you say. I did go to school." Alex got up from the table where we were having dinner. "I'm going to move out and live with my dad." He made this pronouncement, and a gesture with his middle finger I pretended not to see. I held my tongue, listened to his fourteen-year-old rage tramp down the long hall from the dining room, past his bedroom, mine, and bang the door to the living room where he'd watch TV. It was October. He had barely graduated from intermediate school. Now he was a freshman at Abraham Lincoln High School in Coney Island, but only the intervention of a friend in the system got him admitted there.

I poured myself another glass of wine. I had done exactly what Mila had suggested: not get into arguments about who is telling the truth. I had stated my case clearly and shut up. "I called the school today; they told me you weren't there."

Lingering at the table was comforting as I was more at home in this apartment than any place I'd ever lived. After Don moved out in 1980, seven years ago already, I'd lined the paneled wall to my left with photographs—my women's group, my family—to keep me company when I was alone. I studied the brightest picture, Alex and I standing on brilliant green grass, bent forward, ready to sprint off in a race against each other in happier times. Now this beautiful boy needed a therapist, only Alex wasn't talking to him. Dr. Cohen suggested that Alex was exploiting the differences between his father and me. Well, duh! Dr. Cohen said Alex needed a job, or tutoring. If those things didn't work, we should think about a private school. As if we could afford one.

I got up and carried everything to the kitchen. Don had told me that Alex said I was always wanting to make up with him. He doesn't want to make up with me because I'm a bitch. Don just listens. He thinks Alex is scared because he's doing badly in school. He thinks maybe this is just what adolescent boys do, reject their mothers.

I eased my wine glass into the soapy water and washed it carefully. This was not just normal adolescence. If we let Alex live with Don now, we'd be rewarding him for bad behavior, letting him run from what troubled him. He had to learn to take responsibility. I thought Don and I had agreed about that.

It was Alex's job to do the dishes. Tonight, I didn't have the energy to make him. It would have prompted yet another version of the now boring conversation.

"I am going to live with my dad."

"When you demonstrate responsibility, only then will you be able to make such choices."

Hot water on my hands as I scrubbed the frying pan. It's the same conversation I had with my father when I was Alex's age. "When are you going to stop treating me like a child?" I yelled at him, tears streaming down my face.

"When you stop acting like one," he said.

It wasn't the same conversation. Even if I had a two-year-old temper, I was doing well in school.

I was paying attention to Alex.

My father ignored me.

But it had come to this.

"I want you to live with me. I love you, enough not to let you ruin your life. I love myself enough not to let you treat me with such disrespect." I'd said this with anger, tough.

"Well, then, I will be so awful that you will want to throw me out."

"You cannot do anything that would make me throw you out."

"This is going to be interesting. I am going to make life miserable."

Finished with the dishes, I dried my hands. He was doing a pretty good job of it. I didn't know what more to do. Tears came to my eyes, as I began to lose the battle to keep the dangerous stuff at bay: I can't love anybody well. I couldn't love Don in a way that made us work. I can't love Alex in a way that makes him happy. It's my job to make the people I love happy. Which is bullshit!

I was being afflicted by my own young self. I had been like Alex at fourteen, only nobody engaged with me. It's terrible to feel such rage. It hurts me that he hurts like that.

I sat at the kitchen table, talking myself calm before I went down the hall to encounter Alex again. I wasn't angry like a two-year-old anymore. Mila said Alex lies to me because it is so important to me that he tell the truth. What the hell am I supposed to do with that?

Money started disappearing. Alex insisted he needed a beeper. Who needs a beeper? Kids dealing drugs. I called Rick and Muriel, my best friends in Brooklyn. They'd known Alex since he went to nursery school with their son Heath. "He's stealing money, from me, from Don and Tim. He lies. He cheats. He's angry all the time, and he isn't going to school. Do you think it could be drugs?"

"If it were my kid, with this behavior, I would assume so," they both said.

Hearing this, I was oddly relieved. The problem had a name. Nobody could say I wasn't paying attention. I flew into action, calling every substance abuse treatment program for kids in Brooklyn and beyond, explaining Alex's behavior, but then I had to ask the tricky question. "What's the racial make-up of the kids in your program?"

"Black and Puerto Rican. This is downtown Brooklyn. What did you expect?" The voice on the phone was hostile.

I would not send Alex to a program where he was the only white kid.

And then I had to provide the tricky information. "His father's gay."

"We'll take your son. But his father can't participate. Homosexuality is not a moral lifestyle." The voice was sanctimonious.

Finally, with Rick's help, I found The Family Foundation, a residential treatment program for people like Alex in western, rural New York. When

I described his behavior, the woman on the phone, Helen, was kind. "Your son needs us. We take people regardless of race, though most are white."

I made an appointment for the following Saturday. Let Don tell them he's gay.

Alex went to get a haircut. He told the barber, "I'm going to a new school. Maybe it will be a better place for me."

The barber told Tim who told me. It gave me courage, this most positive statement from Alex in many months. It helped me do that hardest thing I'd ever done, send my son away. We got lost on backroads that first trip, stopped to ask directions at a cabin in the woods where five deer carcasses hung by their hind feet, waiting to be butchered. It was easy to believe that the man who came out of the cabin to shoo us off his property had shot them.

"Never heard of it," he said, when I asked about The Family.

Finally, on a dirt road, there it was, a big red barn, a pond, bucolic. The intake procedure was brilliant, with Helen in charge and a boy Alex's age explaining the rules. For Alex to break from his former life, there would be no contact with him for a month. He would be in group, facing his problems, and he would be in school. No TV. He would work in the kitchen and in the barn with the hogs, with the chickens. Contact with girls was forbidden, unless it was work related.

When they tried to get Alex to say what he was addicted to, he said he wasn't addicted to anything. Helen told us this was typical of kids at the beginning, and it was time for us to go.

I can still see my heavy, overwrought boy, held back by two strong adults to keep him from running to my car. I can still feel the white-hot curse he shot at me as we fled the building. "You fuckin' bitch." Shaking as I drove away, I said to Don, tears streaming down my face, "Talk to me." I have no idea what he said, but he did talk, all the way, and without him I never could have made it back to Brooklyn.

I was in my office at *C&C* when the first phone call came from The Family. It was Larry, one of the counselors we'd met on that first visit.

"We don't believe that homosexuality is a viable lifestyle."

Every muscle in my body clenched. "What does that have to do with…?"

"Maybe we can't work with your family."

This was not possible. I had exhausted my leads. We'd known The

Family followed a twelve-step model and had been founded by recovering alcoholics. I had been impressed by Helen, her world-weary kindness. We hadn't known before that first visit that she and the other counselors were conservative Roman Catholics.

Why wasn't Larry calling Don? Because it was easier to talk to me. Because I was the one who had made all the arrangements and, truth be told, I would have objected if I'd been excluded from this conversation. I'd just written an editorial on the wrong done to Rosemary Denman, a United Methodist pastor who, after four years of ministry, fell in love with a woman and was defrocked.

> It is not practicing lesbians and gays who threaten the church, but the acts against them, their exclusion from fellowship and ministry that endangers the church which was called to be an inclusive community of love.

I mailed Larry a copy of the journal with the editorial. It was a mark of how desperate and delusional I was that I thought if he read my editorial, Larry would change his mind.

A month later we set off from Brooklyn to see Alex for the first time, with Don in the passenger seat and I at the wheel. Exiting from the Thruway, the road narrowed to two lanes and my little Mitsubishi was dwarfed by the semis that crowded the road, kicking slush and muddy water onto the windshield. Why was everything so hard?

As soon as we arrived at The Family, we went upstairs. The classroom was bare, with a crucifix the only adornment. We were seated at a small table, Larry, Helen, Don and me. Before they would let us see Alex, we had to discuss whether or not they would work with our family.

Dressed in a red-checked flannel shirt, and rugged-looking, as if he spent time out of doors, Larry shook his head. "Your journal, it reads like '60s propaganda. We have to return to the old values, like we had in the 1950s."

Helen held up her hand to stop this conversation. Older than Larry, in her late forties I guessed, she wore a plain black sweater over a simple, pale blue blouse, her dark brown hair framing a pleasant face. She began the formal meeting with prayer. Then she explained to us that the program had a resident Catholic father who listened to confessions and led mass.

"We take the Protestants to town for church."

"But homosexuality is not a viable moral choice," Larry said.

I began to see how they played good-cop/bad-cop as they laid out their positions. Determined not to rage at Larry's stupid assertions, I tried to think of what to say.

"Let me speak," Don said. Pulling down on his new brown jacket which he wore over a dress shirt and tie, he straightened in his chair, and his voice was calmly authoritative. "I can't hide my God-given nature. I believe that sexuality is a gift from God, and I have come at last to affirm myself, proudly, as a gay man."

I wanted to applaud. It had taken him such a long time to claim who he was.

I saw that Helen and Larry didn't know what to do with Don, a Baptist minister who was partnered with a man, who spoke their religious language and who was happy to pray with them.

Finally, after we went back and forth, Helen came to a decision. "Alex can stay. We will work with your family. The Church doesn't approve. But AA teaches that you don't have to agree with someone to respect and love them."

"Can Tim come with us?" Don said. "If you want family, Tim needs to come too."

I was pleased when they said yes. Don had become passive and permissive, immobilized by Alex's behavior. Tim was my ally and I welcomed his participation.

"Their alcoholism trumped their Catholicism," I said impishly to Don as we drove home. "Thank God for that. You were brilliant."

Despite all the ironies and limitations, and because I knew of no other options, I clung to the belief that The Family could help Alex. The place was a farm that raised animals and the kids had real chores. Maybe, working in the kitchen, he'd learn to be a chef. He'd go to school and learn the twelve steps. Dumisani was a recovering alcoholic. He'd taught me about the power of AA to save people's lives.

For The Family to succeed, we all had to come under its authority and play by its rules. At intake and the first session, Helen and Larry had explained how addiction and abuse run in families and we were asked for full disclosure. I had answered no to alcoholism, drugs, physical or sexual abuse in my immediate family. I told them about Dr. Cohen, Alex's therapist. I told them about Mila, and I told Mila about The Family. Not just their take on homosexuality, but how Larry had dismissed the value of individual therapy.

"You can always lie," he said, "when it's one-on-one. In a group, somebody will catch you out."

Mila didn't hide her skepticism about the level of their skill and training and cautioned me to be careful about what I shared. Despite her warning, I had to tell them about Georgia. Not telling felt like lying, though at that time, *abuse* was not a word in my vocabulary. It didn't begin to convey how I had loved her or why I had to banish her from my life.

Don and Tim sat together, opposite me. Helen and Larry took their chairs. They had intended for Alex to meet with us, but I asked to begin without him.

"There's something more I need to say. When I was sixteen, our church hired its first director of Christian education. She was charismatic and taught us a lot." I tried to keep my voice steady. "Her name was Georgia. When I was sixteen, she seduced me, and we were involved for quite a while."

Helen, wearing the same simple clothes, sighed. She nodded her head, as if all the pieces were finally beginning to fall into place. "Now I understand," she said, "why you are so accepting of Don's homosexuality."

I looked at her wide-eyed. "No," I said, but Larry interrupted me.

"How can you say you were seduced? You were sixteen already. You got just want you wanted."

He didn't have to say the rest, but I knew what was going through his mind. I was a slut. Loving Georgia made me a slut.

"You have to tell Alex," Helen said.

"What?"

"Alex knows about his father. He has to know about you too."

"No," I said again, more forcefully. "I will not tell him." The demand was outrageous. It strengthened my spine. They would not make me a slut. I would not tell.

"I have discussed this with my therapist," I said, sternly. "Alex's therapist agrees with her. Alex already has too much on his plate." *Adoption, divorce, a gay and passive dad in a macho neighborhood, a mother too much in need of closeness and control.* "My story will just drive his troubles deeper and make him even more inaccessible."

They shook their heads. "If you are going to work with us," Larry said, "you have to follow our path. No secrets from anyone."

Desperate, I looked down the table at Don for support.

"What about Simone?" he said, plaintively, as if he were the injured party.

If Don had stood up, reached across the table with his long arm, and slapped me across the face, I wouldn't have been more shocked. It was not his prerogative to speak about Simone, this proud gay man with his partner, Tim, sitting right next to him. Yes, because of Georgia, I had been confused about my sexuality. Yes, I had a brief affair with Simone. It had hurt him. It had helped me know I wanted to stay married to him.

"Your marriage was never fulfilled," Helen said, grimly. "You were always at cross purposes."

"That's not true." If she only knew how hard I had tried to stay married. Now I wanted to kill Don. "We were not always at cross purposes," I said.

"Alex knows about his father," Larry said again.

"I'm not a lesbian. If I believed telling Alex would help him, I'd tell him in a second. I don't believe that." I was almost shouting.

"It's always the loud one who is most vulnerable," Helen said. "You need to tell Alex. He sees you as powerful and controlling. He never sees you vulnerable."

My voice shook. "That's not true. He sees me cry. He sees me at my wit's end. And I will not tell him."

I left The Family that afternoon shaken and alone. I had been fool enough to think Don and I were allies. I thought we were all in this together as a family, to do everything in our power to help Alex. I drove Don and Tim to The Family because they didn't have a car. Not anymore.

Alex ran away from The Family. It was birthing time for the sows and the men and boys had rotating shifts through the night. When he was poked at 2:00 a.m. to go on duty, he snuck around and turned off all the alarm clocks, started the old Ford with a screwdriver. He'd watched how this was done when he'd been driven to the doctor's in town. He'd never driven a car in his life, but he had watched. At Christmas time, stuffing envelopes with invitations to the holiday party, he had memorized the directions from New York City to The Family. He told us later he just reversed them, and he did okay until he hit the Harlem River Drive at rush hour. Shifting in stop-and-start traffic for the first time, he got all the way to East Harlem before the engine started to smoke. He opened the door and got out, abandoning the car in the center lane. He walked to the nearest subway station and made his way to Brooklyn. For eighteen hours we didn't know where he was.

I was at work when Larry called.

"Stay at work," he advised. "Don't organize your life around your son's bad behavior."

I thought of the other young men who had run from The Family; they'd ended up in jail. I wondered where Alex would go. Unable to work, I stood in my office, part of me hoping that he was having a hell of an adventure. At the end of the day, Dumisani drove me to the police precinct where I reported Alex missing. They asked if I had X-rays or dental records. To identify his body.

Late that night, Don got a call from Alex. He was at a friend's house and her mother had insisted that he call his parents. His plan had been to drive to the stables in Jamaica Bay, where he went horseback riding, and live in the car. Without a car, he'd finally gone for shelter. Next morning, we went to get him and took him back to The Family. He ran away a second time on foot, but a state trooper spotted him and took him back.

We went every weekend to try to keep him from running. He seemed to be making real progress. It was three hours up and three hours back and at least two hours of session. I was beaten down. They insisted, rightly, that Alex take responsibility for what he'd done, the lying, cheating, stealing, truancy, and big bad attitude, which were the only things Alex would admit to.

I couldn't escape their logic. If Alex was responsible at fourteen for what he did, then surely, I was responsible at sixteen for what I had done. I was responsible for everything I did with Georgia.

Alex ran away a third time. He discovered where The Family kept its keys and took a car in the night. Stopped in New Jersey near the George Washington Bridge, he was arrested for car theft when the cop asked for his papers. At the juvenile detention center, he declined his right to call his parents. He was not trying to get home.

When I called The Family to report what I'd learned from the Jersey police, Larry said immediately that they wouldn't take him back.

"We thought he was doing better. We can't read him. I'll have to discuss this with Helen, whether we press charges on the car." It was their standard practice to press charges.

The next morning, in court, Don and I watched as Alex was brought in, handcuffed. He didn't look at us. He was lean now, and I thought that he'd grown taller. I had laryngitis and asked Don to speak to the judge for us. He just sat there. I stood and in my croaky voice made a futile plea to the judge, to find another place for Alex as we couldn't handle him. But the State of New Jersey entrusted Alex back into our care as the law required since he was a New Yorker.

I had sent Alex away in November. It was now late March. What had really changed? Before I let Alex into my apartment, I stopped him on the landing. Though it hurt to speak, I made a pronouncement. "You come inside on one condition. You choose this, put yourself back in our custody. You have chosen to be obedient to us."

"I understand that," Alex said quietly, appropriately, without any trace of victory in his voice.

"You do nothing without permission from your dad or Tim or me."

"I understand."

At first, he did. At first, he was a model son, setting the table before meals, washing up without being asked, like he had at The Family, like he had at home, before he stopped. He went to AA meetings, because The Family had taught him to do that, though he still insisted that he was never addicted to anything. I got him a job in my office stuffing envelopes while we hunted another placement for him.

I did not sleep well. I did not know who I was living with, if he'd try to run away again, or steal from me again. Regular high school wasn't an option anymore, but what was?

In the evenings, it was sweet to have him back. We were shy with each other, careful, watched TV, *MacGyver* for him, *Cagney & Lacy* for me, *Magnum P.I.*

I did the ironing while I watched.

"If it wasn't for The Family," Alex said, "I'd be dead or in jail."

Out of the blue. I set the iron on its end and looked over to him, relaxed on the couch, wiry and muscled from the physical work that The Family had required of him.

"Say what? Did I hear you right?"

"Yeah."

I was afraid to believe it. It was the best thing he could have said. Maybe I hadn't made a terrible mistake, sending him there.

Later, when we talked about this, he told me that The Family had taught him the difference between right and wrong. How had he not known? With Don and me as parents? I was incredulous. In my effort to avoid the simplistic moralism of my parents, had I gone that wrong? Still, what he told me gave me courage. I investigated every possibility: residential psychiatric evaluation, special education, private boarding school, classification as a child in need of supervision. That last one we rejected immediately when we learned we would lose control of him once he was in that system. Other programs wouldn't take him or we couldn't afford them. None of them seemed right. Finally, Alex agreed to make the two-hour commute by subway and bus to a day program I found on Staten Island called Camelot, for kids with substance abuse problems. He had the attitude, if not the addiction. He got what he wanted, to stay in Brooklyn.

The Family had kept Alex alive and un-incarcerated, no small successes. The behavior that sent him there—lying, stealing, no respect— slowly reemerged because what was really wrong had not been touched. Once again, Don, Tim, and I found ourselves in parent groups, this time on Staten Island where, thankfully, Alex was not present and the three of us were placed in different groups. Over the next two years, we barely held it together. Until he was old enough to drive a car legally, Alex stole them to go joyriding in the night. A counselor at Camelot told me that Don's passivity could get Alex killed. As much as this worried me, it vindicated me. Alex still wanted to live with his dad. His dad would let him get away with murder.

But then another counselor asked me why I disciplined Alex. I looked at him like he was crazy. What kind of question was that? He wanted to know why I disciplined Alex when it hurt me so much to discipline Alex. There went my vindication.

Alex was just a month short of sixteen when I had an unexpected phone call with the director of Camelot. I'd been trying to reach someone else who wasn't available and he insisted that we talk. He gave me an earful.

"Ninety percent of Alex's ego strength comes from you," he said. "Better it were 50/50. He doesn't behave because of internal strength but because of you."

I hardly knew this man. Why was he telling me this on the phone? While I struggled to figure out how to respond, he continued.

"Don's home is not a healthy place for Alex to live."

"Wait a minute."

"I have nothing against being gay," he said. "But Alex has not dealt with this. That's why it's unhealthy."

"You're not making sense." His tone as well as the content annoyed me.

"It's something that you and Alex have to deal with. Alex sees you as powerful and strong and so important to him. Why the hell, Alex thinks, didn't you figure out how to prevent his dad from being gay? That's why Alex is so angry at you."

Whether this was true or not, I wouldn't believe it unless Alex said such a thing himself and he wasn't talking. I hung on for another whole year. Not till March 1990 did I finally conclude that Alex and I could not live together anymore. He was enraged. His best friend, Earl, warned me that he was afraid Alex would hit me. I was not afraid of Alex, but he was almost seventeen. After talking it over, Don and I agreed that Alex, at last, would live with him and Tim full time. We knew he'd think he won.

Thursday night, I got home from work early. Alex was in the living room with a girl I'd seen before but didn't know.

"What are you doing here?" I asked.

"I'm waiting for Earl."

"Give me your keys. You're moving to your dad's. You're out of here."

His expression passed quickly from surprise and disbelief to anger to glee. "How will I get my things?"

"You will have to call and arrange to pick them up." I had intended to say more, to make explanations.

He was gone.

That very night, and for the first time in years, I dreamed of Georgia. It was a complicated dream about sex with no pleasure, the fear of exposure, about who had and who did not have power in the world, and my failure to please. The dream astonished and confused me. Only later would it dawn on me that whatever else it meant, it meant that my valiant act—taking away Alex's keys, to save us both from something unthinkable—somehow brought me back to what had begun with Georgia, so long ago, when I was just Alex's age.

# 30

## Gather Stones Together

On a Friday night in June, and for the first time in some weeks, Dumisani and I went for coffee at Cousin John's on Seventh Avenue, not far from where I lived.

"These places are getting ridiculous," I said. "*Mousse du jour?*"

I ordered it anyway, raspberry. He ordered cheesecake.

In a minute, I was completely captivated by what he was telling me. It was 1989 and the U.S. government was trying to negotiate a deal to end the conflict in South Africa. War weary, it seemed that everyone was going along—the ANC, the United Democratic Front, the unions, and the churches.

"I talked to my friends in the PAC," he said. "The State Department has called them in, afraid they'll throw a monkey wrench into the whole thing."

He spoke of the Pan Africanist Congress, a rival to the ANC. He was worried that there would be a sellout, what the United States would call a reasonable middle-of-the-road deal. But instead of genuine majority rule it would actually require a deeply compromised power sharing that disproportionately preserved white privilege and power.

I had been making sure that *C&C* reported on unfolding events and was intensely interested in what he told me. I had kept in touch, all these years, with Francois and Molly from my time at Lemana. Francois had been arrested and held in solitary confinement. The offices of the South African Council of Churches where he worked had been bombed. And now, here in New York, his colleague and head of the Council, Frank Chikane, had almost died of poisoning. No question but that the apartheid regime had tried to kill him. We could not be sanguine about talk of change.

"We've fought too long and too hard," Dumisani said, "to have it end in some sellout."

Maybe because we hadn't been together for a while, making love that night was especially intense and waking with him sweet. At breakfast, he told me that the South African government was beginning to issue more visas. He was going to apply.

"But they jerk you around," he said. "They don't grant the visa until the very last minute."

In early July, my old friend Pat from Berkeley flew to New York for a week's visit. She took me to The Anchorage, a vast, vaulted space at the base of the Brooklyn Bridge made available each summer for artists' installations. We entered first one called *Resonators*, its sounds activated by an electric eye—a rubber sledgehammer banged a large metal barrel, sirens screamed, and wind blew through bottles. Sitting opposite Pat, I studied her unsettled face. She looked like a Berkeley person with her long white hair parted in the middle and pulled back into a bun, her big earrings that were planet Earth. She wore a white blouse with turquoise stripes, horizontal on one side, vertical on the other. Her deep-set inquisitive eyes were sad.

She was in the city to borrow textiles from the Jewish Museum for an exhibition she was curating in the fall. But the news she brought, what made her fragile, and filled our conversations, was that Bill had asked for a divorce.

It wasn't what Bill did that upset me, but how he went about it, choosing their twenty-fifth wedding anniversary in June to tell her he was leaving for good. When I first learned from him that he was quitting his job at UC Berkeley because he was dying there, I found it brave. Walking away from a tenured position at the age of fifty to keep one's spirit from withering was no small gesture. I hadn't realized that he wanted out of more than his teaching position. Pat, ever sensible, had started looking for a full-time position for herself some months before. She was flying to Honolulu for a final interview in August to teach in the art department at the University of Hawai'i. She'd asked Bill to come with her; he'd declined.

Pat and I were shopping for Dumisani's birthday present when she said to me, "Let's retire together."

I had just selected a bright red terrycloth bathrobe for him, picking the color because he would look stunning in it. We were meeting him, and Rick and Muriel, for a picnic in Prospect Park. Pat already knew the ups and downs of my life with Dumisani. Laughing, we added a caveat to Pat's idea. If either of us was partnered when we retired, we would not hold each other to the plan. I was surprised by how right it felt. Not to age alone. And we already knew we could live together.

Now Pat and I made our way through the dimly lit cavern under the bridge to an installation called *Horses* by an artist named Viva.

"Horses," I said. "Alex has given them up for horsepower. He has his heart set on an '85 Cadillac."

Pat rolled her eyes. She made it easy for me to say how distressed I was.

We tripped the electric eye and, on a narrow walkway, entered a huge black space that we could feel more than see. The sound of horses started up, horses running faster and faster as light began to play. She took my arm, and we walked in the darkness to the sound of galloping horses, flashing lights casting strange shadows on the walls and floor. We stood close and listened. I put my arm around her shoulder, felt her bones. The divorce had her down to a hundred and fifteen pounds.

Standing in that mysterious space, something opened inside me and she entered the inner chamber of my heart. I pulled back. There was a time to speak and this was not it. I would not burden her with my rushing emotion or the sudden realization that I would want more in retirement than she might want to give. But there in the alternating light and darkness, to the sound of thundering hoofs, I acknowledged it to myself for the first time. This was my old friend. We were still teenagers when we met. I could fall in love with her.

Pat went back to California and accepted the position in Honolulu, which she would take up in January. I called her often. Since I'd already survived a divorce, I could help her avoid the mistakes I'd made, especially about money.

In August, Dumisani and I sat in his car in front of my apartment. He had not gotten a visa and his trip to South Africa was still up in the air.

"Will you move back there," I said, "once you can?" It was hard to believe that this might actually become possible. Jennifer, Suzette, and Stephanie talked about it a lot now: who would stay in the United States and who would go, and how their kids would react. The excitement was palpable. I tried to imagine what it would be like if my friends left. I imagined being with Dumisani in South Africa.

"I have to visit," he said. "But I won't go back."

"Why not?"

"I belong in Brooklyn."

It wasn't the answer I expected. Wanted. I wanted him to say we should go to South Africa together. Hearing this, I thought with some disappointment, that Dumisani would not be the one to keep me from retiring with Pat.

I called her on Thanksgiving, remembering my first Thanksgiving without Don. I'd gone with Alex to be with friends in Boston and a terrible sadness had blindsided me.

"I called because the radio just played," I said, lightly, "I Just Called to Say I Love You."

She told me she had friends coming over, was trying to make the best of it. "Dare I ask?" she said. "Could you imagine coming for Christmas? I'm flying to Hawai'i on January 2. I will need help packing that week between Christmas and New Year's. I have so much stuff."

I flew on December 24, and on the plane, I read Pat's exhibition catalogue: *Embellished Lives: Customs and Costumes of the Jewish Communities in Turkey.* She'd postponed the start of her teaching in Honolulu from September to January because of the exhibition and had assembled more than one hundred objects. The show inaugurated events to mark the 500th anniversary of the settlement in 1492 of the Sephardic Jews in the Ottoman Empire, as Turkey was one of the few places that opened its doors to refugees from the Spanish Inquisition. I liked seeing her name in print: "Guest-curated by textile historian and artist Pat Hickman."

When I entered the terminal in San Francisco, I spotted her instantly, her brilliant white hair. "You can never hide," I said, hugging her. "You've cut your hair."

"Do you like it?"

"Yes, I like it. You look ten years younger."

Driving to Berkeley she told me how we'd celebrate Christmas and about the packing we had to finish. She'd made reservations for us Wednesday night in Inverness.

"I want to go to McClure's Beach one last time."

It had been a favorite place of her family's. I worried about getting everything done, but she assured me with a mischievous smile that there was always time to do one more thing.

"And Saturday night I'm having a henna party. I want my friends to send me off with their marks on my body."

Pat was right about time. She'd already packed seventy boxes, and we would fill fifty more. Most of it was art materials and teaching resources, including thousands of slides assembled in big black three-ring binders, images of contemporary fiber art and textiles from all over the world. Her daughter Madelia, a freshman at UC Riverside, helped by making runs to the post office, and her daughter Hilary, who'd postponed college for a year to get her black belt in Aikido, was in and out. By Wednesday afternoon I could see that we'd finish the job by Saturday, and Pat wasn't crazy to have planned a get-away in the middle of this intense time. She was being wrenched away from the place she loved and had lived in for seventeen years. She was going to Hawai'i, where she knew no one.

We drove north to Inverness to stay overnight in the same cabin our two families had shared back in the summer of 1974, only now it was just the two of us, and it was cold. Matching beds in the main room offered warmth, and though I would happily have crawled in with her, I knew better. Sitting across from each other, we talked about what lay ahead for her and about her work, a piece that she was trying to make that wasn't coming together well.

"Maybe this will be a piece I just needed to make for myself," she said. "But I love being able to talk to you about what I'm doing."

"You're not making it easy by going so far away."

We slept, and in the morning, we drove to McClure's Beach, hiked down the steep hillside to reach it. It was not as I remembered—much narrower in winter and the surf dark and menacing. Pat set off energetically across the sand toward a rocky passage that separated the large beach from a smaller, more private one. I followed uncertainly, unwilling to call her back but the waves seemed dangerous, capable of blocking the passage. Not my hesitation but the wet sand on the small beach convinced her to turn back. We walked the long expanse of open sand to the far side where it was dry and we could sit with a log behind our backs. The sun turned the ocean a silver too bright to look at directly, and we watched distant walkers.

"I will not miss the racing around," Pat said. She'd been teaching as a lecturer at four different colleges, twice a week getting up at 5:30 and not getting home until 10 p.m. Her new job was tenure track and she'd get to shape her own program.

We ate our lunch of leftover duck from Christmas, a sausage she'd been given, crackers, fruit and chocolate.

Pat looked away from me. "I'm going to focus on my work. I'm not ready to think about anything else." She started to cry.

When I put my arm around her, she leaned close. She needed what I had needed when Don left. Friends to care for her. I could do that. I could wait. Being with her was all that mattered now. But I did not hide from myself my untimely desire.

"Our counselors sent me to Al-Anon," she said, sitting up and blowing her nose. "They told me they think I have behavior patterns that Al-Anon would help."

"Has it?"

"I don't know. I've been racing from the counselors to the mediator to Al-Anon to the body therapist." She laughed. "My sadness…. I have been frantic to get help."

She told me Al-Anon was full of lesbians. "They were married for years to alcoholic husbands, and when they finally had the courage to leave them, they partnered with women."

"Can you ever imagine doing that?" I kept my voice neutral. "Loving a woman?"

"Yes," she said. "I dreamed of loving you. I even spoke to my therapist about it."

I studied her thin, elegant face with its pale eyebrows over green eyes set in deep sockets. Did she have any clue as to what she was saying or how I might hear it?

"Pat, if nothing else happens, it doesn't matter." I didn't know if I could make her understand. "A long time ago, when I was trying to work out what Georgia meant to me, I kept pushing questions at Mila. *What if* questions. What if I really work through all of what Georgia was about? What if I learn to love and accept myself as a woman? What if, after all that, I was to fall in love with a woman again? What would be wrong with that? To hear you say that you dreamed of loving me. It gives me some kind of completion. There's nothing wrong with what I feel for you."

"Of course not." She placed her hand on mine.

"But I have a strong skepticism," I said, "about those women who divorced their alcoholic husbands." I had mulled over these matters for decades, written about them in my novel, for the journal, discussed them with Mila. "I mean this is a big deal for me. I want those women to choose who they love."

Sure, some women always knew they wanted to be with a woman.

But for the rest of us, I didn't want love to come because of fear or political commitment, not because we had no choice and not because of bad experiences. I didn't want Pat to love me because she thought men were jerks, but because of what happened between us. Of course, what happened between us was possible because of what had happened to us before. It was not something falling from the sky, outside of history, with no emotional antecedents. Still, I wanted us to choose in courage, not because we were avoiding something, scared and angry. I didn't say all this.

Because I was afraid I might frighten her, I said, "I'm not meaning we should be lovers."

"It feels like a huge jump to become lovers."

"Indeed." But something was happening as we sat there, holding each other. It was too intense.

"Why is your nose crooked?" I said, running my finger down it.

"In elementary school, I was playing baseball and somebody threw the ball at me. I wasn't skilled enough to catch it or smart enough to move out of the way." She laughed her almost raucous laugh.

"One thing for sure. We would not have been friends in elementary school."

On Saturday night, Pat had her henna party, a dozen women gathered before the fireplace in the dining room, sitting on the floor, talking about their lives—her daughters and the artists and curators who were her friends. After everyone had spoken, Pat showed us how to make cones out of baggies to apply the henna. She sat with her olive-green pants pulled up to her knees, put on Lillian's lace stockings which became a kind of stencil that could be followed to decorate her legs. She extended her arms out to each side, and I watched while Marcia drew circles of dots on her left hand, lines on her thumbs and nails. I hadn't realized what Pat had in mind. She would disembark in Honolulu with these temporary tattoos on her body and wear them during her first days at the university, until they wore off, the marks of her friends and the life she was leaving behind. Secretly, because I worried about how she would be received, I was glad that the henna didn't work as well as she had hoped and the marks were faint.

"Never has so much attention been paid to these legs," Pat said. The room was full of laughter. Then with tearful goodbyes.

I fell asleep immediately in the bed in the basement. She came in the morning to wake me, and after a moment of awkwardness, climbed in bed with me.

"What a wonderful party," I said. She wanted to go over it, remembering what each person said, ending with Marcia's wish for everyone: big surprises.

"Thank you for coming," Pat said.

I kissed the top of her head. "Of course. I loved it all. My life at home is crazy. You make me calm."

"We should swap qualities," she said. "I'll give you calm and you can give me some anger. I have trouble with anger."

Flying home, I was wound up tight. I couldn't stop thinking of Pat, of her and her friends, and the art they made. They complained that they didn't get the recognition they deserved; they scrambled to make enough money, but they kept making art because they had to. Pat's work had its own strange integrity. Could I say the same about mine? About my invisible writing life? I had revised my novel about Georgia one more time, found an agent who circulated it without success. She told me that the manuscript was too straight for gay publishers and too gay for straight ones. Though I wanted to, I didn't believe her. I just couldn't write it right.

Thinking of Pat's bright smile, her courage to take on this great unknown, I calmed down. She was fragile now; I was too. Alex wanted to quit school and be treated like an adult. I didn't trust him. He wanted rewards without work, privileges without taking responsibility. Navigating our life was exhausting.

A lot would happen in the next fifteen years before Pat and I would be old enough to retire. For the sake of that, it was worth taking great care with what was now my ordinary, creaturely desire. I remembered holding her hand, small in mine, delicate-boned and cold, and covered with henna.

She gave me an idea. I would be fifty in January. I had already decided to give myself a party. Just as each person had spoken at Pat's party, I would ask people to speak at mine. The past year had been momentous and not just in South Africa. In November, the Berlin Wall came down. I had been in Berlin in the summer of 1961 on my way home from Beirut when East Germans were pouring into West Berlin, just before the wall went up. Now it was down. Yes, we had things to celebrate. No, we didn't know what was coming. My close friends were old friends. I would ask them to tell stories and we would learn things we did not know about each other.

# 31

# Time to Embrace

On Sunday, February 11, 1990, a message flashed across TV screens around the world, interrupting broadcasts, even kids' channels: *Children, go and tell your parents. Something very important is about to be announced.* My friend Anne, in Boston, called me. She had just gotten a call from her mother, who was with her grandchildren in North Carolina. I turned on the television. Nelson Mandela was about to be released from prison. To be alerted generationally as I was, from child to grandmother to daughter to me, seemed powerfully right. Millions of people around the globe had been waiting for this day, working for it, for decades. We watched and waited, not quite believing, to see Mandela, alive and free after twenty-seven years in prison.

I called Dumisani and got his answering machine. He called me back from South Dakota and had only a minute before his flight to Salt Lake City. He had to go from there to Dallas and we didn't really talk until he got home. He hadn't seen anything. I got to tell him how Mandela, holding hands with his wife Winnie, walked out of Victor Verster Prison, tall and dignified, their free hands raised in a clenched-fist power salute. I had paid very close attention to what Mandela said, and I got to tell Dumisani. *I am not a prophet. I am your humble servant. Your work has released me.*

"They showed pictures of Mandela's house in Soweto. People were dancing in the streets. Men were on the roof, painting bright, wide stripes of the ANC colors across the front of the garage." Black, green, and yellow.

"Stop!" Dumisani rarely cried but I could hear in his voice he was close to tears. "That was my house. I used to live in that garage."

"Oh my God."

"I knew this was coming," he said. "I didn't know when. De Klerk announced last week that political exiles could return home. I applied right away, but they said they wouldn't give me a visa because I was too controversial a person."

Controversial and well known from his travels around the United States. Reporters began to ask Dumisani when he was going home and he told them he couldn't get a visa. Reporters started calling the South African consulate on his behalf and then the consulate called ACOA and told them to turn off the reporters because they were tired of being bugged about Dumisani.

"If I get my visa," he said to me later in the week, "I will have to ask you a favor. I'm supposed to preach February 18 at Park Slope Methodist. Would you speak for me?"

How could I say no? "My birthday party is the night before. Did you forget? I'll be exhausted and hungover, but of course."

"It will only make you better," he said, laughing. He got a ten-day visa. He would return, briefly, to his home, after thirteen years in exile, thirteen years spent working for divestment and sanctions, pressures that played a critical role in the final release of Nelson Mandela.

The favor he asked, to speak on his behalf, meant that we had navigated successfully the end of our decade-long, our hot-then-cold-then-hot-again, our finally impossible, impermanent affair. We would remain friends. He did respect and trust me.

My fiftieth birthday party was in February instead of January because Stephanie had been overseas and I couldn't imagine having the party without all of my women's group present. But I woke that Saturday of Presidents' Day weekend feeling sad, alone, and annoyed that I was stressed enough to have an outbreak of herpes. Too much was happening all at once—the party tonight, Dumisani leaving for South Africa tonight, and speaking in church tomorrow, something I had not done in fifteen years.

Dumisani came at noon to pick up a video I had. I'd never seen him so wired. We hugged and before I knew it, we were kissing. I pushed him away though I didn't want to.

"Stop," I said, "I'm contagious."

I didn't have to explain, and I saw that if it had been safe, I'd have taken him to bed.

"Are you going to Natal?"

There was heavy fighting in Natal.

"I'll hold my hands up and say, 'Please don't shoot!'"

We laughed. His visa was restricted to Johannesburg. He was in the apartment no more than ten very intense minutes.

Mid-afternoon, Muriel came with pink and white tulips, gold and white balloons, pink and black streamers. We'd gone together the night before with Suzette and Stephanie to a huge celebration of Mandela's release at Riverside Church, and we talked about it as we began to decorate the apartment. I hadn't realized how much I would need company, how anxious I'd be about the party. Muriel was an artist with flowers and showed me how to remake the room. The party would begin at seven and by five we were hanging streamers in the dining room, draping them from the chandelier out to the high molding. We'd almost finished when the buzzer rang. I went into the kitchen, pressed the intercom button and asked who it was.

"Hi. I'm early. I'm a little early."

I hit the button to open the downstairs door. I knew instantly who it was. It absolutely could not be who it was. I raced past Muriel, down the hall, and yes, I flew down the stairs. There she was, coming up to me. Pat had flown all the way from Honolulu.

She had written me almost every day since Christmas. I had written her almost every day since Christmas. January 23, my birthday, I had the flu. Alex, with the generosity I had almost forgotten he possessed, brought me a dozen red roses. I put them on the dresser in my bedroom, smelling their sweet fragrance as I slept. I was still sick in bed when Pat's letter of January 21 arrived, and I read it in bed. She wrote as she often did on brown, textured handmade paper, a newsy letter about her job, wondering what I was thinking about mine, if I could ever imagine leaving the East Coast, if we should switch our long-distance phone service to get a better rate. Then she wrote a P.S.

> I've just awakened in the early morning and I want to make love with you. This is happening now, night after night. On the phone recently, you said something about it doesn't have to be sexual. I have trouble imagining withholding that. I have never made love with a woman, never imagined it, and yes, I feel vulnerable, but I do feel safe with you and trust you. This is so new, and I don't know the way. Are we on the same wave length?

Yes, yes, yes! I had been prepared to wait, for years, if necessary. And I never imagined that she would get on a plane and fly to New York for my party.

Pat followed me into the living room carrying a small bag.

"I have a gift for you." She placed a Micronesian ginger lei around my neck, kissing me lightly on the lips. Even more lovely than the tight, white blossoms, their stems twined and bound by white cordage, was the pungent scent which filled the room.

The lei only made me more agitated. Pat was here! I needed time to take it in before people stated arriving and was completely keyed up when they did, introducing Pat as my very old friend. Stephanie's partner, John, interrogated me. Had she really flown all the way from Honolulu for my birthday?

"That's a friend!" he said. Little did he know but I was not ready to say.

Wine was poured, plates of hors d'oeuvres placed in easy reach around the living room. We filled the chairs, spilling over onto the floor, and I explained what I had in mind, though they knew because I'd put it in the invitation.

Surrounded by sixteen of my dearest friends, I began. "Tell us when you first became aware that the world was bigger than your little family. For me it was the end of the Second World War when I was five..." Then for more than two hours we heard from each other about the coming of our social and political consciousness. Those who grew up in Communist homes talked about the need for secrecy and the sense of being different. The South Africans spoke of growing up under apartheid and the different ways it shaped their lives. The Canadians came to the States. The Americans, almost all of us, had to leave the country and live overseas—Japan, Ghana, Geneva, Congo, Turkey, Lebanon—to see our own country more clearly. I kept looking at Pat, sitting among my friends, my quirky, not easy to know friends. Hearing them speak, she was getting a deeper entrée into my life then I'd ever have been able to give her by telling her about it later. And then it was her turn to talk.

"I don't think chronologically like most of you have," Pat said. She was sitting on the floor where I could see her only in profile, and she wore matching pants and a jacket of soft green silk lined with brilliant rose, the garment in the room I remember. I could hardly hear what she said because my heart made too much noise. She had come all the way from Honolulu.

"I couldn't wait to get out," Pat said. She must have been talking about her hometown. "The week of high school graduation, half the boys in my class were arrested for cattle rustling."

We laughed. It was ten o'clock already and we traipsed into the dining room to fill our plates, then sat again in the living room to eat. Stephanie had brought fish and vegetable curry, Jen rice, chicken and lima beans. Janet brought salad and Suzette brought three desserts. The champagne came out. We toasted Mandela. We toasted Dumisani. They toasted me. The room fell quiet, and I felt my friends were shy.

Muriel broke the silence, and I was able to calm myself and listen. "I respect so much how you have parented."

John said, "When Alex grows up, he will realize that the strengths he has, he's gotten from his mother."

I smiled through my tears, strong enough to hear such words of sympathy. My friends understood what I was going through with Alex. Pat had come from Honolulu. It was after one by the time everyone said goodnight.

Sleep was impossible. Pat and I climbed into my bed. I was extremely tired. I was wide awake. I had herpes so we couldn't make love.

"You were brave to come," I said.

"I worried it might be too much, mixing different worlds."

"I'm glad you didn't ask. I probably would have said it's not practical."

"I know."

We couldn't make love but it hardly mattered. We held each other close.

In the morning, we went to church. Standing in the pulpit, looking out at the congregation before I began, there was Pat, sitting with old friends of mine. I began to speak about how humble and how happy I felt—humble because they were expecting Dumisani, who was at that very moment flying home, and happy because this was one of those rare moments that is unequivocally celebratory. I explained how I'd heard the news, a television show interrupted not for the things we were used to—assassination, the collapse of the stock market, a declaration of war—but for unconditional good news. How rare that is. No matter what comes tomorrow, today we celebrate.

"Did you notice," I said, "that Mandela left prison not in a vehicle but on foot? A long time ago he wrote a book, *Long Walk to Freedom*. He's still walking. The struggle is not over. Remember the words he spoke when he was sentenced to life in prison, the words he repeated as he spoke for the first time as a free man: '...*a democratic and free society in which all persons live together in harmony and with equal opportunities. It is the ideal which I hope to live for and achieve. But if needs be, it is an ideal for which I am prepared to die."*

Mandela played on a larger stage than the rest of us, I said. But that's really the only significant difference. Mandela is accountable to his people, connected to a worldwide community that worked to free him. He is not personally ambitious. He is ambitious for the freedom of his people. He knows what he lives for and he knows what he is prepared to die for.

On whatever stage we play, I concluded, we need community. We need to recognize that the individualism and consumerism that dominate our culture are actually more dangerous than the terrorism or Communism we have been taught to fear. Like Mandela, we need to know what we live for and what we are prepared to die for. I spoke what felt true. I had never been this humbled or this happy, for the largest and the most personal of reasons.

That Presidents' Day weekend, so intense and multifaceted, would live in my memory as a colossal time. Pat had no winter coat; I gave her mine and wore my old one. I could not stop pausing in front of the shop windows on Seventh Avenue to look at our reflection in the glass. Two stunning women in stylish black coats, some inner warmth making their faces radiant. We ate leftovers from the party, which tasted even better because the spices had had time to penetrate. The flowers on the table glowed in the candlelight. We made love for the first time, not in some strange place, but here in my bed in Brooklyn, where I belonged, the sweet smell of ginger in the air.

I had been afraid of this moment, when we would first disrobe completely. Would I find her body desirable, as I must, if I was to love her completely? I asked her to lie on her stomach, took lotion and began to massage her narrow shoulders, felt her delicate bones. Since college she had been teased about her pear shape, small breasts and big hips, as if her body had been designed by two different makers. My hands kept moving, exploring her warm, generous flesh. She turned over and I saw what she was—a goddess, a fertility goddess. I started to laugh and couldn't stop, laughter of exhaustion and delight.

Her body brought to mind an image I knew from Cyprus—flat chest, hips like protruding knobs, thick thighs. I tried to explain. "You can be a goddess—but you can't make me bear children. We can't have children. I have all the child I can bear."

She looked at me quizzically, shaking her head. I bent down to kiss her, and we began to love each other with a tenderness and intensity that was achingly familiar and anciently new. She fell asleep in my arms and my happiness sang me to sleep.

Then, very early Tuesday morning, I had to drive her to the airport.

I fought back my tears. "By coming, you leap-frogged us over so many things, so many unknowns. Thank you!"

"You're welcome."

Her voice was calm, a quality I would come to need, to count on for comfort. Now I needed this unadorned exchange. It took me days to come down from her unexpected appearance. A woman capable of such surprises, well, she made us kids again, like we were when we met, only now we were teenagers in love, that crazy. She wanted what I had to give her—my impetuousness and my humor, my smarts and my seriousness, my devotion and my desire. How we loved each other—giving and receiving. How simple. How extraordinary.

I made an appointment with Mila, but not to get her permission.

"I'm in love."

"Tell me," Mila said, curious.

I got such pleasure telling her the whole story, and I hesitated not a second to say what I finally understood. "I'm not avoiding something, or being hurt by this, or trying to prove anything, by loving Pat. It means I have put Georgia to bed at last."

Mila shook her head at my choice of words, but she smiled warmly.

"You don't judge," I said. "I do. I have. I'm the one who made things problematic."

"Indeed," Mila said simply and with satisfaction.

"You don't tell me what to do," I joked again. "If you were choosing for me, you'd choose a man on the East Coast."

She laughed. "I have only one concern. Pat's great neediness, coming out of a long marriage. You certainly can understand that kind of neediness."

We talked about how this might be an interim relationship for Pat. She could get engaged in her new job, her life in Hawai'i. She might need me less if she did.

"I want her to get engaged in her life," I said adamantly.

"What about your life? Your work?"

"I haven't hit my stride yet."

I told her about Sunday morning, how satisfying it was to speak in public about what mattered. "The things I can do are not in Hawai'i. We will have to live apart for a while. It doesn't matter. The worst thing that can happen is that I'll help Pat get started in her new life and loving her will help me survive mine. I feel as if my emotional life has already shifted. Alex isn't at the center anymore and that's good for both of us." And then I was flooded with gratitude.

"Thank you for helping me get to this place. I am so happy with Pat."

Mila nodded. We both knew how far I'd come and what it had taken to get here.

Dumisani called me shortly after he got back from South Africa, full of stories, but he wanted to tell me in person and we agreed to meet Friday night at the Carriage House on Seventh Avenue where we could talk quietly for a long time. Walking to the restaurant, my mind raced with all that had happened in his absence. I didn't have to worry about what I'd say to him. He'd be full of talk.

For two hours, he did talk almost nonstop, and I loved hearing his stories fresh. He hadn't known who would meet him; his return was on the news; he visited his parents' graves; he left all his clothes because sanctions were working and his family didn't have things.

"I took my nephew to the bank," he said. "The kid pulls on my coat while we're standing in line and says he has to pee. I think, 'Oh no, where can the kid pee?' I go over to this old guy who is sweeping the floor and ask. He says in this big voice, 'Where have you been? It's not like that anymore. We all pee in the same toilet now.'"

He had been embarrassed. Telling me, he laughed, and I did too, delighted.

He'd gone to the South African Council of Churches and my old friend Francois, Francois from Lemana, Francois looked at him. They'd met in my living room. Francois knew who it was but he could not believe it, and then they embraced.

He'd spent a whole half hour with Nelson Mandela. And each event he spoke of at length and with deep emotion. He was exhausted and ordered another cup of coffee.

"I've talked too much. Tell me about you."

I did, carefully. "I've decided to look for a new job."

He leaned across the table and took my hand. "I want you back. I have friends with a house on Martha's Vineyard. They will be there next weekend; it will be only the four of us. We can talk."

"Dumisani, I love you dearly, but it won't work. Nothing has changed. What has changed?"

"Come. We will talk things through."

He tried hard to persuade me. I was high on all he'd told me, the layered, poignant, fraught complexity of what was happening now in South Africa. Why not go with him?

"Let me sleep on it," I said.

He drove me home; I did not invite him up.

"At least a kiss," he said.

I didn't object.

"Ten years is too long to give up."

"We already gave up, remember?"

"We didn't do it properly. It was just a break. Right?"

I got out of the car and went inside, up the four flights of stairs and into my apartment. Of course, he wanted me now, to share his amazing journey. But I believed he was no more able than he ever had been to share his private, vulnerable self or give me the intimate, attentive caring I wanted. I saw how deeply fond of him I was, but I could not go to Martha's Vineyard with him.

I couldn't sleep. I had to tell Dumisani why. I was not ready. Mila and I had spoken about it, the wisdom of circumspection. I didn't know what would happen. Pat was very far away. When I had fallen in love with Simone, I needed to tell. Now I wanted to cherish what Pat and I had begun, and I needed no one's approval and would not expose myself to criticism. Dumisani's invitation rushed me, and I had to ask myself what difference it would make if Pat were a man. Yes, it would be easier to speak if I had fallen in love with a man.

I saw that if it weren't for Pat, I would say yes to Dumisani. I'd already begun to investigate a way to go to South Africa myself and we'd spoken about being there together. He had looked very weary but no less attractive for it. I wondered if I would miss having sex with him, and my mind went back to a sunlit afternoon when Georgia tried to tell me about sex with a man and I wouldn't hear it. It was like the lady said: making love to a man is very different.

I woke at 3:30 a.m. and I knew how I could talk to him.

After church, we sat in his car.

"About Martha's Vineyard," I said. "I was being very protective Friday night. It's not whether or not you've changed. It's that I have. There's someone else for me."

He smiled, defending himself with charm.

"It's hard for us," I said, repeating what I'd practiced in the night. "We don't live in the same place or get to see each other very often, but we're going to live together as soon as we can figure it out."

"Who is it?"

"Do you really want to know?"

He pulled back a little, looking at me curiously.

"It's a woman."

He didn't try to hide his surprise.

"It's Pat Hickman."

He frowned as if he couldn't remember who she was, or else he knew immediately and couldn't take it in. "Oh," he said. "So some things do come full circle."

Quick, I always knew he was quick. I would not say it that way. This was not closing a circle. This was going forward to something altogether new and I didn't need to explain myself.

"You must know how important you are to me," he said. "The only thing that matters is that you're happy."

"I'm happier," I said very quietly, "than I have been in a very long time."

He was puzzled; she was very far away. I said I did not want to lose him as a friend. He said of course not. We hugged goodbye.

I walked slowly up the stairs, the stairs that just days before he'd gone down to get on a plane to go home to South Africa, the stairs Pat had come up five hours later. I had to call her. She had confessed that she was worried about his return. I couldn't help smiling as I dialed. He'd taken the news with such grace and generosity and it pleased me to be able to tell her that.

After we spoke, I sat for a few minutes by the phone, looking into the front room of my apartment, my woven mat from Lesotho that I'd bought in Johannesburg, the chairs and sofa my friends had recently filled, my plants hanging in the windows. I was deeply at home here, but never intoxicated like this before. South Africa: what courage, stamina, suffering, sacrifice, endurance, and, yes, love, had made this moment possible. Who knew what would happen next? But this step, this freeing of Mandela, and

Dumisani's ability to go home, it was the beginning that had finally begun, a measure almost a century in the making, more.

I got up and walked to my front windows, looked out over the rooftops to the south where I could glimpse the top of the Verrazano-Narrows Bridge. Pat had come all the way from Honolulu and she had sat right here, in this chair. I couldn't tell what would come next. I didn't need to. Pat and I, forty-nine and fifty years old, had known each other for more than thirty years. We had known each other for five minutes—it felt that new. Old and new. If you asked how we dared, the answer is simple. We couldn't help ourselves. We had the safety of old friendship and we had falling-in-love euphoria. Realizing these things, the smile that spread across my face was as broad and strong as that bridge out my window spanning the entrance to the harbor.

# Epilogue

## *And Pondered Them in Her Heart*

## *Pat*

Despite my vehement assertions that the work I did was not in Honolulu, and my secret prejudice that Hawai'i was nothing more than a place for the overly romantic to honeymoon, by the end of a year and a half, I could not stay away. The distance between the East Coast and the Mid-Pacific—5,000 miles, five time zones—put us too far apart. Pat had the more secure job. I quit mine and, with nothing but love for her and the optimism it generated, I traveled west. I thought I knew her. I had to learn what I couldn't see before and who she'd grown to be as she came into her own, a teacher and an artist whose mind works in ways it's sometimes hard for me to fathom. Almost three decades in, I'm still learning.

I flew to Hawai'i on August 19, 1991, gripped by news of the coup in Moscow which resulted in the brief house arrest of Mikhail Gorbachev and the beginning of the end of the Soviet Union. Competition between the Super Powers had defined the world for virtually my entire life. Yet the simple assertion that newscasters made, that every person on the planet could be grateful that they never went to war, made me uncomfortable. That was only part of the story. Competition between the USSR and the United States involved meddling in the struggles of colonized people around the globe as they sought independence—prolonging wars, distorting development, and costing the lives of more people than will ever be accurately calculated.

I couldn't know it yet but by moving to Hawai'i I would be isolated from much of my previous life, and I would enter a world that would teach me things I didn't know I needed to learn. But that's another story.

My story with Pat is that no matter how out of my element I sometimes felt, I never regretted my decision to make my life with her. In 2006, she retired from her position as professor of art at the University of Hawai'i and we moved to New York's lower Hudson Valley, renting her a studio and then searching for a home close by. She had lived on the Bosporus in Istanbul and wanted a home on the water, one with ferryboats and a fireplace. To my surprise, we found what she wanted, in a funky little neighborhood, with railroad tracks for freight trains just above our property. I get to chop kindling and build fires again; we take a ferry to cross the river. The things Pat dared ask for shape our lives now. We look at each other in wonder: how did we manage to find such a place to live? Well, why not? We found each other.

It hasn't all been charmed. In May 2007, I was diagnosed with breast cancer and had a mastectomy. Too soon after the end of my chemotherapy, Pat and I traveled to Australia, and on the plane, I watched as my left arm swelled up with lymphedema. For many months thereafter, I wore a black compression sleeve that covered my hand and my arm up to my elbow. Though it made ordinary tasks more difficult, I didn't mind wearing it. It wasn't just that people told me it looked sexy. For decades, I'd lived with invisible pain. It helped me that what I was going through was not hidden.

To break up the long journey to Down Under, we rested overnight in a friend's home in Berkeley. The walls of our small bathroom were mirrors. I could study my now lopsided self, more fully than I ever had. I saw it first in those bathroom mirrors, and the image made me laugh. My body finally suits me. If I hold my right arm over my single breast and stand at an angle, I have the slim chest of the boy I wanted to be when I was young. And if I turn the other way and hide my left side, the soft-breasted older woman I am smiles back at me.

At first, I hadn't wanted to move to Hawai'i. Now I knew the islands were not just beautiful beyond description but a complex, multi-dimensional place that had taught me as much or more than any place I'd ever lived.

In 2011, New York State legalized same-sex marriage. When we fell in love, it was against the law in every state for us to wed. At first, Pat didn't want to marry until it was legal everywhere, as she couldn't stand the idea that we could wed and then have our vows disavowed.

When we did marry in 2013, we placed Micronesian ginger leis over each other's heads, just as Pat had done for me when I turned fifty. A year later, what else? We returned to Hawai'i for our honeymoon.

## *Dumisani*

In 1994, I flew from Hawai'i to South Africa to be an official international observer for the election of the century, the one that made Nelson Mandela president of all South Africa's people. Dumisani was already there. We had very little time together as I was working with Jennifer in KwaZulu-Natal and he was in Johannesburg. Still, it was thrilling to be with him and he took me places I'd never have gotten to without him. Dumisani joined the new government and married a South African woman. In 1999, he came back to New York for a decade, serving as ambassador and permanent representative to the United Nations. He told me that, at first, he had to pinch himself to believe it.

In 2009, just days before he was leaving to return home for good, I went to the South African Mission at the UN and got half an hour of his time. We sat in his office, a room as large as his Brooklyn apartment had been, on a green upholstered couch and chair. I asked if he remembered who Georgia was. I said I was going to write about her impact on my life, which would include writing about him.

"Yes, I remember," he said. And we talked about what had happened.

"I can't say that I wish I had never met her," I said.

"In my belief system, we have the life we were meant to have."

This was not the time to debate these things. He had annoyed me by repeatedly speaking of Hawai'i as *lala land*, when he wrote occasionally. I'd brought him a book that, with text and photos, showed the Hawai'i I'd lived in, a book I'd contributed to. I hadn't known if we'd get beyond formalities and was grateful for his careful listening to what I needed to say. Now I wanted to inscribe the book.

When I looked up, Dumisani said, "In the rural areas, you walk, you walk a lot. And walking in the rural areas you come to a crossroads and meet someone who walks with you for a while, until you come to another crossroads, where you part company."

I handed him the book, open to what I'd just written. "I am so thankful that you and I walked the same road for a while." We hugged. He kissed me on the lips, a discreet kiss, but reminding us.

# *Don*

When Don moved out in March 1980, he left me a letter.

You have offered me more than I have been able to receive... I am so very tired of being terrified and feeling inadequate in my own home. I am exhausted with feeling uncomfortable... I will always love you.

Did Don find what he longed for by moving out? He had that brief moment, when we were still married and he was going to the baths. He became a sexual animal, and once, just once, we came together, uninhibited, as I had always wanted. I can't help but wonder if it didn't last, this new male passion. Seven years after he moved out, I walked behind him and Alex down a school hall, father and son, and they were creatures from different planets. Alex was not as tall, but that wasn't what made him closer to Earth. Even if his soul was in turmoil, he was at ease in his body, grounded, his macho stride carrying him along with a kind of grace. Beside him, Don was all tense angle and awkwardness, belying any assertion that he had finally found comfort and acceptance in his physical self.

In 2011, at a Union Seminary alumni event, I met an old friend I hadn't seen for decades. Tom told me of three men he knew when we were students, men who married, had children, and then came out as gay. One was Don. The other two men died of AIDS. What would I have done if Don had tested positive? Of course, I worried about it, not just for him but for myself, fantasizing the worst. Don lived to be sixty-six. He died in 2006 of leukemia, not AIDS.

Before he died, Don planned his own memorial service. When Tim called to ask if I would speak about his years in South Africa and in East Harlem, the years that only I knew, I didn't hesitate. The service was in Judson Memorial Church in the Village where his friends, the oldest of whom were also my friends, would gather. After the stories about Don's work, the courage he had and the people he'd helped, I had one more thing I needed to say.

When Don married me in 1964, it was still five years before Stonewall. It was a time when it was not okay in his family or in his culture to be anything but true blue, Eagle Scout straight, and it took Don until he was almost forty to acknowledge to himself and then to speak out loud that he was gay.

"If you imagine," I said, "that Don navigated his search for himself with ease and grace, free of deep suffering on his part and on the part of those he loved, you would be wrong."

I closed by saying that Don had the great good fortune to meet Tim, and the next chapter in his life could begin. After Don and I divorced and for a long time, I said we never should have married. I don't say that anymore. I was trapped and troubled when we wed, and so was he. However clumsily and inadvertently, we helped each other. With Don I started growing up; I began to confront what had happened in my life.

## Simone

In early December 2011, I met Simone for dinner. We sat at a table for two in the dimly lit restaurant where, because it was early, we were essentially alone.

During my years in Hawai'i, we'd communicated infrequently, and now we lived very different lives. Hers, she said, had not turned out the way she had expected. She wrestled with the notion of God and the meaning of human existence. I wanted her to be happy. Truth, she said, not happiness, was what mattered.

After we'd ordered, she pulled from the inside pocket of her dark jacket a very small package.

"It's an icon," she said. "I have just painted it, from the Ducci Madonna and Child."

She was surprised that I didn't know about the fourteenth-century painting purchased by the Metropolitan in 2004 for an undisclosed sum said to be about $45 million. Simone's icon was tiny and, unlike the original, she told me, the hand of the child bore the mark of crucifixion. I had to hold it up on the brick wall, above the small table lamp to see it at all, and it was alive and compelling in the soft light. She sat with her back to the window, her shaved head silhouetted, and I thought she looked like a Buddhist nun.

"If God does not exist, I am betrayed," she said fiercely.

My stomach knotted. What good was belief if it gave no comfort?

She knew what I was thinking. We had had these conversations before. She smiled. "You can't argue about faith."

I agreed. We would never see eye to eye. I did not grapple with these religious questions all the time and did not want to. But no one else talked to me like Simone did, and she reminded me of where I'd come from and the limits of my affirmations. More than that, I couldn't forget that this was my friend who, long ago when we were both in a kind of agony, let me love her. We rarely spoke of it; it existed in another time. Walking to the subway, we linked arms. I pictured us as old women, meeting in the city, sharing a meal, looking at art, until we couldn't anymore.

## *The Women*

Jennifer Davis, Janet Hooper, Stephanie Urdang, Suzette Abbott. Did it require four women to take the place of Georgia? I once joked that it had. If I believed for a time that I couldn't live without Georgia, I didn't want to live without my women and, during my decade and a half in Hawai'i, I came east almost once a year and saw them. Now we live from Boston to Washington, D.C., we gather quarterly, and we still talk about our lives.

In 2010, in Stephanie's warm, welcoming New Jersey home, we sat amidst her African art—paintings of dense urban scenes, complex woven baskets and sculpture both playful and statuesque—and reported on what we were up to. When it was my turn, I had reason to mention Simone and the events of the 1970s.

Suzette squealed, "I forgot you had an affair with Simone!"

"I did too," Stephanie said.

Janet and Jennifer had not forgotten.

"Half/half," I said, amused. "About what I can expect from this group."

Before I would have been devastated that they forgot something of such importance. Now I laughed. They did not define me solely by my convoluted search for myself. None of them had understood at the time what was at stake for me in that affair.

Stephanie coined the term *conscientious observer* to talk about her work in Guinea Bissau and Mozambique. Maybe it's what we were to each other, conscientiously observing each other's lives, witnessing, remembering, and even forgetting as acts of sisterhood, which is how we talked when we began.

Were we always there for each other? Of course not. Did we have rows? Absolutely. Were these differences worked through thoughtfully and to mutual satisfaction? Not necessarily.

I can't help but be aware that the youngest of us is now more than seventy, the oldest more than eighty. We've witnessed already birth, adoption, and gravely ill children. We've married and divorced and partnered, had affairs both casual and not. One of us almost drowned, one has had debilitating migraines, three of us have had cancer. And we've witnessed not just the deaths of all our parents but the death of a three-month-old grandchild.

I sometimes think of death now, that one of us will be the first to go. We talk about it sometimes, getting used to the idea, as if one could. We've shared our lives for more than forty years. Perhaps the next years will be the hardest, the ones in which we help each other age and hold each other as our group grows smaller.

## Mother

My mother died in Ohio, age eight-four, on July 23, 1991, just before I moved to live with Pat. My father had died the previous October, age eighty-three. I have always been grateful that they did not die young and I had time to become a good daughter, traveling to where they lived, caring for them briefly after surgery, arranging for a nursing home after a terrible car accident. Their last year coincided with my first year of loving Pat. They thought of her as my old friend.

Our love was new; I had an extremely demanding new job; my parents were frail and needy and thrived on my energy and my good humor when I visited them. If I had told Mother I loved a woman, what might have happened? Maybe Pandora's Box wouldn't have opened. The box was mostly filled with Georgia. In one corner was Mother's damnation of Don's deviant behavior, and hiding underneath that, her own outrageous washing of herself when I was in the bath. Maybe the lid would have stayed sealed. In time, I would have told her that I loved Pat, and maybe she would have been happy for me. But I'll never know because she died.

Near the end, I got a phone call from one of her nurses. "If this were my mother, I'd want to get here as quickly as possible." I got on a plane. Mother was in pain, and I sat by her bedside, reading aloud whatever she wanted, mostly from the Bible. She was deeply distressed because she could not feel the presence of God, a presence that others in her church proclaimed. Blaming herself, she asked me what she'd done wrong, why

God was silent. I was her daughter who had gone to seminary. I should be able to tell her.

She slipped into a coma, days before she died. Pat was with me, and we were making plans to live together. I wanted to get on with my life. Maybe Mother's unresponsive presence resonated with things unspoken. Maybe it took me back to that impossible time when I had to choose between my mother and the woman I loved. Even if true it's no excuse.

If I could erase just one day, suck back into my mouth one utterance, I would choose the day I stood beside my mother as she lay as if asleep.

I would take back my angry declarations. "Give it up. Die already."

They say that the auditory powers are the last to go. I have no way of knowing if she heard. But it shames me deeply that at her death, I could not put my needs aside for just a little while longer and stand by my mother with love in her final hour.


# *Alex*

Alex stood next to the cab of his newly purchased flatbed truck parked in front of our house. It was 2009; he had just started a towing company and wanted to show off his vehicle. Seeing him by his big black truck, I wanted to believe that this work would be different from previous endeavors and would allow him to make a decent living. He had been married for ten years. He had a GED. He was thirty-six, alive and un-incarcerated. I'd had such dreams for him. He'd made different choices. What mattered was that he had an adult life.

This realization led to another. The conversation I had been waiting to have with Alex for twenty-two years could finally take place, the conversation about Georgia. I asked him to come up again on a Saturday in November when Pat was away. I asked him to come alone. He entered the house without knocking, came directly to where I was working, and picked up the book on my desk, *Sniper: Inside the Hunt for the Killers Who Terrorized the Nation.*

"This is about those guys in D.C., yes?" Alex said.

The older man, John Muhamad, had been executed earlier in the week for the killings. I was interested in the other man, Malvo. John had become the family he'd desperately longed for. He would do anything to please John. Even kill. "The younger man was seventeen. How responsible is he for what he did?" I said. "When do we become responsible for our acts?"

Alex put the book down. "How many people did they kill?"

I could hardly believe the day's first conversation. We went into the living room.

Alex sat in the olive-green chair by the fireplace; I sat on the soft brown, leather-like couch across from him, my feet tucked up under me, my racing heart happy to be at this moment at last. Alex wore a white and gray T-shirt and hadn't shaved in a couple days. At ease, he seemed ready to hear whatever it was I had to say.

"I have been thinking about this conversation for twenty years," I said. "It was Helen and Larry at The Family who brought it up first. Remember them?" I said it mockingly, as of course he remembered them. "They insisted that I tell you. I refused. You weren't old enough. I need you to know this. When I was sixteen, my father hired a woman to be Christian education director in our church." I told Alex a bit about her, that she was the most interesting person I'd ever met. "She did to me what all those priests you've heard about did, engaged me in a sexual relationship that was completely wrong." I didn't hesitate. "I was so under her spell that I was completely complicit."

Comfortable in his chair, Alex listened intently, making it easy for me to continue. I explained how long it had gone on, how disturbed I had been when I first entered seminary and met his father.

"Your dad was the first person I ever spoke to about her."

"Mom," he said quietly. "I'm sorry this happened to you."

Maybe there was a touch of embarrassment in his voice. Maybe he felt he had to say something. What he chose to say was exactly what I needed from him. I looked across the room at this grown man, sober and attentive. I'd never seen him quite like this before. He didn't flinch when I continued.

I spoke about Don's difficulty in accepting that he was gay, and that sex was a scary thing for me because of what had happened. I told Alex I was too angry when he was a little boy.

"My parents never knew what happened, and I was irate for years about many things, including their inability to protect me."

"Not to defend them," Alex said, "but they couldn't have suspected it. It would be the last thing they'd think of."

We smiled, remembering my hear-no-, see-no-, speak-no-evil parents.

"Your father and I loved you dearly, but we were not mature enough to keep our crap out of parenting you."

It was quiet in the house, the fan on the wood stove making the only sound as it pushed warm air into the room. A large copper tray-table from Turkey sat between Alex and me, giving us just enough distance from each other.

I said as straightforwardly as I could, "I'm sorry, Alex, that you had to live through the aftermath of all this. I wish I could have been a better mother to you."

He sat up in his chair. "Don't say that. Would I have been better off with a sixteen-year-old in Pennsylvania?"

"Maybe not," I said, smiling. "Maybe not."

He went on insistently. "You know what I'd have done if you'd told me when I was younger? I would have found her and I would have punched her out." He laughed easily.

I had called the years of our estrangement the war years. Now he was saying he would go to battle for me. I could hardly take it in. We went on talking for a long time, with no B.S. charm on his part, no false humor or effort to placate on mine.

"So where is she?" Alex said. "What happened to her?"

"I haven't had contact with her for, I don't know, more than twenty-five years. I did Google her once, and again not long ago. Now I couldn't find anything. But a few years ago, a woman with her name, so it might have been her, was working for an organization sheltering runaway youth. I like to think she's doing penance for her sins."

He frowned, disbelieving. "You are much too kind."

It startled me that he assumed the worst and it brought me up short. It had not occurred to me that Georgia was in that position, if it was Georgia, in order to prey on vulnerable kids.

It was time for him to go. We hugged at the door. I watched him descend the stairs to the street and disappear behind the huge hedge where he'd parked. He'd given me more than I'd ever expected.

I put another log on the fire and took the chair that Alex had just vacated, turned it to the hearth. Mother and son. Both of us making choices in our teens, when we couldn't know the consequences, choices that would color the rest of our lives. I didn't expect Alex to think of it like this. What mattered was that he now knew more of my story. Over the next years, as we each dealt in our own ways with what began when we were teens, he helped me gain a bit more wisdom about change, what can and what cannot.

## *Georgia*

Was I too kind, wanting to give Georgia the benefit of the doubt? After our last encounter, in 1982, I thought less and less about her. Then, back when I lived in Hawaiʻi, I looked her up and took the information I found to invent a life for her. I was volunteering at the time for the suicide and crisis line in Honolulu, and I imagined a life for Georgia based on the life of a woman I met there. This woman's daughter was an addict living on the street and the mother knew that, at least for now, she could not reach her. She volunteered to help strangers in the hope that some stranger might help her child. I wanted to believe that Georgia's work with runaway kids was like that. There was nothing she could do for Amy or Louise or me, but she could, as penance, help other kids.

In August 2010, Amy called. An upcoming reunion had put us back in touch, and I invited her to visit. We talked about Georgia for the first time in four decades.

"What did she think she was doing?" Amy spoke as if she was mad at me, as if I had to make a reckoning. "We were young. We were trying to figure ourselves out. Sexually. Why did she do it?"

I hadn't expected such raw anger, not after all this time. "I think," I said quietly, "that she was trying to figure out what had happened to her." I thought of the last time I'd seen Georgia. She had made herself heavy to hide her attractiveness. Amy had made herself thin.

"I've never told my husband," she said. "I never did therapy, though maybe I should have. My sister calls her a pedophile."

She ranted, and from her ranting I learned things I had not known or had remembered differently. Georgia had taken both Amy and her sister to bed, though Amy didn't know the extent of what happened to her sister, and she had never asked. Georgia always made it clear to Amy that I was her first love. Georgia told Amy repeatedly that her sexual response was not adequate, not like mine. Amy insisted other girls were involved, naming them.

"It was all so terribly confusing," she said. "Georgia had us reading Tillich and Niebuhr. She told me I had such a good mind, that I got these big theological ideas amazingly well for someone my age. She took me to McCormick and I got to hear Hulda Niebuhr." There was almost awe in her voice, and then only anger. "She used God to seduce." She added, softly, "I could never trust anyone again."

It was the priests, all those predatory priests whose behavior was brought to light in the press beginning in the early 1990s that made me hunt for information about Georgia. By the time Amy came to see me two decades later, the worldwide exposure of these priests and the Roman Catholic Church's efforts to protect them was common knowledge. I followed the story with unrelenting interest because it was my story too, and I was often outraged. Then I read of an occasion when the church did the right thing. In early 2011, at Saint Mary's Pro-Cathedral in Dublin, Ireland, at the start of a liturgy of lament and contrition for victims of sexually abusive priests, an archbishop and a cardinal prostrated themselves before a bare altar. I pictured them in brilliant robes of red or scarlet. Later, on a video, I saw that they wore cloak and cassock of brown and black, sackcloth and ashes.

The act of prostration was accompanied by essential words. *When I say "sorry," I am in charge. When I ask forgiveness, however, I am no longer in charge. I am in the hands of the others. Only you can forgive me; only God can forgive me.*

Georgia never asked forgiveness. I never gave it. But the comparison is wrong. The archbishop and the cardinal were not perpetrators but took on themselves, in their deeds and words, the failure of the church to protect the innocent and act against the guilty. Would that it had been the pope.

My church has no archbishops or cardinals. Who could perform an equivalent rite on behalf of me, on behalf of Amy, on behalf of all the invisible victims, boys and girls, women and men, of sexually abusive religious workers in the Protestant churches, including Georgia herself? Georgia who was both preyed upon and predator. Mostly the exposés have targeted men. What about Georgia and women like her? And did I hunger for some rite of recognition from my church? I'd stopped attending decades before. I still had ties, standards, and irreducible expectations, some of which I'd learned from Georgia.

Catholic, Protestant, Orthodox: Christianity is a communal faith— love your neighbor, even your enemy. You can't be Christian all by yourself. Though I am part of no congregation, I've come to see that my way of being in the world has been shaped by the practice, by the stories, in ways both sacred and perverse, to such a degree that any operation to cut the faith completely out of me would kill the patient. I remember the story about hypocritical believers who pray in public to be seen and the admonishment to enter the closet, close the door and pray in private. It amuses me, given the nature of the secrets I've carried in my life, that the closet might now be just the place for me to entertain my enduring, perplexing questions about God.

Rites of lamentation and contrition, yes. But also action to bring those who are guilty to public attention and accountability. For any church to use its institutional power to protect and hide perpetrators instead of seeking justice on behalf of the victimized is as outrageous a sin as any which a priest or nun or minister or Christian educator commits abusing a child.

Does this mean I want Georgia to be identified and prosecuted, if that were legally possible? I don't like thinking about it. Why? Because she's *my* perpetrator and therefore deserves special treatment? She'd be in her eighties. What would be gained by exposing her now? And yet I write this story. I am not writing to expose her. I don't want her troubled in her old age. Unless. Unless, she lied to me when she said I was her last. Unless she worked with homeless kids to hurt them.

The uncomfortable truth is that for many years I wouldn't have been able to say which was worse: that she lied to me or that she hurt other kids. If she lied to me it meant that I was not her last, her chosen, her special beloved. Now it's the other children I wonder about.

Georgia's Janus-faced nature stymied me for decades. I had language for just one side: charisma, ecstasy and, yes, love. The other side had no adequate name, which made me all the more vulnerable and subject to her. Amy and I called it seduction. We both said it was not traumatic, not sudden or violent. Amy said she was confused. Amy's sister called Georgia a pedophile. I said she colonized my mind. Once I had a dream in which I raped someone. Relating this to Mila, I said, plaintively, "I never raped anybody." She said, "No, quite the contrary." Later, she called it assault. Both of Mila's assertions helped me because they verified the wrong done to me. But assault makes me think of a young girl in New York City who is pressed into the sex trade; rape brings to mind an Afghani girl who has to marry her rapist for her child to have a life. Names do matter though they can also over-simplify and trivialize.

Georgia did what we would now call grooming, subtly setting me up over seven months before she risked having sex. I had no idea what was coming, but by the time it came, she had prepared with such care that I was more than willing. Coming out of her embrace took decades. If asked now, I would say I had been abused, not assaulted and not raped. But I would also have to say that subtleties matter and that all abuse is not created equal. When Amy asked why Georgia abused us, I said she was trying to figure out what had happened to her because of course she was also sexually abused. Georgia said she loved Virginia. Georgia said she loved me. I would say that in the beginning and for a long time, I loved Georgia.

Do I wish I'd never met Georgia? Yes, of course, when I consider the price paid not just by me but also by my son. But without her, I would most likely not have gone to seminary. I would not have married Don. I would not be Alex's mother and the folly of such thinking becomes completely evident.

Do I want anything from her, even now? Nothing I might get from her would do me any good. I imagine her reading my rendition of what happened. Nothing she could say in praise or blame is anything I need to hear. I want nothing from Georgia. No contact. No information. Nothing but the impossible: irrefutable proof that she never harmed another child.

When it all began, I didn't feel harmed. I felt chosen. Being chosen carries privileges I didn't want to give up. For too long, I couldn't see the cost. But no one could save or separate me from Georgia. Though many people helped me, I had to do that myself. I had to learn what was wrong. Not that Georgia and I were both female, but that she was an adult and I was a child. The worst abuse was not the sex. It was her use of power, her betrayal of trust, her manipulation, her lying, her secrets and her capture of my mind.

What I can't know is how my life might have played out differently without her. Would I have loved a woman sooner, become a lesbian in my teens or twenties, or not at all? What I do know is that I didn't let the guilt and shame I carried because of Georgia keep me from ever loving a woman again. Thank God for that. Until the end, I have my beloved Pat.

Almost daily now, I walk through the woods near my house along a path that runs parallel to the Hudson River, below the steep, faulted sandstone cliffs of the Palisades that rise up to my right. What happened to me keeps teaching me, even after all this time. I puzzle over the fact that what I believed was the best thing that ever happened to me turned out to be the worst. The river is an estuary here, moving with the tides, and I feel an affinity with its upstream flow. Though it has taken me a decade, walking and writing, writing and walking, I have finally been able to tell what happened in my life. By choosing to write about Georgia, I have made her not less but more important. No, I have made what was hidden visible. The writing comes to an end. My story continues. It's a story about love, after all. It won't be finished until I take my final breath. Not even then.

# Acknowledgments

In 2005, on Oʻahuʻs North Shore, I attended a silent retreat led by a Zen Dharma teacher. In one of her talks, she spoke of a religious teacher, his serenity and power for good. Later, she asked us to think of the first person we fell in love with—the joy of that first love—as a way to imagine what enlightenment might offer. What the Dharma teacher gave me that morning was a new way to think about my experience because my religious teacher and my first love were the same person. I made the decision to write this memoir.

At Haystack, Deer Isle, Maine, Baron Wormser led a writing workshop and Elizabeth Garber was a fellow student. From them, I learned about the MFA program in creative writing at Stonecoast, University of Southern Maine. If, I thought, the faculty and students at Stonecoast are as good as Baron and Elizabeth, I would learn such a lot. Indeed. In addition to Baron, Richard Hoffman, Ted Deppe, David Mura, Jaed Coffin, Suzanne Stempek Shea, and especially Debra Marquart, formally and informally, shared their rich knowledge, experience and enthusiasm. I worked most intensely with Barbara Hurd, whose rigorous critiques and attention to detail helped me learn to read and to write with keener observation and awareness. At Stonecoast, I met the novelist Carolina De Robertis. Years later, her final reading and critique of my story attended to my large themes of gender, sexuality and race, and challenged me to go even deeper as I brought my story to a close. I remain deeply grateful to these generous people.

A few words about the church of my childhood. Yes, it launched the story I have told here. It also introduced me to a visionary leader in the Presbyterian Church (USA), Margaret Flory (1914–2009). Margaret founded the Junior Year Abroad program, one of the first of its kind, that sent me to Lebanon in 1960. Because of my involvement with the

Southern Africa Committee, I wanted to live and work in South Africa. I went to Margaret and joined her Frontier Internship program. Founded specifically to foster new ways for the church to be engaged in the Cold War, post-colonial world, it provided the structure and support for Don and me to spend two years at Lemana. I am one of countless individuals whose world expanded exponentially and whose life was changed forever because of the work of this remarkable woman.

The Frontier Internship program provided the resources for the first meeting of the Zambia Group, mentioned briefly in my text. The members of this group, in addition to Don and me, were Ruth Brandon, Anne Crane, Marylee Crofts, Eileen Hanson, Bill Minter, Carolyn Wilhelm McIntyre Minus (1941–1994), Sarah Perreault, David Robinson, Chris Root, Charles Wilhelm (1942–1968), and David Wiley. All of them have engaged in different aspects of activism and scholarship related to Africa. They have inspired me, taught me and helped keep me involved in the work that first brought us together in Zambia in 1967. Their friendship has been an immeasurable gift.

The FI program introduced me to my most important writing companion, Linda Lancione. We met for the first time in the mid–1970s when she was briefly in New York, and we discovered we were both writing novels. We agreed to exchange manuscripts, which we have continued to do, now for more than 40 years. Linda's commitment to her writer's life has encouraged and sustained me through productive and difficult times. The writing of this book has been accompanied throughout by her unfailing support and constant, cherished friendship.

One more bow to the FI connection. Ada Focer received her PhD from Boston University in 2016, with a dissertation titled "Frontier Internship in Mission, 1961–1975: Young Christians Abroad in a Post-Colonial and Cold War World." Ada interviewed me in 2009, and her thoughtful questions prompted me to reengage with my experiences in South Africa and to write about them more accurately. A conversation that began as an interview has never stopped. She has been an energetic source of encouragement throughout the writing of this book, and it is through a friend of hers that I made contact with my publisher, Exposit.

Moving to Rockland County in 2006, I looked for fellow writers. I thank Shawn Behlen for helping me understand that my manuscript needed one more major revision and for helping me see how to begin. For encouragement throughout and for hosting me in their home in Las

Cruces, New Mexico, Shelley Armitage and Deborah Moore were present when I wrote the final words.

In 1994, I traveled to South Africa to be an official observer at the election that made Nelson Mandela president of all South Africa's people. I experienced the election with my indispensable friends Dumisani Kumalo and Jennifer Davis. In 2019, both of them died, Dumisani in January and Jennifer in October. Dumisani was able to read and critique an early draft of my manuscript, and I saw him last in South Africa in 2015. Just days before she died, on a walk with Jennifer, we talked about the coming publication of my book and I was able to thank her for the many ways she helped me, including giving me language to bring the story to a close. I can't imagine my life without either of them.

To all the people in my story—my family, my women's group, my lovers and friends—I thank you for being in my life. I can only hope that this memoir does justice to the experiences we shared. My son Alex, thank you for your unstinting support for my writing, for assuring me that this is my story and I can say whatever I need to say. E Pat, mahalo nui iāʻoe me kuʻu iwihilo nei. Piha loa me kuʻu aloha iāʻoe!

# Index